The Complete Book of Practical Camping

The
Complete
Book of
PRACTICAL
CAMPING

JOHN JOBSON

Winchester Press

For

ANNA MARIE D'OLIO JOBSON

Contents

Acknowledgments

My deep gratitude to Ted Kesting, Lamar Underwood, Captain Earl F. Hammond, Weldon B. Hester, Red Higgins, Erle Stanley Gardner, Donnie Johns, Ned Frost, W. W. Phillips, Jr., and especial appreciation to my dear editor friend Lois E. Wilde, without whose efforts this book could not possibly be.

The Complete Book of Practical Camping

1

The Anatomy
of Camping

Who/Where/When/How It All Began

Camping is a subject with no beginning and without end. It is loaded with romance, yet starkly simple. In prehistoric times camping was the life-style—as it is today for such peoples as the Bedouins of northern Africa and the nomadic Mongols of northern Asia. Early explorers such as Marco Polo, circa 1266, camped. In the course of world history, many ethnic groups have exchanged worthwhile ideas and then adapted techniques and equipment to fit specific requirements.

Much of our camping lore stems directly from the military. Armies on the march and in the field have to camp. Our GI's camped out across Europe using basically the same methods Caesar's armies did. Through the centuries, much military equipment has been tailored to fit civilian recreational needs.

So, speaking grandiosely, worldwide camping is a homogeneous yet heterogeneous (one has to mull this a bit) art with countless roots like those of a giant redwood reaching deep into antiquity. Or, we could say all kinds of people have been camping in all kinds of places for a long time, and some have learned from others.

The first white stalwarts of North America to practice wilderness camping and survival were the Western mountain men, Eastern pathfinders and similar frontiersmen. They learned it by directly emulating procedures long known to the Indian tribes on this continent.

Survival techniques varied greatly among our Indian nations. In the East in deciduous forests with their indigenous flora and fauna, survival was one thing. It depended upon quite different techniques on the high plains of the buffalo-eating Horse Indians. The dwellers in coniferous forests had other time-proven and unique ways of comfortable existence. So did Eskimos on the shores of the Arctic Ocean.

Camping activities such as cooking game meat (above left) or fish
(above right) can be performed much as they were by Indians—America's original
Campers. Sense of accomplishment and self-sufficiency turns wilderness
chores into fun. Author (below) even seems to be enjoying himself as he dries
out after thorough soaking on rainy, windy, choppy canoe trip.

So the first white men who learned how to camp in order to survive in North America were our hardy frontiersmen in the East, the mountain men in the West, and trapper-explorer-prospectors in the North. They learned camping either directly from the Indian, or second-hand from someone who had, or acquired their knowledge as a combination of both. They slightly adapted many trifling details to suit their individual preferences, but the entire picture—and a panoramic, sweeping, colorful canvas it is—remains one thing: Indian.

Garnering provender and other of life's necessities from the land under wilderness camping conditions is Indian-inspired. The kind of fire, method of cooking, which woods to use for what, how to acquire game, choose campsites, tan leather, make shelters, combat illness and injury, stalk-track, navigate by dead-reckoning, predict weather—in short, most any aspect of woodcraft which is effective has roots (or rather, a main trunk line) running right back to the Indian. At the same time, we must bear firmly in mind that the white man, once having mastered these outdoor skills, quite often vastly improved them.

The Indians have never been excelled in some things. An example is the Plains lodge (teepee, tepee or tipi), which remains the world's best tent design for comfortable living in the wilderness, provided one has horses or other means to pack it. Another design hard to beat is the birchbark canoe. We've improved the *material*, but not the design.

So, my friends, your campfire—if you have made it correctly—has romance, nostalgia and historic significance far beyond what you might casually imagine. In appearance, warmth, type of wood, location and convenience, that fire is similar to campfires enjoyed far, far in the past.

If you've chosen a campsite with skill, the chances are excellent it was camped upon so long ago that no evidence remains. For, you see, we choose the proper campsite a great deal of the time with the same logic used by those past-masters of the art, the North American Indians. Nowhere does this more strongly manifest itself than in old books and magazine articles written in the 1880's and 1890's—and on through the hectic years of World War I, on past the Roaring Twenties, into the 1930's to the present day. The truth is, little of significance that is really new, startling, or revolutionary to basic camping technique has been written in the last 30 years.

The early writers, having learned camping skills from Indians and frontiersmen, put the knowledge on paper well before, shall we say, 1920. Discerning students of such matters marvel at the beautiful jobs of rehashing and interpreting and the different approaches used by writers of later decades who arrive at much the same conclusions as camping writers did back in the 1880's. The reason is uncomplicated: If they do a good job, they *must* tell of proper wilderness procedures laid down by the Indian. I mean, back in 1680 a bone-dry willow fire burned fiercely hot but was not long-lasting. It will burn the same way in 1980.

The area of revision and improvement for the modern writer is not in changing the basic woodcraft but in taking advantage of the astonishing strides we have made since World War II in design of equipment. Our new tools, shelter design, fabrics, insulation and just about anything you can name is more often than not better than it ever was. Consequently, camping can be more fun and more convenient than ever before. I constantly seek new and worthwhile items and techniques of horse-canoe-backpack camping and wilderness survival with the tenacity and dedicated enthusiasm that a pal of mine used (before he got married) to discover honey blondes who were 5′ 2″ tall and weighed 110 pounds. But I never forget that a lot of worthwhile wilderness camping techniques, styles, and procedures stem directly from the mountain man, who got it from the Indian. So the pompous pontificating of some "experts" occasionally gives me the fantods. When the subject of wood-

Above: Camping in Jasper
National Park, Alberta, has
acquired new look since
World War II, owing to improved
designs and materials for
packframes, tents and
other equipment. But basic
techniques of woodcraft
are still vital and have not
changed much. Left: Many
experienced woodsmen
still prefer to "rough it,"
relying on traditional,
simple but time-tested gear.

Methods and gear are influenced by locale. This Yukon campsite, reached by packtrain, is being set up with A-wall tents and woodburning sheepherder's stoves.

craft is pursued, invariably there arises the question, "Why is there so much conflicting advice on the outdoors from duly constituted 'experts'?" The answer to this is a trifle complex.

To begin with, experts on the out-of-doors are humans and have strong and weak points. Each man bases his work on a series of opinions, adjustments and balances. With a sensible person, acquired knowledge is constantly checked against experience. If a person has an open mind (as every writer should) he is not afraid to revise opinions that he previously felt were as firm and enduring as Mt. Rushmore. Alas, there are some who never can or never will revise, alter, change or adapt anything.

Another important facet of this problem concerns the degree of experience a chap has had and the versatility of that experience. No matter how talented a guy is, if he has had only five or ten years of camping background, when he takes pen in hand he is going to make a lot of mistakes. It takes more like three decades to learn that you don't know it all. Or take the matter of locale: A White Hunter from Africa could not write knowledgeably about hunting and camping in northern British Columbia. Much the same applies throughout North America. A fellow whose total or nearly total experience has been in the lowlands of Virginia or the Carolinas would be presumptuous to create an essay on camping in the desert. Yet this is not uncommon.

Five different writers could have five different opinions on any aspect of woodcraft and give five widely variant sets of instructions—*and all could be right!* Or all but one could be wrong; or *all* could be incorrect. There's an example in the wonderful books that have become camping "classics"—*Woodcraft* by Nessmuk (G. W. Sears) and Horace Kephart's *Camping and Woodcraft*. One of these volumes dates back more than 70 years and the other about 50 years. If these wonderful men were around today, I am positive they would revise large sections of their works. Yet many keen outdoor enthusiasts consider their books to be camping and outdoor "bibles," something which would likely appal both Nessmuk and Mr. Kephart. To the best of my knowledge, neither of these gentlemen had wide experience over many different types of terrain. Many beginners today disdain modern advice on the technique of backpacking and follow the advice of Nessmuk and Horace Kephart, neither of whom had much experience at the game. Nessmuk toted a backpack on one ten-day jaunt in Michigan or Wisconsin; the rest of his packing was short portages in New York State. Kephart's packing was confined to the southern Appalachians and the lowlands of the Mississippi River. They were hardly in a position to advise on the Rocky Mountain area. Nevertheless, I still enjoy reading those books on stormy nights when the wind is howling around the eaves.

To many people, camping means weekend backpacking. Every state has scenic destinations like this one at North Carolina's Savannah Headwaters.

As a youngster, I was a dedicated reader of all things outdoors. My parents strongly encouraged me in this, purchasing every known book on the subject and subscribing to every contemporary outdoor magazine. I pored over Nessmuk, Kephart, Seton's *Two Little Savages*, *The Book of Woodcraft*, Townsend Whelen's writings, the Boy Scout Handbooks and many, many others, and enjoyed them all. I formed strong opinions, some of which are still with me today—and others which definitely are not. For I learned long ago that there is no substitute for experience. Long, hard experience gained not behind a desk but in the wilderness. The best teacher of all is Nature.

I learned, so very long ago that the exact year escapes me, not to accept as gospel the advice of a chap who has experience in only one region. He may be prejudiced by what he has learned there and turn a deaf ear and unseeing eyes to the way things are done in other areas. I am exceedingly fortunate in having for many years been constantly assigned to far-flung, remote areas all over this continent and abroad. But I know I don't know it all. With that out of the way, let me tell you what I have learned.

To Start Out Camping

There is no "mystique" about learning to camp. It is not necessary to ponder some bulletin titled "An In-Depth Projection Into the Motivations of the Modern Camper." (If there were such a pamphlet, that is—and I would not bet there isn't because of late I have read some pretty fruity stuff designed to "aid" the beginning camper.)

One conservative big-city newspaper, not noted for rash statements, has referred to camping as a national "craze." I am not fond of the word "craze" in connection with my beloved lifelong hobby, but that there is a steadily increasing boom in family (and other kinds of) camping there is no doubt, and no oracle can accurately predict when it might level off, let alone recede.

The primary reason for the current mass desire to camp is exceedingly uncomplicated. It isn't that we are a nation of lemmings and that we are prepared to follow any "in" trend. It simply is the unvarnished, apple-pie-logical, American-know-how proposition that camping is the greatest bargain of all worthwhile vacations. There is no doubt about that.

Still, some people seem to be mighty timid about getting started camping. They are afraid they might appear ludicrous the first time out, something akin to a golf duffer on an overcrowded municipal course or that feeling the first time on the dance floor.

I assure you these little apprehensions are groundless. It is human nature

Ever-increasing mobility has much to do with the steady rise in camping's popularity. Vacationing by pickup camper is economical way to see this country.

to be at least a bit fearful of the unknown. So if you haven't camped as yet, don't imagine it is akin to mastering championship snooker or learning to win at sudden-death pangingi. It would be glorious, indeed, if everything in this world were as easy to learn as how to camp!

Let us assume that you are a young married man and, come vacation, you want to take your wife and kids camping. What is the procedure? What will it cost? Where will you go, and what will happen when you arrive?

The first thing you must have is a sense of well-being about the adventure: confidence that, as far as the actual family tent camping is concerned, all will go well on the first, or shakedown, camping trip. The next thing you ought to have is an automobile. I am not being flip, and I will hastily add that it is possible to enjoy really good camping without a car or pickup truck. I have done plenty of it. Some years ago, residing in Manhattan where a car is a nuisance, my wife and I used to put our gear aboard sundry trains and we easily and conveniently camped all over New England. But, obviously, if you have a vehicle, so much the better.

Your gear? Even getting the best, you should come in somewhere under $250 to $300. I mean for all the basic and necessary equipment for solid, healthful comfort afield. Bear in mind that gear of good quality can easily last 20 years or more. Actually, you can amortize this as an expense for the *first* vacation—from then on you're using it for free. Take a family of four on a two-week vacation and see how far $300 will go when you must pay for motels or hotels and restaurant meals.

Amount of gear to pack depends on such factors as transport, distance to campsite and length of stay. Man pictured below is using excellent tent, propane cook stove and lantern, but no excess gadgets are in evidence; man at right plans longer stay, with much gadgetry to assure fun and comfort.

You'll need a family-style tent. Popular models are versions of the umbrella, the prairie schooner and the pop. Be leery of any design that seems too far out. These look good in artist's drawings and they are peachy in color photos (particularly with fetching bikinied models), but some are a pain in the clavicle for living afield.

You will need a stove, either gasoline or LP; a lantern, likewise either gasoline or LP. A folding oven is nice to have and is practical. You will need a camp cooler (or refrigerator) and, especially if you have youngsters, a safety-approved tent heater. The best way to sleep afield is in the proper-weight sleeping bag. Under the sleeping bag you must have either an air mattress or

foam mattress. Cots are a matter of personal preference, but if you prefer to sleep on one you'll need lots more added insulation under the bag. A food box is convenient—the kind that has folding legs and a work space. Sooner or later you will require a nested cooking kit, so if your equipment budget hasn't run out, get it now.

Before you go, practice erecting the tent. Learn to do this expertly. Also, squirt the garden hose on it a few times to tighten it up. Become familiar with the new stove and lantern.

And don't worry. A wise lady in North Carolina recently told me that family tent camping in organized campgrounds is merely an extension of sub-

urbia. Besides, there are always experienced campers at any reasonably busy campground who are happy to help with advice or muscle, if need be.

Before it slips my mind, a tip: Carry along, if economically feasible, either a miner's tent (the best for the purpose), a cabana-type tent or a backpacker model as an adjunct to the big family tent. Use it for storage, keeping the living tent from clutter. Beginners often buy too small a family tent—it has to accommodate all the sleeping bags *plus*. A crowded tent is miserable when you must stay inside because of rain.

I can't tell you where to go on your first camping trip, but I can tell you how to make it all a lot easier: Buy a guidebook to campgrounds. The one I use lists 9,000 campgrounds with 150,000 campsites. There are many variations and they are available at your local newsstand, book store, state conservation department, federal agencies, etc.

Tenting Tonight

Recently I read a statement (the enthusiasm of which was only matched by its ignorance) that—due to the immense popularity of trailers, camper coaches, vans, motor homes and so forth—very few "moderns" (whatever they may be)

Couple at left will enjoy roomy, durable umbrella tent, set up
beside clear mountain pool, with fireplace located at safe distance and
slopes shielding site from prevailing wind. Campers above sit on
their closed-cell bedroll pads outside ultra-portable backpacking tent.

camp with tents. Getting a grip on myself (it caused a wave of vertigo), I faltered to my old typewriter for rebuttal. I refuse to say that this lofty camping oracle has rocks in his head, as that would be impolite. I will only remark that he doesn't know what he's talking about. It is true that recreational vehicles (trailers, coaches, vans, motor homes, *et al.*) have swept the land like a prairie fire. I have on many occasions used all these RV types for big trips. Let us pray the gasoline "shortages" have faded into limbo as you read these lines.

But modern tents are better than they've ever been and more are being sold. There are several types of camping (like a Yukon pack trip or an African safari) where the only practical method of living comfortably, healthfully, and pleasantly afield is with tents. If you are a serious backpacker who leaves the trails and proceeds into the high, wild, free mountain basins, you will live in a tent. If you take lake and stream camping trips—come night, you'll be sleeping in a tent.

There are purists who claim if you are not camping with a tent, you really are not camping. They have a point, at that. You do not need roads to camp with tents. Search the wide world over and you'll come upon mighty few more rewarding experiences than having a good tent for your wilderness shelter. Then smell the oddly nostalgic, heady mixture of clean canvas, uncontaminated air, woodsmoke, the scent of conifer or sage or lush early-summer prairie grass. Listen to the soughing of summer breezes in towering cot-tonwoods or the steady, rhythmical patter of rain on dependable canvas. A great many people who are able to camp any way they choose still camp with tents. One foremost attraction of an expensive Northern pack trip or a top Af-rican safari is this camp life under canvas.

Tents have one big disadvantage when compared to recreational ve-hicles and that is, if you are traveling fast, covering a lot of country, making one-night stops, the tent is a bloody nuisance to erect each night, strike and pack the following morning. I once did this on a fast trip over the Alaska Highway. We had fun where we stopped for several days (as on the Kenai Peninsula) but the daily work, on the road, got tiresome. A pickup and coach would have been much better!

But these new tents are really getting to be something. I have one now that is not only lightweight but far, far tougher than tents used to be. The floor is so waterproof it will stand in four or five inches of water indefinitely. And, of course, it is snakeproof and bugproof. However, let us begin at the beginning—with the tepee.

2

Under Canvas

When I was a youngster, my father arranged for me to spend a portion of two summer vacations at an isolated cattle ranch in South Dakota. He surmised it would be "good for me" and he was right.

This spread was remote and as lacking in frills as a pioneer homestead. The machinery consisted of a Model T touring car, a cream separator and a windmill pump or two. The ranchers were practically self-sufficient. Living from the land, they wove wool fabric from their own little band of sheep and constructed most of the buildings from cottonwood logs. Midday thirst was slaked by drinking from gourds. Hank, the owner, remarked that his ranch was so isolated he'd finally had to buy his own tom cat. The daughter, who must have been in her early 20's (but to me, at my tender years, seemed middle-aged) said she had never had a boy friend or seen a locomotive. I think the ranch was in Gregory County—at least, I recall passing through the town of Gregory.

That ranch was adjacent to property controlled by Plains Indians—the once mighty, fierce, and often intelligent, generous Sioux. At that time they had a respectable settlement within a reasonable horseback ride from the ranch. Hank treated me the way all small-boy guests were treated in those days. He absentmindedly saw that I had enough to eat and that I was "in" every night with no broken limbs; with deep understanding, he left me to my own devices. He furnished me with a spirited but easily controlled mustang which I rode bareback. I soon discovered that by cutting across country, carefully noting a few unmistakable landmarks, I could reach this Indian settlement. It got to be a habit.

After breakfast, while the shadows were still long, I was furnished with a flour sack containing enormous hunks of lavishly buttered corn bread. (I drank from creeks.) I roped my steed, which was kept in the pole corral, and was off for the day. Each furlong my pony galloped over that unbroken, virgin prairie of buffalo grass dotted with wild rose shrubs was keen enjoyment. I shall never forget the feel of that Dakota wind on my cheek. The sweet song of the meadowlark made me nearly burst with the joy of living and each badger, coyote, rattlesnake and eagle I saw was an adventure. Diamond willow and cottonwood bordered the creeks and I would dismount and study the bark and the leaves, for I never wanted to forget a tiny infinitesimal detail of those happy days. With the intuitive insight of a quite small boy, I knew the experience was exceptional and not likely to ever be repeated.

At the Indian settlement were several youngsters in my age group, and we became fast friends. Oh, we had the usual scuffles and such, as children will, but after my third or fourth visit I was not only accepted, I was one of them. The elders ran me through the chow line and baths scarcely noticing (and caring less) if it was one of their own brood or me.

The Sioux are kind and tolerant toward children. I never saw one of those Plains Indian children severely reprimanded. But then, come to think of it, I don't recall ever seeing them give cause, either, for there wasn't a disobedient or disrespectful youngster among them. Doctor Spock was not yet on the scene.

The adults, even the old people, took me to their bosoms and I was one of the family. To this day I get palpitations every time I read that the Plains Indian is "stoic" and "inscrutable" and "can endure pain." To my notion, nothing is further from fact. This group did an extraordinary amount of laughing; and believe me, if one of them bashed his thumb with a hammer, he hollered like hell. Possibly this erroneous idea got about because the Indian learned to be reserved in the presence of a certain type of white man.

Among the old people were many whose personal experience went back to the days of the buffalo, the Plains grizzly, buffalo wolf, prairie elk, bighorn sheep, Sitting Bull, the first repeating rifle and the coming of the U.S. Cavalry for, mind you, this was years ago. They instructed me in Plains lore (the straight McCoy, not nonsense). In family discussions, I even heard tidbits that aren't ordinarily shouted from the housetops—among them some little pearls about the Custer shindig and the Wounded Knee massacre—for these people occasionally reminisced about events the same way southerners still occasionally talk about the Civil War. I also learned a few words and sketchy phrases of the soft, muted Sioux language which, alas, I have now forgotten.

"My" Indians lived in two types of shelters. The younger or "jaycee" set mostly lived in small wood-frame structures but the older generation, for several reasons—including the primary one that they had more experience and thus better judgment—mostly resided in magnificent, towering, beautiful lodges (called tepees, teepees, tipis, too).

  *   There are, by the way, places where the Plains Indians still do this. The other day I read a fatuous remark that it is difficult to find an Indian who has

seen a real tepee for 75 years. It is little things like this that nearly give me a seizure, for my wife and I seem to find the opposite true. Not long ago, in the Shoshone reservation of Idaho and the Blood Indian (Blackfeet) reservation of Alberta, we drove past many tidy, neat, efficient Indian farms and frequently beside the modern farmhouses were genuine Plains tepees. My guess is that they were occupied by old-timers.

Other Plains Indians utilizing the tepee included the Blackfeet Confederacy, the Cheyenne and the Crow. Their tepees may differ in detail but not in principle. Anyway, about the *name:* my Indian friends at that time called a tepee a "lodge." Without question, this structure is the best shelter ever invented that can be assembled, disassembled and transported by horse, if your purpose is comfortable year-round living in the wilderness. For healthful, enjoyable outdoor living, it is the world's best tent design. To this date, to my knowledge, no scientist or engineer has been able to improve the pattern originally used by our Plains Indians.

Right at the moment there is in this country a rapidly expanding clique of tepee aficionados. Interest is fairly widespread and growing. Any lover of the outdoors who actually has lived in a tepee is an enthusiast. Owning one does have its problems (which we'll get to) but many feel the disadvantages are compensated by the pleasure of ownership.

The nearly-conical Plains lodge is exceedingly roomy and well-ventilated. It is cool in warm weather and cozily snug in bitter winter. It withstands the heaviest downpours and snowfalls and it is remarkably stable in high winds. I have read it will withstand any wind, an exaggeration because a wind that will levitate a roof off a barn will demolish a tepee. The Indians used to strike their villages if a tornado threatened. But a lodge will withstand gales and blizzards that would quickly flatten most tents, no doubt of that. It is one tent in which it is customary to have an open fire for cooking, heating and illumination.

Right here I shall reveal a little tip that I have always closely guarded. In the early spring, when the grass is just starting to grow on virgin, unbroken prairie, you can distinctly see the circles where lodges were pitched over 100 years ago. The grass, for a short time, is a different color. Thus, by using small aircraft, you can easily locate ancient, forgotten village sites. My theory is that the great bubbling pots of meat cooking for hours inside the tepee gave off a grease or a residue that changed forever the chemical content of the soil—but I could be wrong. I learned this from my Indian friends. By the way, these lodge sites are often circled with rocks.

Exit of smoke from the open fire is assured by two ingeniously contrived smoke flaps, easily adjustable via two poles to create the proper draft condi-

Right: Sioux-type tepee is still among finest designs for large outdoor shelter. Close look at bottom of canvas reveals inner lining staked down for cold weather. Far right: Jamboree of tepee-users proves Indian tents not only are picturesque but remain popular, at least in some Western regions.

tion. Of course, even if the flaps are adjusted precisely, under some atmospheric circumstances smoke will hang in the upper portion of the lodge, sometimes even so low one has to sit to escape it. We have all seen days when smoke from a chimney will not rise but flows along in a horizontal pattern until it dissipates.

During exceedingly hot weather, with no apparent breeze, a tepee can (sort of) manufacture its own gentle flow of air. The bottom of the tepee is astutely raised, like an antebellum debutante daintly lifting her skirts when crossing a puddle. Usually (but not always) it is raised a bit higher on one side than the other. The sun's hot rays beating on the tepee warm the air in the top which rises and, thus, there is a mild but perceptible air movement. In a wood structure of the same inside dimensions, you'd be stifled.

Even though it is an impressive, towering structure, a lodge can if necessary be erected by a single person. Indian ladies customarily put up and struck the lodges. And speaking of ethnic customs and all that old baloney about how the poor Indian women were dreadfully abused, put upon, nearly worked to death—I would like to point out that the women were in charge of all domestic duties and anyone who imagines the wife was not boss (of not only her home but largely the entire camp and the upbringing of the children) doesn't know whereof he speaks. The males' primary duties were acquiring game meat and making war.

Tepees afford such downright comfort and sense of well-being that we cannot stress the point too strongly. There is also the pride of ownership: They are so beautiful and impressive they are a constant joy. Why haven't

they been more popular? A good question and a jim-dandy answer is that, first of all, a tepee requires long and relatively heavy poles. Poles must be several feet longer than the diameter of the lodge. Say you have a tepee 18 to 20 feet in diameter. Poles should be 25 feet long. For a lodge this size, they should be about two inches (or a trifle more) in diameter at the point where they are tied (upper portion) and about four or more inches at the base. A lodge 30 feet in diameter will need poles 35 to 40 feet long and proportionately heavier. As to how many, a 20-foot tepee (good size for sportsmen) will require 15 to 20 poles for the lodge cover, plus two for the smoke flaps. Larger tepees require more, smaller ones fewer. Obtaining poles is not always easy. One cannot just dash out and harvest them when the mood strikes. First, you have to find some lodgepole pine. (Red cedar is okay but almost always has to be trimmed down on circumference if the proper length is to be obtained.) Next you have to obtain permission to cut the poles, and some way has to be devised to transport them from campsite to campsite. Some western lumber yards sell lodgepole pine. Indians in pre-horse times used to tow small ones travois-fashion behind dogs. Tepees were smaller then. But after they had horses, towing ceased to be a problem. We solve it these days by constructing a stout rack on top of our automotive vehicle. The poles are placed with butt ends alternated so the load is leveled and then firmly lashed down. And we're on our merry way—albeit a bit slower than normal. Poles, incidentally, have to be cut straight and kept straight. Rude presses can be made to do this.

Another disadvantage (some feel) is that a tepee requires lots of space—

both at ground level and in height. One cannot be pitched at any old camp-site. However, usually the type of guy who likes a tepee would not consider erecting it in busy conventional campsites. He explores farther afield and lo-cates his own spot where he and his family can really Get Away From It All.

Tepees, and pretty good ones, too, can be purchased ready-made. They may differ in small respects from an authentic Plains lodge but the differences are not apparent to the casual eye. It's fun and worthwhile to make your own, particularly if you let some tent manufacturer do the heavy sewing. As to de-sign, I'm always reminded of the tale related by Ernest Thompson Seton about the Old Timer who was asked if he could make a tepee. His retort went something like, "Well, I've lived in them. But I've also worn a suit of store clothes but that doesn't make me a tailor." As the yarn progressed, the old boy did finally come up with a good tepee.

If you have a pattern, the project surely is not beyond ken. Before cut-ting a full-sized one, make one to scale out of cheap muslin, about six feet in diameter. Heed my words—as you progress with it you'll see why. Many people think the tepee is a precise, symmetrical cone. It is not. It looks that way but actually, if pitched properly, the rear side is steeper and the entrance

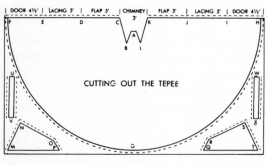

CUTTING OUT THE TEPEE

Making your own camping tepee can be an enjoyable and successful project. Patterns show how cover and smoke flaps are cut and put together. But author warns that shaping can be tricky, so its advisable to start with expendable six-foot scale model.

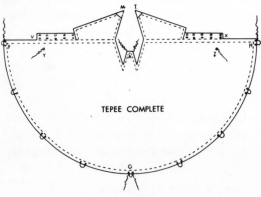

TEPEE COMPLETE

and smoke-flap side (front) is gentler. The floor plan is not round but slightly elliptical. As all patterns for tepees I have seen show a true half-circle (which is mighty close, at that) I urge you to build an inexpensive six-foot scale model before taking on the big boy.

Always use gleaming white canvas for a tepee cover. Originally, from all I can learn, the Plains Indians preferred hides of the cow buffalo—hair removed, scraped thin and otherwise processed so that they remind me of the clarified calfskin on drums. The hides were tightly sewn together before the pattern was cut. Thus the hide lodges were not only as lightweight as possible, they admitted a soft, translucent light. I have closely examined several of these ancient hide lodges, now brittle with age, and while I am impressed, I prefer white canvas. Indeed, when (via the traders) white canvas hit the Western frontier, the Indians fell upon it with glad cries, and the transition from hide to canvas was rapid. Some stubborn types remark that this conversion was coincidental with the extermination of the buffalo, but to those True Believers I say that canvas predated the end of the buffalo herds by quite a bit. Besides, a few Indians jumped the gun on the traders by commandeering wagon covers from the prairie schooners. And, as a clincher, all old Indians I've talked with say canvas is better in every way for lodges.

To erect a tepee you first securely tie (with a clove hitch or two) and then tightly wind a few coils of stout rope around three tepee poles. Some tribes used four, but three is best. Experiment until you get them up so the rope is tight and will not slip. The other poles are laid round consecutively, with most of them lying in the front crotch formed by your tripod. This places the bulk over the opening and smoke hole so the mass doesn't bulge the tepee cover. Leave a long length of rope dangling down to form a tie-down or anchor rope, which is securely staked *inside* the tepee. The cover is raised with the last pole and unfolded and adjusted around the poles. The front is secured with a dozen or more large dowel pins. Then go inside and further adjust the poles until the tepee is nice and taut and pleasing to the eye. The first time you do it is a formidable occasion. Until you learn to estimate all steps of the procedure, you are going to have some trial-and-error; expect plenty of error at first. After you learn how, you can erect a tepee so ruddy-fast it will astonish not only bystanders but yourself. The bottom circumference is staked, of course. You should hang a waist-high or head-high inside lining for cold-weather use. This lining can be fastened to the poles from the inside.

When you have mastered this, how you'll enjoy your tepee! Especially at night, with the dancing light of a campfire reflected on the cozy canvas walls. There is nothing quite like it.

Here are two good A-walls. Tent at near right, shown on winter evening, is comfortably roomy, well-lit and warm. Lashings on tent at far right are secured to convenient trees.

The A-Wall Tent*

A great many things in this life that appear to be logical are not. Take the case of the ancient A-wall tent. These were popular before the Greeks and Trojans battled. I don't know exactly how old the design is, for I've never delved into the subject to that extent. I have a photograph of General George Armstrong Custer on the Plains back in the 1870's, seated in front of an A-wall tent. A-walls were popular in South Africa during the Great Trek. I once had the privilege of examining a portfolio of sketches and drawings (copies) said to have been executed at a Green River fur rendezvous of the mountain men about 1840 or so. In one, among the scattered tepees, was a shelter that looked mighty like an A-wall tent to me.

I am not exactly a spring chicken, yet the first tent I can remember was an A-wall. My dad used one on camping trips back around the close of World War I when my goal in life was to toddle around on rubbery legs and see how many garter snakes I could catch and present to Mother. So it would appear that in this age of modern, scientific tent design, the old A-wall should be as dead as Kelsey's aspidistras (they froze in the blizzard of '88, you know). The only thing wrong with this view is that it is not true.

A-wall tents remain among the most practical and popular of wilderness shelters. They are still serving sportsmen from Mt. Kilimanjaro to the slopes of Mt. McKinley. I would wager 95 percent of Rocky Mountain outfitters select them. Their use is "standard" with many varied groups, including summer youth camps, oil-mineral exploration parties and the Far North Indians and Eskimos.

A-wall tents are eminently suited to comfortable, healthy outdoor living. For one thing, they nicely accommodate a woodburning stove. Always specify an A-wall with an asbestos-ringed hole for the pipe of a woodburning sheepherder stove. The best color is a glittering white, not brown or green (which can make the interior gloomily dark and does not reflect heat as well). A good A-wall is rugged and long-lasting and it can be erected in many different fashions. The three "poles" are usually furnished with the tent (two upright and one ridge pole).

In obtaining one for your own use, it is better not to get a sewn-in floor. There is nothing wrong with having an 8-to-12-inch sod cloth attached to the circumference of the inside bottom, however, as this is great for eliminating drafts (and in some cases, moisture). More than likely, you will sleep toward the rear of the tent, so place a tarp on the ground there. It is usually not necessary or even desirable to cover the ground in the cooking area, around the stove.

I have spent a good deal of time in A-walls. I would venture that in the true wilderness they've been my bulwark against the elements at least 70 percent of the time. Add 20 percent for the times I've slept under a basic fly or hastily rigged tarp and the remaining 10 percent should cover the other types of tents I've used in the wilds.

I would not say the A-wall tent is the best for auto camping, or for conventional family camping. There are other tents much better for these purposes. But for the wilderness, far from roads, where the Northern Lights streak across the frosty sky and the wolf howls, having an old-fashioned A-wall tent is never a mistake.

Above: With awning thrown back over ridge pole to let in sun, author relaxes and tends to some leather-mending in his Whelen campfire tent. View at right, with rain awning extended, shows how tent is erected and secured.

The Great Whelen Wilderness Campfire Tent

Among camping *cognoscenti* there is absolutely no question whatever that Colonel Townsend Whelen was the greatest, most knowledgeable sportsman-camping-expert—and this is taking nothing away from such popular, accepted woodcrafters as Horace Kephart and Nessmuk. Colonel Whelen's expertise transcended theirs, in my opinion, for he knew all that was best and most worthwhile in the contemporary camping scene, and he took intuitive, uncanny looks into the future. Indeed, Townsend Whelen was a camper's camper. If there were facts he had not learned about tents, assuredly they were unimportant.

He loved certain types of tents, and he particularly doted upon wilderness shelters suitable for one or two persons who do all their own work. Whelen never owned a closed tent, though during 40 years of Army service he had much experience with them. Early during his many trips to lonely lands, especially the Canadian Rockies, he learned that the ideal portable woods shelter is a "campfire" tent, and the best of these is some form of lean-to, as op-

posed to Nessmuk's "shanty-tent," the Baker, the old "Tom Sawyer" or, believe it or not, the so-called commercial "campfire" tent. Skirting redundancy, we'll mention ol' Nessmuk again, who put it nicely when he said the best wilderness tent combines the essentials of dryness, light weight, portability, inexpensiveness, ease of erecting and striking; *and* it must admit light and warmth from a campfire, day or night.

A lean-to form (without a low wall in the back, which adds more problems than virtues) reflects, or "bounces," light and heat from the campfire off the back wall, onto the shelter's floor, keeping it dry and warm. With most campfire tents, a person has to sleep with either his feet or his head toward the fire. This had been going on for hundreds of years, but the Colonel did not like it at all. He believed it was much smarter to sleep across the front of the shelter, with the fire keeping not only the head and feet warm but—more important—the vital organs such as the kidneys, etc. This way it is easy to reach over in the morning and throw fuel on the coals. And most pleasing of all, the camper is not closed in from the pure air, the sights and sounds and smells of unspoiled wilderness and the comforting warmth and sight of an open campfire. The Colonel used to tell how fond he was of looking from his cozy nest up through the treetops to a velvety blue-black sky ablaze with diamond-bright, glittering stars, as he dozed off.

I often get letters and phone calls from Whelen tent aficionados, including the district attorney of a large city, a vice president of a car company in Detroit, a wealthy Washington wheat farmer, an industrialist in Spain, a guide in Alaska, and a good many average guys. All have one thing in common with regard to their Whelen tents: They *use* them and look upon them the way an old-car buff looks upon his mint Locomobile roadster.

The Whelen tent was born in 1926. Following suggestions from the famous big-game hunter and naturalist Charles Sheldon, Colonel Whelen designed the shelter and, as I recall, had the first one made up by Dave Abercrombie in New York City. Whelen modestly called it a "lean-to," which I guess it is. But saying the Whelen tent is a lean-to is akin to observing that Mary Tyler Moore is a girl. Like most superior things, it is simple, yet ingenious. It is effective and versatile. I'm describing the one-man model (which is good for two), but it can be made in practically any reasonable size.

Starting with the basic lean-to, instead of leaving the sides open or bringing them down straight, they are splayed outward and forward. Thus, the sides extend three feet forward and three feet outward from ridge perpendicular. About these sides: We fans of the shelter do not always splay them out as Whelen intended. Sometimes I have mine straight, and in other instances I toe them in, depending upon the weather. From Plains Indians I learned that you can do amazing things with canvas by a bit of adjustment here and there. The awning is usually thrown back over the ridge tape, out of the way; in case of bad weather it extends forward at a slight angle and effectively keeps out rain, sleet and snow. Guy lines are not necessary, as two poles, sharpened on either end, and about seven feet long, hold the canopy in place—one end of each pole in a grommet, the other inside the tent.

To erect the shelter, lash a ridge pole about 15 feet long to a tree, and use shear (or "scissor") poles to hold up the other end. The ridge pole will be outside the tent—above it, holding the canvas up by tie loops extending from the ridge tape. A strong sewn-on tape serves as the ridge of the tent, with loops on either side, plus (generally) some tie tapes. Affix the ridge-tape loops to the pole—for the one-man model I simply use two short lengths of rope, with clove hitches. If you can find two trees suitably spaced, forget the big ridge pole and simply run a rope between the trees.

Under the tape ridge are two loops for insertion of a stick upon which to hang wet clothing. On the back there are two loops so that in a heavy, wet snowfall you can run ropes out to help support the weight. Other inside loops aid in holding a mosquito "bar" over the bedroll while sleeping. This tent does not lend itself to a mosquito net on the front, but you seldom require one during the day or evening as the fire keeps them away. Your fire, serving for cooking as well as for light, warmth and companionship, should ideally be rather elongated and about five to seven feet from the tent. Whelen used to cut a log for a "Deacon Seat" and sometimes I do, too.

My first Whelen tent was made by my wife from a sketch sent to me by the Colonel. An outfitter in the Yukon said he could not live without that tent, so we gave it to him. My present one was bought for a modest price and is of excellent quality.

This tent is not for a public campground nor for timberline backpackers. It's unsuitable for a big-time packtrip where you're waited upon by plenty of hired help. It is a one-or-two-person wilderness campfire tent that works best in unspoiled, virgin-type forested country. For that kind of camping, it cannot be beaten. Until you experience the glorious security and freedom of your snug, dependable Whelen tent, until you watch the glowing coals slowly fade and hear the mysterious hoot of the great owls and the mournful cry of the loon, you have not experienced top-echelon camping.

Here is Ann Jobson's pattern for Whelen wilderness campfire tent, which was modestly called a canvas lean-to by its inventor, Colonel Townsend Whelen.

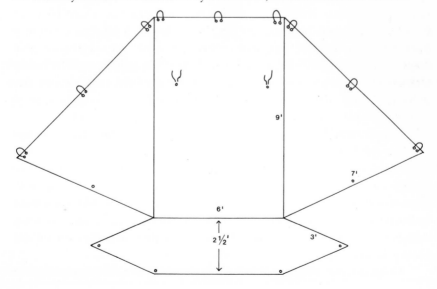

Family Tents

It's fun to poke about among the wide selection of family tents before buy-ing—an umbrella (there are countless versions, practically all of them good), quonset (Prairie Schooner), pop-up (igloo), cottage—and a fellow should, for peace of mind if nothing else, know a little about fabric and "waterproofing." Knowing material weight (7-ounce, 10-ounce, or whichever) is not so impor-tant these days. But in the old days it was common practice for quick-buck artists to mail-order shoddy goods to unwary buyers. The cheapest fabrics were soaked in all manner of mixtures including stuff like clay, for heaven's sake. Weight per square yard is now determined before finish is applied to the fabric. Tent materials are categorized by type: duck, drill, twill, duo-ply, poplin, palina cloth. Thread count means the number of threads of warp plus number of threads of woof, per square inch. Often a manufacturer or retailer will slap his own cunning sobriquet on his tent material, calling it something like "Rhino-Lite." There is no harm in this, that I can see.

A tent of heavier fabric should last longer than one of lighter fabric but this is not necessarily always true. The heavier fabric, of equal quality, will stand more abrasion and scuffing, and it has greater tear-strength. Why, it is asked, are not all tents made of heavier material? The answer is that there are practical limits, just as there are limits on the weights of automobile fenders. It would not be in your best interest for a manufacturer to make your um-brella tent of the same canvas he would use to make a tarpaulin to cover a football field. Generally, smaller tents (backpack models, say) are made of lighter-*weight* material than a family umbrella tent meant to be carried in the trunk of an automobile. There are rare exceptions. I have seen little bitty tents made of 3.4-ounce Egyptian cotton, but these were special-purpose items made on custom order and not suitable at all for general use. The family tent should be strong enough to withstand years of hard use and do all it has to do, yet lightweight enough for ease of handling and small enough to com-press into a totable package.

A family tent should not be totally waterproof, yet it should not leak wa-ter. Two things keep a tent from leaking water. One is that water possesses surface tension and, if the spaces between the threads of the tent fabric are small enough, a droplet of water actually bridges the threads and helps pre-vent other water from entering. A close-woven tent with no water-repellent treatment whatever will shed water like a teal's back if the pitch is steep enough. Secondly, threads swell when damp, further deterring water from passing between them.

All good family tents should be treated with a chemical preparation (often known as "Extra-Dry") that makes each thread water-repellent, yet leaves microscopic air spaces between the threads so the tent will "breathe." No family tent should be waterproofed to the point where it is unable to pass vapor, or air. And while we're on this subject, all good family tents should have ample screened windows and (perhaps) other means of ventilation. There are other tent finishes called "Semi-Dry," "Oil Tempered" and even one called "Waterproofing." Whichever, be sure that it *adds very little to the natural weight of the canvas,* is mildew- and flame-resistant, soft, flexible, won't "rub off" and won't crack, peel, harden or melt into goo.

Most family tents are of the "umbrella" type, an anachronistic term dating back to the Roaring Twenties (at least) when this kind of shelter was erected by means of a miserably heavy iron or steel pole that stood in the center of the tent, smack in the way; from this radiated iron rods like an umbrella's ribs. The new tents are about as much like these primitive models as a snowmobile is like Admiral Peary's sledge. And the frame is now of light-weight alloy, spring-loaded, and usually outside the shelter.

When you get your tent home from the store, unpack it and check to see that you have all the parts (packers are human and sometimes err). Check to see that no enthusiastic freight handler has fiendishly impaled the fabric with a steel hook, or some such. At the first opportunity, well before the initial campout, erect the tent on your back lawn if you have one. Or in a park. Follow the directions carefully and take your time. Be sure the zippers are all closed, and when you stake out the bottom, don't tug or pull on the tent. Don't have the floor exactly *loose,* but definitely do not have it tight. You can irreparably harm the shelter by doing this.

When the tent is fully up, my advice to you is this: Wherever there is a joint in the frame, mark it so it can be instantly identified. The time will come when you'll have to set this baby up in some campground long after dark, and it is a source of immense satisfaction to be able to do it with a facile grace by the feeble light of a run-down flashlight, and so get the tired wife and kiddies to sleep fast. Some fellows match color to color with plastic-coated tape. Others use a stripe of paint across the joint, using a different color each time (if you do use paint, then dry-wrap that with transparent tape, as paint has a habit of coming off alloy poles).

Take the hose and, using a fine-to-coarse spray, thoroughly soak the outside of the tent. On some tents, this activates the water-repellent treatment— the cotton threads swell, needle-holes at seams will (or should) close. The shelter will "shrink" as cotton fabric (usually the choice for family tents) changes its characteristics when wet. Finally, check for leaks.

Don't roll up or pack a damp tent. This will ruin it, if left damp. There

Top: Pop-up, or igloo, style
of tent if comfortable, durable, and
probably fastest of all to
set up. Above: Family model
incorporating umbrella
and cottage features has generous
fly plus rear extension and
height enough for anyone to stand in.

Below: Family-sized quonset, or Prairie Schooner, design is an
ingenious tent that can be erected quickly and is reasonably compact
when struck and stowed away. Bottom: Some variations on
cottage-tent theme are spacious enough to accommodate visiting relatives.

Sturdy, light,
easily transported
and erected,
cottage tent gives
ventilation and
shade in daytime,
warmth at night.

will be occasions when you must strike camp in the rain, but unfold the tent as quickly as you can and dry it before storing. This prevents mildew, probably the number-one hazard to a tent's long life. At home, store the tent where it is dry (this knocks out most basements).

Don't worry if your tent is not sleek and svelte like the pictures in the advertisements. With spring-tension frames, in a day or so the wrinkles disappear, much like those in a sports coat when you hang it in the closet for a few days. But regardless of the type of frame, an expertly pitched tent is never a taut, over-tight one.

Don't pitch your tent under trees that exude sap or will drip interminably in the rain. If you have a choice, try for sun on the tent in the morning and into early afternoon—then shade. If you attain this, along with a prevailing breeze, you are on the way to the ideal campsite. It's always a good idea to check beneath the ground in advance for small but highly annoying sharp roots and rocks. They are a bloody nuisance for many reasons, one being that when trod upon they pierce the fabric. Many experienced campers lay a stout tarp on the floor inside. Others place overlapping sheets of building paper *under* the tent floor (the kind with a tar-like substance sandwiched between heavy water-repellent paper).

Generally it is not wise to pitch the tent too close to the campfire. Many tents have been ruined by so doing. Keep it back out of danger of heat and flying embers. A toy broom is useful for sweeping out pine needles and such.

The high-impact plastic tent stakes are great, but if you must stake down a tent in flinty, rocky, rooty ground, I have yet to see any device surpassing the big "bridge" 12-inch spikes. They twist in, around unyielding objects, and hold. And they can be restraightened.

When you strike camp, be sure to meticulously clean the tent bottom. The top portion of the tent will be folded loosely atop the floor. With two people (preferably) working, fold over about a third of the bottom of the floor, and clean to beat the dickens. Do the same with the other two-thirds, before rolling it up. Your tent will appreciate this.

If it ever leaks, see the nearest tent-and-awning dealer for a supply of his best grade of canvas dressing. Repair (at once) any little rips or tears that develop.

One final word on buying your first tent: When the neophyte asked the leathery veteran outdoorsman how much film he should take along, the veteran's frosty blue eyes twinkled (as they do in all these yarns) and he answered, "Figger the amount you think you need and then quadruple it." Within reason, tent size can be "figgered" the same way. Get 'er bigger than you think you need.

Backpacking Tents

A tent I remember fondly is one that my dad and mother made for me. (People did things like that in those days.) My dad, a manufacturing jeweler by trade, had an inventive turn of mind with camping stuff. This tent vaguely resembled some of today's backpacking models, or "mountain tents." The floor measured about eight by six, and the front was a peak about five feet high running back to about a foot above ground. You erected it by staking the four corners and throwing a line over a tree branch, if in a hurry. If you wanted to be fancy you could add more stakes and, with "Y" branches driven into the ground at strategic points, expand the rear and sides a bit for more room. This simple shelter was a joy. Made of muslin and soaked in naphtha and paraffin, it had a fascinating redolence that I still can recall. That was a real hiking tent, believe me, and I have just talked myself into getting a new one. Mother put on a bobbinet with tie-tapes to bugproof the openings, but I'll get a tent with zippers.

The two-man mountain tents introduced in recent years seem to have reached a lofty plateau of astute development. They're versatile enough to be used at a campsite anywhere, from real wilderness to public campgrounds where one must have privacy. Most of the small, light backpacking models these days are made of nylon or partly of nylon, but with designs that

"breathe" and therefore overcome a former disadvantage of synthetic materials. No one will ever convince me that more than one full-grown man can
be comfortable sleeping in the smallest "two-man" models, but for backpackers and occasional overnighters—an enormously important and growing
segment of the camping public—they're great. Many of them weigh less than
five pounds (including aluminum or fiberglass poles and plastic stakes) and
take hardly any space when rolled up, jammed into a stuff bag and carried on
your packframe or, if you're not carrying much else, right inside the pack.
Some of the roomier ones—even those that feature insulation—weigh substantially less than 10 pounds. In addition to durability, water-repellent nylon
has the advantage of lighter weight than comparably water-repellent cotton.

Water*tight* nylon has the disadvantage of being too efficient. It keeps
moisture *inside* a tent until your own breath condenses and makes it unpleas-
antly clammy and damp. But a compromise—a nylon-cotton combination or a
weave that's tight enough but not too tight—will breathe while also keeping
the rain out. And there are ingenious "tent-in-a-tent" designs that employ
easy-breathing fabric plus a generous outer waterproof fly to keep you dry,
and even these tents are very light in weight.

Some of the backpacking tents, both imports and American-made
brands, have futuristic exterior skeletons (but are nevertheless quick and easy
to put up once you've deciphered the instructions, often written by foreigners
who haven't quite mastered English). Other models employ more traditional
designs and look like the little old two-pole pup tents you may remember

Left: Author's mountain tent, intended to
sleep two, is very comfortable for one large man
like Jobson. Above: Backpacking model
has waterproof nylon fly pitched over fabric that
"breathes" so interior won't collect dampness.

from your most cramped and miserable Boy Scouting days, yet are surprisingly comfortable. They all deserve at least an inspection if you're thinking about buying a shelter for backpacking expeditions.

They are widely available. I examine a lot of them, and I haven't run across a lemon recently. Bear in mind that such a tent should be tough, longlasting, extremely light in weight and, preferably, of a size to accommodate two campers and their gear. What's big enough depends, of course, on your camping life-style. For some backpackers who go it alone, something with a four-by-seven-foot floor and only a little head room may suffice. For other campers, a five-by-seven or six-by-eight floor and enough height for comfortable sitting might be the minimum. In any case, the tent should have a waterproof floor. The front should open wide for campfire enjoyment and should be bugproof. Heavy-duty, easy-working zippers are desirable, and a fitted waterproof fly will not go amiss.

A question I increasingly receive from readers is what the difference is between a mountain tent and a backpacking or hiking tent. Purist-wise, the mountain tents have a lower profile on account of high winds often encountered at mountain-climbing altitudes. They are confining, a nuisance to dress in, and even to sleep in. They hold warmth a trifle better. A backpacking tent can be made lightweight, yet still have respectable headroom. Each of my favorites—both sleep three or four, thus are really adequate for two—have seven feet of headroom, making it more convenient to dress and undress, and if need be, to cook to a reasonable amount.

Basic Two-Man Camp

A discussion of the wonderfully improved two-man mountain tents leads inevitably to a discussion of the two-man camp, which is American as Coney Island redhots and which every camper has to use (comfortably and very pleasurably if he knows how) sooner or later. The term "two-man," of course, just means two people—as often husband and wife or father and son as two old buddies. It's wise for outdoorsmen to know the mechanics and techniques of this particular phase of camping, for while in some ways it resembles other types of camping it has peculiarities unique to itself. Traditionally, the style is highly useful for *true wilderness* camping, though any good campsite lends itself to this versatile way of living afield.

In general, the two-man camp is a highly mobile outfit that can be set up and struck easily and rapidly. The equipment and supplies are lightweight,

Below: Four-way ventilation minimizes condensation of moisture
inside this 5-by-8-foot backpacking tent. Bottom: Tent
with low profile is sensible in high country or windy regions.

often exceedingly so. Thus, most modes of transport are workable: a canoe or other small water craft, light aircraft, bicycle, trail cycle, horse (without the need of an added packhorse), dog team, snowmobile or four-wheel-drive. Finally, it can be carried on the camper's own back by means of a packframe or packboard.

The tent itself weighs only a few pounds, and the maximum weight of the whole outfit is elastic but, ideally, should not exceed 50 pounds for two (exclusive of food), which means 25 pounds for one person's share of the gear, including the weight of the packframe or saddle bags. This is maximum, mind. Most experienced wilderness campers go lighter, and their camps are by no means spartan. Experience teaches the value of eliminating nonessentials. The result is field living as comfortable as one could wish, and at least as healthful as life in the average American home.

Naturally, individual requirements differ. While we have to conform to

Below: Young couple of average height and girth will sleep comfortably in this light backpacker's tent, which can easily be crammed into compact stuff bag and toted with other gear on pack frame.

certain proven·and established procedures, the rules stretch and bend enough to compensate for reasonable personal preferences and a modicum of variation. Take the matter of shelter. In the two-man technique of camping, ideally it's a tent, and I included the weight of a light backpacking tent in my suggestion regarding the maximum poundage to be carried. But some chaps get by with no shelter as such (though they may hastily rig one in an emergency). They lay the old bedroll under the stars and, inhaling the heady fragrance of balsam, drift off to dreamless sleep. This theory is fine, and actually workable under some circumstances—but not for long periods under rigorous North American wilderness conditions.

For summer camping or in regions of very mild climate, some campers use a plastic "tube tent." As the name implies, it's simply a big, long tube of very light plastic, held up by a rope that's run through the tube and tied to a couple of trees. A few strategically placed stones will hold the tube open, giving it a triangular shape as viewed from either end. The transparent ones are most popular, since they let you look up at the trees and stars, and give the illusion of sleeping in the open. Some fellows depend on an even simpler expedient—an extremely lightweight tarp, rigged in one of many fashions. Tubes, tarps and the like do work, but not too well over the long haul. Wind, rain and cold can cause problems, and the average camper sees no need to simulate an emergency when he can have the comfort of a tent.

Many enthusiasts are fond of the Whelen lean-to open-face shelter. This is a wonderful wilderness shelter, as I think I intimated—one of the very best. Its limitation (for me, anyway) is that its most successful use depends upon an elongated fire for maximum comfort in cold weather. It makes for a jolly camp—this lallygagging under cozy shelter, the mellow light of the fire bouncing warmth off the rear of it and onto your back. Snowflakes hissing as they strike cheery flames. I'm very fond of the shelter, as are most who have tried it. But it is seen at its best only in areas with an ample wood supply. Another requirement is a reasonably dependable prevailing breeze.

As a lot of my camping is near or above timberline, where the wood supply is not inexhaustible and a prevailing breeze swaps ends until it seems to prevail from all compass points, and furthermore as I sometimes manage to get into swarms of insects and as I camp in so many different kinds of locales—I prefer a two-man mountain tent as my all-around, multi-purpose shelter. It's generally the basis of the two-man camp.

If a fellow spends much time above timberline, his outfit should also include a small but efficient mountain stove with a spare flask of fuel. Primus is a good make, and there are others. Sleeping bags for this type of camping are of the mummy shape or tapered style and insulated with prime goose down.

(I'll go into more detail about sleeping bags, stoves and other gear in later chapters.) A light plastic ground sheet is handy, and likewise a lightweight rain parka. For this setup, when in timber the best all-around axe is the popular three-quarter size with sheath and small Carborundum stone. Your knife can be the pocket type or a sheath model with its own sharpening stone in a pouch on the sheath. Many feel that an air mattress is superfluous. I do not— and I carry a three-quarter size for this kind of camping. Extra clothing for a week-long trip should include a change of underwear and socks. Enhanced by a down-insulated jacket or vest, the average type and amount of clothing you ordinarily wear in the wilderness ought to suffice. (Again, I'll go into detail about clothing in due course.)

Your packing list should include map, compass, pen light, sun glasses, light binocular, plumber's candle, basic emergency sewing kit, hand mirror, nylon cord, Chap Stick or similar balm, sunburn lotion, first-aid kit (small and well-thought-out), bug repellent, matches in waterproof container, windproof cigarette lighter with spare flints and fuel, soap-impregnated scouring pads, water-strength facial tissues, toilet kit including soap, a few paper towels, small notebook and pencil stub, canteen (optional in some areas, mandatory

Youngster watches and learns as his dad drives stakes; but unless wind is
up, solidly built exterior-frame tent like this doesn't really need stakes or lines.

in others), an old lard pail for tea, plastic cup. A short length of wire is some-times worth its weight in gold. All of these items are considered necessary by a great many experienced go-light campers.

Cooking and eating equipment should be dual-purpose, nested, made of lightweight alloy. Grub will be freeze-dried and dehydrated, mainly—ampli-fied with items such as fruit drink, dry milk, candy, and so on. A wire grill is often useful.

The old notion of going out with a handful of beans, rice, corn meal, oat-meal and a slab of sowbelly is romantic. It sounds like fun, and it *is* fun. I ought to know; I did it for some decades. But in terms of nutrition, the new foods have it all over the old to such a degree it's ludicrous to compare the two. I'll have much more to say about cooking, but here and now I urge you never to consider augmenting the menu with game, fish, fowl or wild plants. That, too, is fun, but counting on it can result in severe hunger pangs. Garner and harvest what comes your way, of course, but *plan* on eating what you bring with you, just as you have to plan on living in a comfortable tent even though you may decide to sleep under the sky some night.

Other Tents

We have by no means exhausted the subject of tents. Another of my favorites is a canoe tent (so-called because it is popular with old-time canoeists) known as the "Explorer." This is an exceedingly picturesque tent—sometimes a bit balky to erect just right, but a faithful, dependable shelter. It is my feeling that every outdoorsman should at one time or another camp in the wilds with an Explorer tent.

As a youth, in the undulating sage mesas, valleys and flats of Nevada, Wyoming and southern Idaho, I slept many a night in the so-called "miner's" tent. This is a fine professional tent, probably the most used (after the A-wall) by knowledgeable men making their living in the field, off-road. It looks just like an Egyptian pyramid: square on the bottom, four corners rising to a sharp peak. It can be pitched, quickly, by tossing one rope over a branch, af-ter staking the bottom. Or one pole in the center, inside, will keep it taut. Outside scissor poles work, too. It is a most adaptable and versatile tent. I keep one around and these days use it on big-game hunting trips to keep spare gear and supplies out of the A-wall cooking and sleeping tents.

Modern tents are great. The very best-designed and -made of all time. A few years ago my ol' hunting partner, the late Tom Billiard, and I, after an ex-

Pyramid-like "miner's" tent (top left and right)
is old-fashioned, perhaps, but still one of the most
adaptable and versatile designs. It can be
pitched fast by tossing rope at top over a tree branch,
then staking the bottom. Alternate methods are
to use scissor poles, as shown, or single interior
center pole. Multipurpose fly (above) is
rigged as deep lean-to, in classic manner of Baker
tents, forming airy and spacious shelter.

At beach campsite on lee side of bluffs, family has pitched commodious pop-up tent that combines features of long quonset and bubble-shaped igloo styles.

pedition into the Barren Grounds, for some reason decided life would not be worth living if we did not travel the length of the Yukon's mighty Tagish and Bennet lakes in (get this) a 17-foot canoe. These lakes are *not* canoe lakes. Maybe we had dined too well, or something. Anyway we had a pal, bush pilot Captain Ray Simcoe, fly us to the end and leave us. We made it, after some harrowing adventures (some of which actually turned Tom's hair noticeably whiter), but the point is we had one of those igloo-shaped pop-up tents made with an integral fiberglass frame. It was a joy to erect and strike, and was bug- and weatherproof. We had some terrible winds, with rain and sleet lashing that little tent bitterly. It came through like a thoroughbred.

While most folks think of the umbrella or cottage family camping tents for only conventional public campground use, don't get the notion that is all they're good for. There is so much quality designed and fabricated into these tents that they can take unbelievable abuse and do it like a champion. And those spring-loaded alloy frames! Well, a few years ago my wife and I went into Bonnet Plume Lake in the north-central Yukon Territory near the North-west Territories border. For testing a new conventional family-type tent, we fetched one at great expense, air freight being what it is up North. There was

Outside their safari tent, author and wife examine wildlife bones found
in African bush. Jobson notes that he should have tied bright rags on guy ropes.

a storm with winds of hurricane force which leveled most of the tents in
camp, ruined the rest, tore some to shreds. Our little family tent with spring-
loaded frame took it in stride. It gave like a lithe young willow that still
stands after the mighty oak has fallen.

Not long ago, the safari operators with whom my wife and I hunted in
Africa in 1968 asked me to design and/or recommend the ideal safari tent for
their cherished clients—no more than two persons to a tent. As they wanted
some 15 of these units, and as they said "ideal," you can see it was a responsibility. By ideal I took it that they meant best for their area. Anyway, I had at
it, and what I arrived at was very similar to the traditional old British East Africa safari tent. The tent was akin to a common wall or A-wall, but with five-
foot six-inch wall height, and an eight-foot ridge height. With 843 cubic feet
of livable space, the shelters measured twelve-feet six-inches wide, ten feet
deep, with a door five by seven feet. Three 60-inch-by-20-inch nylon screen
windows provide excellent ventilation. Of 8.53-ounce high-quality cotton
fabric, with 10.10-ounce floor and heavy-duty zippers throughout, it is one
rugged outfit. In the rear of the tent is a small private roomette for portable
toilet and folding bath tub. An outsize fly (tarp) is rigged over the tent, ex-

tending out just a wee bit in the rear, but a full eight feet in front, making a shady "veranda" under which one can loll about in safari (director's) chairs, play cards, read a pocket mystery, or simply watch game with a binocular, and glory in the wondrous acacia trees silhouetted against the incredible opalescent African sunsets. We specified spring-loaded aluminum framing for these safari tents, and at last word the tents are performing nobly in the midst of Cape buffalo herds, prowling pachyderms, nosy hyenas and inquisitive lions. I am relieved it is over. The air freight alone was over $1,500!

I mention this caper for the reason that I am fairly certain that for heavyweight camping (car, boat, 4x4, plane) a safari-type tent has got to be among the world's best, provided you have room to pitch it, the necessary muscle to erect and strike it (not beyond the abilities of a young couple), and the means to pack it around. The British of East Africa are among the world's most proficient campers, if you are impressed with efficiency, total field comfort, healthy camp conditions. We might take a page from their book. I would like to see more of these authentic safari-type shelters complete with extended fly for those who can use them in North America.

Cunningly designed tents often are a compromise and have definite limitations. An *ideal* tent would be so versatile as to be perfect for camping in the Arctic, the Amazon jungle, Dismal Swamp, Washington rain forest, Sonora Desert. It would be inexpensive and durable. You could pack it on your back for sleeping one or two; or you might toss it into the family sedan for sleeping a family of six. What with all this newfangled technology, I would not collapse on the floor in giddy surprise if such an ideal tent eventually came about. Until then, I am going to keep on buying tents to fit the distinctly different types of camping. But only one at a time.

3

Other Shelters, Permanent or Wheeled

The Log Cabin

If all of your camping is highly mobile, then you probably don't even think of cabins in connection with it. But at a permanent campsite a log cabin can be a delight, and constructing one is not as difficult as you might imagine, although for the average guy it certainly was difficult prior to the advent of the hand-held chain saw. This marvelous tool, easily held and controlled by a single man, cuts logs into sections, rips them lengthwise (half-sections often are useful in cabin-building), saws lumber on the spot for flooring, roof sheathing, door and window frames, and so forth. Fitting logs together by truing their parallel lengths is a cinch for a chain saw, and being able to closely fit the logs is of great importance.

With close-fitting logs, the only chinking required is a thin, narrow strip of fluffy insulation (fiberglass is good) to accommodate the slight expansion and shrinkage of the logs through the years. Many chaps still prefer to chink with some type of mortar, on the exterior expecially, but it's mostly for appearance's sake.

Log cabins are a unique sort of structure, and even with a set of cold, hard blueprints you can improvise and revise here and there. But you should prepare a detailed sketch of your log cabin-to-be or acquire a set of professional plans from which to work.

Some fellows like to build a cabin on a concrete slab; others prefer massive wood beams resting on concrete "pillars" or rock pylons. Either way, it's important to get your wood up and off the damp ground to prevent rot and discourage termites.

Level the first tier like a billiard table. Then make certain each following tier is level before proceeding with the next. This will save you a world of trouble for a quarter-inch discrepancy can finally add up to a full 12 inches of vacant atmosphere. When you go to add the roof, a thing like this could discourage you. In a region of exceptionally heavy snowfall it is best to have a sharp, chalet-type pitch to the roof.

During the 30 years my tiny wife and I have been consorting (with benefit of legal and ecclesiastical wedlock, of course) we have grown inordinately fond of log cabins. We have contentedly set up housekeeping in a great many of them during those happy years: in New York's Adirondack Mountains, the Appalachians of northern Georgia, the Berkshires of Massachusetts-Connecticut, a moss-covered duo in Ontario. Plus a veritable cornucopia of them in the West: the Black Hills, Wyoming, Colorado, Arizona, California's Sierras, Oregon, Washington, British Columbia, the Yukon Territory, and Alaska.

It's hard to decide which cabin we liked best, but a nice span of wilderness life was in one on the bank of the Big Minam River in the Eagle Cap Wilderness of Oregon's Wallowa Mountains. We would sit on the porch on a cool evening and listen to the tinkle of the glass-clear Big Minam. We'd watch weary salmon—300 long miles from the sea—and Dolly Varden and steelhead trout. On a few larger rocks above water we observed the little gray water ouzels pump themselves up and down, then casually walk into the swift water and feed on the bottom, still walking! They emerged as dry as a Mojave dinosaurian bone. On the far bank, two "tame" mink passed several times a day, with their peculiar rolling gait, and eventually we saw their offspring, too. In the cliffs 300 yards or so back from the river, bull elk bugled in the frosty months of September and October.

There were no phones, no roads, no radio, no TV, no city noise, no interruptions, no fret, fuss, or bother. Months slipped by. One way to fully enjoy life is in your own cozy log cabin under the big sky.

The Shake Roof

Many discerning outdoorsmen feel that the finest and most appropriate topping for a cabin is that ultimate of roofs, the genuine shake roof. It blends in with woodsy surroundings but is pretty and practical most anyplace. Its durability is astonishing. It easily outlasts corrugated steel. Years ago I ran across abandoned cabins so old the sidewall logs had rotted away—but the shakes were intact.

There are shakes and then there are shakes. I feel that the best shakes are split of Western red cedar, called by some arborvitae, and by botanists *Thuja plicata*. It is a durable, light, strong wood, with a rather fine grain and a pleas-

Above: Handsome log cabin, with stone chimney and shake roof, is chinked with mortar and insulated. Such a structure is more than permanent camp in the woodlands; it's comfortable enough to become builder's home. Left: At Canadian log camp, woodsman disdains mortar but chinks walls with moss.

antly aromatic odor. Its complete lack of pitch or resin makes it resistant to fire. A sort of yellow-brown when fresh-split, it turns an appealing silvery gray in a year or so. It absorbs very little rain water because splitting separates the fibers while leaving the wood-cell walls intact. Also, the many grooves act as water-conducting channels, so a shake roof sheds downpours. It even insulates your cabin. The peculiar cellular structure retards passage of heat and cold. Now the good news: Shakes add tremendously to your roof's strength. Overlapping and interlacing, they become structural components of the building.

With froe and mallet, I have split so many shakes in my time that I now take a spectator's view of personal shake splitting. I make do with commercial shakes that are handsplit and resawn. These are beautiful shakes to work with and give a rugged texture to the roof, with heavy butt-lines.

Other types of shakes are taper-split, which means you split from alternate ends of the block with your froe and mallet; and straight-split, meaning the shakes are split from the same end of the block. It may be my personal preference (and I advise you to examine several types) but I think you'll find the handsplit and resawn best for up-to-date wilderness roofs.

Shakes are not uniform like other types of shingles. Generally running from 18 to 32 inches, they vary in width and, to a lesser degree, in thickness. Some have a slightly different color or texture, giving the roof a fetching handcrafted appearance. Shakes should always be of perfectly clear stock—no pins or knots and all heartwood (no sapwood). They should not be narrower than four or five inches nor wider than 14.

The roof deck, or sheathing, can be either solid or spaced one-by-fours or one-by-fives. There should be sufficient roof pitch to insure drainage and prevent wily mountain zephyrs from sneakily blowing snow or rain under the shake ends. The minimum pitch must be one-sixth, or a four-inch vertical rise for every 12 inches of horizontal run. It is not advisable to expose to the weather more than 13 inches of a 32-inch shake, 10 inches for a 24-inch, seven for an 18-inch.

When starting to lay shakes at the eave line, a 36-inch-wide strip of 30-pound roofing felt should be laid over the sheathing. The starter row of shakes can be doubled or even tripled. After each row of shakes is completed, an 18-inch-wide strip (at least) of 30-pound roofing felt should be installed over the upper portion of the shakes, extending over on the sheathing, too. Shakes should be apart about one-quarter inch to allow for expansion, with spaces off-set, of course. There are special shakes to cover the ridges and hips—usually two shakes cemented to form an angle.

Proper nailing is vital. Always use hot-dipped zinc-coated nails, never ordinary galvanized nails. And never drive them until the heads are into the shakes. Just have the head meet the shake, no more. Two nails to a shake, they should bite at least half an inch into the sheathing boards. Two-inch (6d) nails usually suffice.

It's best to lay a temporary board (plank) over your shake roof if you must walk on it. Roof coatings (many vended as protective coatings) should never be applied to a genuine shake roof. Shakes need no coating and, in fact, it could shorten the life of cedar roofing.

Station-Wagon Camping

A few years ago my wife and I took a 26-state, 11,000-mile fact-finding reconnaissance of camping facilities in our central and north-central states. We drove and camped in a station wagon. Where conventional auto camping is concerned, they are extremely versatile, particularly with family outdoorsmen. With the rear seat of our wagon folded down flat to floor level, it has a neat cargo space eight feet by five feet four inches, excluding the fender wells.

When we bought it, the first thing we did was to have a custom mattress made to cover the rear from the back of the front seat to the closed tailgate, with slight cutouts for the fender wells. This is a foam rubber covered with light canvas, and it set us back nearly 50 bucks. I recoiled when I got the bill, but have never regretted buying it, for it has payed for itself many times over. When we decide to go light and fast (and often we do), we merely toss a couple of sleeping bags over the mattress for Real Good Sleeping.

Toward the tailgate, out of the way, we set up our station-wagon cooler or sometimes a little 12-volt refrigerator. A small grub box, a one-burner and a two-burner camp stove, a small cutting board, a tarp, a lantern, etc., and we're all set. More often than not we use the opened tailgate for both work space and dining table. For privacy at night we simply put up a few sheets of newspaper secured with plastic tape. If I encouraged her, my hard-working wife would make curtains, but the newspaper is satisfactory, what the heck. We had a set of window screens for insect protection, but they wore out; now I carry either a roll of fine copper mesh or bobbinet and, when we need a bulwark against ravenous mosquitos and such, we cut generous panels to fit outside, and we fasten them in place with tape. We have a reading lamp with an extension that plugs into the cigarette-lighter socket. By and large we always arrive home as rested as when we left. This all may sound a bit spartan and bleak to some, but it isn't, really.

With mattress of proper size, station-wagon camping
can be almost luxurious for one or two people,
and there's room to stow clothing, gear and provisions.

Other trips, for example over the Alaska Highway, see us carrying tents. One favorite of ours is the station-wagon umbrella-type which closely fits to the opened back of the wagon. We are exceedingly fond of this setup. In the tent we cook, eat, and lounge around in canvas folding chairs with arm rests. It is quite an elaborate setup, with a folding table and plenty of bright gas-lantern illumination. We sleep in the wagon, as it is so comfortable and convenient it would be foolish not to use it.

On other trips, where it is impossible to get the wagon all the way into the desired camping area, we use other types of tents and pack them along with the bedrolls, grub and other equipment—on our backs if it isn't too far. If it is, we arrange for horses or other labor-saving devices. For this type of camping, we have one tent for sleeping and a smaller one for storage, which keeps things tidy and uncomplicated. If it rains frequently, I sometimes rig a tarp to cook under. In cold weather we use an A-wall tent with a wood-burning sheepherder stove and sometimes a flameless tent heater.

A station wagon is ideal for a lengthy wilderness trip where you are going to have an impressive load of gear and supplies to be taken in far from road's-end via bush plane, pack train or boat. It will carry a tremendous amount of weight if it is equipped with the proper springs, shocks and tires.

Another good feature of a modern station wagon is the relatively large space available on the roof. There you can install an outsized luggage rack.

Station-wagon lunches can be elaborate if you turn tailgate into kitchen
featuring cutting board, one- or two-burner camp stove, plastic
food containers and cooler chest or small 12-volt portable refrigerator.

You can carry a boat or a canoe or install a folding car-top tent. Canvas boots
are available that fit onto the back of the open wagon, affording even more
interior room. There are over-the-counter pads, mattresses and air mattresses
to fit most wagons, so there really is no need to have one custom-made. Indeed, many campers use the air mattresses from their camp bedrolls. If, with
all this, you have a little too much luggage in the back for a comfortable bed,
transfer it to the front seat during overnight stops.

The items needed either first or most frequently will be more easily
available if loaded last. This is something every individual has to work out for
himself, and getting "shook down" may take a day or so of actually doing it
on the road before things are efficiently organized.

Most modern station wagons are built low to the ground, with little road
clearance. They're generally meant for hard-surface or good gravel roads. If
you have to go a short way on tough dirt roads, avoid the ruts. Get the wheels
up out of them, if you can, as it is easy to lose the transmission or rear end.
Expert drivers with much back-country experience can take a modern station
wagon into some surprisingly rugged country. Three pals of mine from Washington, in their annual quest for coho salmon and steelhead trout, drive a station wagon over the casually maintained 300-odd dirt-and-gravel miles from
Williams Lake, B.C., to Bella Coola on the coast. When we went over it I
used a Land Rover 109.

52

Camping trailers like those pictured at right and below have many advantages. Self-contained, they fold up simply and compactly, and they're easy to tow. By comparison with pickup coaches and full-sized travel-trailers, they're also inexpensive.

Camp Trailers

One of the deservedly popular easy-to-tow "camp" trailers is the folding-tent variety. (I refer here to the general type with a metal-alloy or fiberglass body and fabric shelter section—not the expandable type which, though good, is something else.) Among its advantages is convenience in towing and handling. You don't need special rear-view mirrors, brakes or a complex hitch. Such trailers are remarkably light in weight and usually present no towing or handling problem for the family-size automobile. This is a delightful feature while cruising open turnpikes, on long hill ascents and descents and in negotiating rough back-country roads. Folded for traveling, they are no larger than the average utility hauling trailer, so the camper doesn't have to go to great lengths equipping his automobile for heavy-duty towing. You can take them where you can take no standard-size travel trailer or lofty pickup coach.

For what you get, these camping trailers can be considered inexpensive.

The camping trailer is part house trailer and part tent. Many people appreciate the convenience of having their hauling trailer and a well-designed, commodious tent in one inseparable, functional unit. If you enjoy family-style tent camping, chances are excellent you'll be happy with a camping trailer. For family auto camping, they are generally more convenient than the straight tent setup. All you need is *self-contained in one superbly engineered unit.* The canvas portion (the main living quarters) unfolds from the neat trailer "box" and everything is at your fingertips. Full-size beds or bunks are immediately ready for use, the bottle-gas stove ready to go. There is an ice box or refrigerator. Some models have private toilet facilities and water-storage tanks. It is not exactly conventional tent camping nor is it travel-trailer or pickup-coach camping. It is a way of life of its own.

Of course, the folding tent takes a few minutes to erect and to strike

Right: John and Ann
Jobson pose for
snapshot at entrance
of camp trailer.
This one is
single-level, or
"off-the-ground,"
type. Below:
Interior of roomy
model holds cupboard,
sink and stove.

when you leave. On the other hand, it is much faster and more convenient than unloading the old family sedan, gathering all the related gear, setting up a separate tent and so forth. The average camping-trailer family can be halfway through its evening meal while the straight family-type tent campers are still struggling to set up.

Camp trailers come in a variety of designs, so examine as many as possible. Most are good and not overpriced but they do differ in layout, especially in the matter of storage. Entry doors can be from the side or rear; window placement varies. The choice is something that should be talked over with the Little Woman, for she is usually the one who does the major portion of the household chores. The ladies are shrewd and far-seeing on these matters.

In general there have been two basic types of camp trailers. One is the "off-the-ground" (one-level) plan. The whole living portion of the structure is literally off the ground. These usually are the most expensive and are generally far easier to erect and make level. Some models are up to 15 or so feet wide and can sleep 10 people! They usually afford more storage space, and the trailer body is a bit larger than that of other models.

The "on-the-ground" (split-level) models are generally lower priced— some amazingly so, for what you get. Bed (sleeping quarters) and living space is off the ground, contained in the trailer body. But the rest of the structure resembles a conventional tent. Though the canvas portion is attached, making one integral unit, you still require a tent *site* because it is erected, for practical purposes, just like an ordinary tent.

Great things, the camping trailers. They have come to fill a special niche in our scheme of living afield.

Pickup Camper Coaches

I recall a good many years ago when, on goose-hunting trips and such out on the Dakota prairie, we enthusiastically lashed a haystack tarp over and around the stake body of a truck, tossed in our odoriferous bedrolls, a crude ice box, lantern, gasoline pump-up stove, an incredibly ill-assorted collection of provender swiped from the kitchens of our long-suffering mothers, and merrily took off just as if we had good sense. That was our "coach." (I might add, the male parent who owned the truck would have taken an apoplectic view of our creating an outhouse structure on the rear of his working truck.)

Since those carefree days I have camped with most specimens of manufactured pickup coach. The first were a bit rudimentary. They weren't designed as astutely as current ones: There was waste space; some weren't insulated properly; most were far too heavy. So we had to beef up a regular pickup truck to carry them. We'd install heavier springs and shocks, truck-type wheels and tires, and so forth. We got by. Now, "Detroit" has heeded the call. You can buy a pickup truck specifically engineered to carry a camper coach. The tires, wheels, springs and shocks are correct. The engine is a *bomb!* The radiator and fan are extra-capacity. More important, the gear ratio and drive train are so proper as to be diabolically clever.

Because the coach is self-contained, you are not necessarily dependent upon organized campgrounds. You can stop and can go as you see fit. Right now. If darkness should overtake you, a reasonably wide, legal place in the road will serve as an emergency stop. Or a residential street. Or the parking lot of a supermarket. A time or two I have driven into the parking lot of the state police and was made welcome.

A typical modern pickup coach is a weatherproof, insectproof shelter designed with the same skill a yacht builder uses to compact luxurious surroundings in *minimum* space. The skin is metal alloy, the interior often wood paneling. Windows are plentiful, screened, with crank-operated opening like metal casement windows in modern homes. The coach is insulated so it is comparatively cool in hot weather and snug in cold temperatures.

For a 15,000-mile camping trip through New England, the South and several Midwestern states, I designed and tailored to my needs the ideal "package" coach and pickup truck. It had to fulfill several requirements. For one thing, I knew that occasionally I'd be in the heavy traffic of the great Eastern metropolitan centers. In these circumstances I do not like to drive

Here are two camper-coach
models mounted on the truck beds
of pickups. These are both
of the slide-in kind,
which can be taken off standard
pickup bed so that truck
can be put to non-camping use.

Above: Midway between station wagon and pickup coach in terms of space, this rig turns light truck into miniature home. And it can be mounted with boat rack. Right: Chassis-mounted coach, though less popular than slide-in type, is rugged and spacious.

something that lumbers along like a milk cow with the colic. When I tromp down on Old Nellie I want to feel that seat hit me in the back. (I think being able to do so is much safer—that's my theory, at least, and I have driven a lot of miles in my time.) We were going to travel now and then on fast toll roads and I wanted to keep up with the traffic flow. But I knew I'd be spending more time on relatively narrow, winding and deceptively steep roads and lanes of the Appalachian Mountains.

I picked a 10½-foot slide-in coach for the living quarters. (Two types of full-size pickup camper coaches are currently popular. The "slide-in" is just that: It can be slid in or out of a standard pickup bed, freeing the pickup for other uses. Another type—less popular now but preferred by a few—is the chassis mount, which is a coach permanently secured to the truck chassis.)

Interior view of luxurious chassis-mounted coach shows stove and oven, sink, refrigerator, lamp, cupboards, end of one of the bunks, and curtained extension at front (over truck's cab) which contains one of the other bunks.

You can bet mine is comfortable, for on a journey of such magnitude I like to sleep and eat "like at home" with no cutting corners. So in this 10½-foot coach we have a full kitchen with gas refrigerator and oven range (exhaust fan and canopy with light above the stove), shower and toilet with holding tank for wastes, thermostat-controlled heater (a safe one), twin propane bottles with gauges, electric automatic-pump water system, hot-water tank (not a gadget), twin glass-lined water tanks (one in reserve), gasoline saddle tanks for truck fuel totaling 55 gallons of gasoline, electric and propane lights inside the coach, twin sinks—and sleeping space for six. The truck is air-conditioned, with a boot cut-through to the coach. The coach has more cabinet-closet space than we need (and I took along five hunting rifles, a shotgun, a full-size office typewriter and a modest library).

Here are two early-vintage pickup coaches. Home-built, picturesque
log-cabin coach at right was woodsman's rolling hunting camp.
The other van, still older, was Erle Stanley Gardner's famous "house car."

Travel Trailers and Motor Homes

Years ago, when they were largely homemade, we called them "house cars."
It was an art, the converting of a truck or heavy-duty automobile into a walk-
through, self-contained and self-propelled home on wheels.

The most intriguing one I ever heard of, a rig that still sends me into a
giddy euphoria of vicarious warmth, was a house car owned many years ago
by my friend, the late Erle Stanley Gardner. It was a picturesque outfit. To
the best of my memory, the base was a Model T or Dodge truck, a sort of
walk-through type that might well have been the prototype of the splendid
vans of today, although to compare them would be akin to saying a Ford tri-
motor plane is like a 707. Erle's unit was by no means streamlined, being a
lofty affair that rose to commendable heights, with a terrific road clearance.
It had plenty of nonsafety glass windows, and Erle equipped it with an ice
box, means to carry lots of water, groceries and other supplies. It had a camp
stove (as I recall) and a bed (convertible, I think).

At that time Erle was living in Ventura County, Calif., and had a thriv-
ing law practice. Whenever he could escape, he would top-off supplies, check
the gear and head for his beloved California desert. By day he'd explore.

Come evening he'd camp. Parked in the purple shadows, he could watch the beautiful, bizarre Joshua trees etched against a glorious Mojave sunset (of which, incidentally, there is none more vivid unless it might be an East African sunset). Erle had room in that cozy, secure, self-contained nest for a typewriter, and it is my feeling he created some of his early stories camped by a remote waterhole in the vast, lonely, colorful desert.

So many worthwhile goodies have blossomed on the camping scene in the past decade or so that terminology and definitions are getting away on us. Old-fashioned "house trailers" are now "travel trailers."

A modern *motor home* is not a pickup camper coach, van home, mobile home, travel trailer, camping trailer or expandable trailer. It is a unique outfit superficially resembling a bus. (Alas, it eats gas like one.) However, inside, the better ones are as plush and self-contained as a suite at the Greenbriar Hotel. The exterior can be from approximately 20 to 30 feet long.

I am often asked how these units drive. Are they difficult to maneuver? The answer is no, I do not find them so. In fact, now I would as soon drive one as a car, or pickup. They are full-power—power steering, brakes—and they have automatic transmission. The truck chassis on which they're constructed is the cab-over type, with the engine underneath, between the cab seats, which are the comfortable aircraft or bus type. The windshield is a big wraparound, like that of a transcontinental bus, and as you are seated close to it (no engine or hood in front) you have an extraordinary view. The rigs cruise very stably. My wife carefully walks back and forth in ours, in transit. The ride is exceedingly comfortable. You have no sensation of a "truck" ride.

A good motor home will have a fiberglass or alloy body, a complete kitchen, large refrigerator, gas range, twin sinks, stove-canopy with exhaust blower, hand water pump, pressure water lines and hot and cold faucets in the kitchen, worlds of cabinet space, a bathroom with flush toilet and shower, holding tank for wastes, enormous gasoline tanks, air-conditioning both from the truck engine (12-V) and a separate air-conditioner powered by the big self-contained light plant (115-V). This plant is started by pressing a button on the dashboard and is fueled from the truck's regular tanks.

It also has a separate bedroom, a lush divan in the living room, dining nook with picture window, at least two full-sized closets with full-length mirrors. Also, either twin propane tanks or a single "gigantic" one. You can use the twin 12-V lights instead of bothering with the big generator plant and the 115-V lights or air conditioner. You will probably have one or more propane lights, too. You also get a forced-air automatic gas heater and thick, resilient carpeting.

Such splendor does not come cheap. With the current trend toward

These photos show several popular versions of the largest homes on wheels. Full-sized "motor home," which looks somewhat like a bus, may be 20 or even 30 feet long. It eats gas, but is surprisingly maneuverable as well as luxurious. Travel trailer is, of course, less costly and can be hitched to family car and unhitched when not in use. It can also be coupled to a "4WD" truck that may serve as detachable rolling spike camp.

small, gas-saving rigs, what the future holds for these big gas-gobbling lovelies is anybody's guess. A lot of the plants making them have drastically cut production, and some have folded.

I learned a long time ago that the most rewarding driving for me, with a motor home, is away from any sort of hardtop. I'm not kidding. You take a modern rig with duals on the rear, anti-spin drive, a good powerful engine, proper transmission plus a high center, and you can go some surprising places! Not only on back-country gravel and dirt single-lane wagon tracks but off *any* sort of road or trail. An example: Not long ago Fred T. Huntington, a big-game hunter and president of R. C. B. S. (which manufactures reloading equipment), invited my wife and me to a little-known area in northeastern Wyoming out near the "town" of Recluse, to shoot prairie dogs. Fred spoke in glowing terms of a dog town that had not yet been found by government poisoners. We went there straightaway, in a 30-foot motor home which we were using at the time. A regular safari left the ranch of Bill Matheney—a procession of four-wheel-drive vehicles, with the Jobsons tagging along. They solicitously invited us to ride with them, explaining that we were going into

"4WD country," but I demurred, saying we'd go as far as we could, and that way would have our rest room, ice, cook stove and, if needed, air conditioning. When they angled off a cow track leading through virgin sage, they politely pulled up but I waved them on. The upshot was we all went (as I figured we would) miles from the nearest road, up and down, and arrived unscathed at the dog village. Only one place gave me pause—a dry wash—as I thought I might get hung up not from lack of traction or power but from the steep banks. The rig took it in stride. Many years ago I drove a similar outfit to the end of connected roads in North America and did not stop there. We went over frozen tundra, at times through eight inches of snow, smack into our big-game hunting camp—the first time it had been done. I only give these examples to show that it *can* be done.

There is no need to baby a good motor home. If you're not familiar with off-highway and off-road driving, believe me, there is not a whole lot to it. I am not referring to the sort of hoodlum-type "driving" wherein irresponsible sophomoric types ruin hillsides and watersheds with various RV's (recreation vehicles), causing ecological damage. Begin at first by leaving the hardtop and trying gravel roads. After you see how easy it is to manage on those, learning to do without the white center line and shoulder markers, try some narrower gravel ones, and then dirt. Then pull off 100 yards or so for a campsite. About dirt roads: If it looks like rain, best forgo them because on some (especially Western gumbo) a few drops of rain can turn the surface and subsurface of a dirt road into something beyond belief. Even ranchers can't get out, with a tractor.

Whether or not you plan to forsake freeway-type roads, buy yourself a couple of good jacks for tire changing, if and when. Get a "handyman" jack, first of all, as these have multiple uses. With a length of cable, you can use one as a winch to pull your rig from a tight spot. When changing a rear wheel, use the handyman to hoist up the side of the rig a bit not only to make it easier to jack up the axle, but to clear the wheel-well area. There are hundreds of cases where a good fellow has jacked up his motor home and found (after taking off the wheel lugs) that he couldn't remove the wheel. For the axle, obtain a big hydraulic truck jack with a much higher rating (safety factor) than the salesman may think you need, because a fully loaded motor home is *heavy*.

Ladies tell me their number-one hint is to coddle the refrigerator. Don't depend on the door-fastener the factory furnished. Use it, but contrive another, because it is an awful mess to have the door fly open on a rough road. Use cardboard or plastic boxes to hold food, and fit them snug to prevent undue jostling and banging about inside the fridge. Carry lots of spare water in

GI-type cans (either metal or plastic), folding plastic containers or milk cans. When parked at campsites, place them outside in the shade and use the conveniences that you've paid for.

There is no harm in carrying a bucket and a dipper to sample uncontaminated stream and lake water; if doubtful of its quality, run it through the filter or use a purifier. (About filters: Some years ago I saw a filter salesman take a bucket of fluid from a Mexico City open sewer, process it with a little filter he had, and drink it! That may be carrying things a bit far.)

It is a wise investment to buy one or two extra propane tanks, to take "back in" when you reach a wilderness area. In transit, put your spare propane tanks in cardboard or wooden boxes and leash them down. One of these juggernauting around on a steep, winding grade is sort of like looking up at the Empire State Building and seeing a 500-pound safe plunging right at you. In camp put them outside in the shade. All this is for a really long stay—normally, the two filled propane tanks will see you through. It's just that if you do run out, far from a source, in the middle of the night, you will wish you had the third tank. As for my emphasis on having plenty of water—like money, it is hard to have too much.

With trailer unhitched at National Forest site, part of family can laze around camp while others use car for errands or sight-seeing drive.

4

Sleeping Gear

Sleeping Bags

I don't know who invented the sleeping bag but I suspect it was the ancient
Eskimos who discovered that if they made an enclosed bag of caribou hides it
was far warmer than an equal weight of hides used as blankets. I learned early
that when I commandeered a couple of Mother's wool comforters they
worked about five times as efficiently for me afield if I likewise borrowed
oversize safety pins (we called them horse-blanket pins), then folded over the
bottom and side edges of the comforters and pinned them securely. That way,
body heat was largely retained or, depending upon how you look at it, the debilitating chill was effectively barred from entering. And that is the simple
principle of the modern and highly efficient sleeping bag.

Once you have the shelter of your choice, probably the next most important item of general camp gear is the sleeping bag. The matter of obtaining
solid, sound sleep cannot be too strongly emphasized. My own experience has
taught me that a person can endure certain appalling inconveniences in camp
and along the trail and still have a reasonably good time. He can be cold and
wet and experience extraordinary physical stress, for days on end, in an emergency. He can exist on the most primitive food in insufficient amount and still
enjoy himself to a degree—provided that each night he gets his full quota of
comfortable rest. If he doesn't get this rest, he will be knocked out in a couple
of days. These harsh conditions are, of course, rather unlikely as far as the average camper is concerned, but they are not impossible.

If you must economize on some item of camping equipment, do not
make it your bedding. I don't mean to suggest that a person should run hog-
wild and buy the most expensive models available. It would be money wasted
to purchase an arctic-weight down-filled bag for desert, beach or other sum-
mery, warm-weather conditions. But likewise it would not be prudent to hit
the Yukon with a $9.98 cotton-filled wonder. In choosing the proper bag,
specify a filling of fluffy man-made fibers (such as Dacron fiberfill II) or North-

ern waterfowl down (goose down is best) in a weight that will give you a margin of safety for unexpectedly low temperatures.

If you plan to be camping in Jackson Hole, Wyo., in August, you could reasonably expect the nights to sometimes hit 32° (or freezing). Select a bag the makers say will assure warm sleep at 20°, *at least*. There are good reasons for this, among them the fact that some individuals sleep warmer (or colder) than others. There are all sorts of chill-factor variables, even including humidity and altitude. Then, too, some folks sleep in the raw, some with heavy flannel pajamas or nighties and wool socks. Again, you might experience an unseasonable change to unusually cold weather (it happens often in the mountains). So, as the Scouts say, "Be Prepared."

In general, the larger a bag is, the better. You can shift and turn at night without having the whole bag roll with you.

Your bag should have a slide fastener along one side; some zippers run clear around the bottom and this is very good. Check to see if the bag has an insulated tube or flap running inside along the entire zipper length. Zippers without this added feature admit cold air. In camp, try to air your bag daily, or at least every other day—as in use the bag will acquire moisture, the deadly enemy of effective insulation.

Here are two rectangular sleeping bags, both with full-length side zippers and other typical modern features. Bag at top has flap that can be propped up as fly over sleeper's head. Bottom bag has removable down-filled liner.

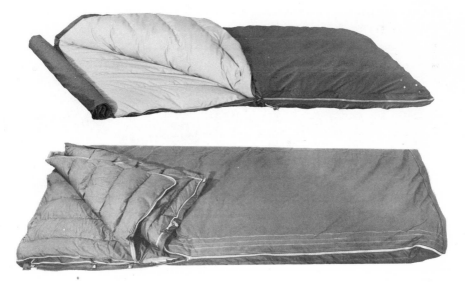

Bags insulated with Kapok—or even wool batting—are about dead. The man-made fibers employed today for popular sleeping bags are very good indeed. They are nonallergenic, mothproof, mildewproof, relatively inexpensive, durable, and capable of keeping you sufficiently warm even under rigorous conditions. For average camping they are simply ideal.

The Queen of Fillings for cold-weather bags remains prime northern goose and certain other waterfowl down. It is the warmest, weight for weight, of any sleeping-bag insulation. Among its disadvantages is that it's expensive (original cost), it can mildew, and one of life's more frustrating chores is trying to thoroughly dry, in the field, a down bag that has been completely soaked. Just the thought of it makes me crochety as a folk singer without his guitar. The experience is enough to give a brass Buddha the shingles. Nonetheless, I would be doing you a disservice if I did not strongly advise you to consider down for northern and high-mountain fall and winter use.

Where camping requires minimum weight, such as backpacking and mountain climbing, the lighter semi-mummy-shaped bag is popular. On these the zipper is often short and in the center of the bag rather than along the side and bottom. New designs zip together in pairs. Some of these bags merely cover the legs and hips, and you sleep in your down jacket.

About blankets: Some may prefer them instead of a sleeping bag, but personally I think this a sour notion. If you do use blankets, get the fluffy,

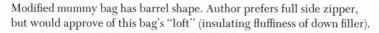

Modified mummy bag has barrel shape. Author prefers full side zipper,
but would approve of this bag's "loft" (insulating fluffiness of down filler).

long-napped ones—not a hard weave such as military surplus that is designed for long wear rather than maximum warmth.

Let me describe my own fiber bag: I like about five pounds of improved Dacron fiberfill II, a heavy 12.22 duck cover and a flannel liner. My bag is 39 inches by 85 inches, has a full-length weather-sealed zipper, so the bag can be aired daily, and it has box edges. The box edges are important to adults and tall teenagers because they prevent cramped feet. (There are campers who dislike the mummy and even the semi-mummy styles because, to them, sound sleep means plenty of leg room for tossing and turning.)

For storage between trips, I unroll our bags, fold them loosely (over about twice), sprinkle with moth flakes and dot with a few moth balls. Before leaving on a trip I air them thoroughly. I spoke previously of airing afield, and (this cannot be stressed too highly) most bag failures occur afield because they weren't aired. Unzip your bag and air every chance you get—either draped on a rope or over a branch or bush. A dry bag is a healthy bag and a perspiration-soaked bag is an abomination. You can be miserable (and can get ill) in a damp sleeping bag.

Periodically, your sleeping bags should be cleaned. In the case of the expensive down bags, I send mine back to the manufacturer for dry-cleaning. But these enlightened days most dry-cleaning establishments can clean your man-made fiber family camping bags. Many models are even machine-washable. Before buying a bag, read the label or tag for the manufacturer's cleaning recommendations.

Mattresses

The first mattress afield was the earth itself, and if you're tough and lithe it is possible to sleep a night or two on the ground without becoming a basket case—if you know how. The first thing you *must* do is to contour the earth to fit your anatomy. Scoop out hollows for the hips and shoulders; if you have tender feet, make a hollow to accommodate your heels. Make a small mound for your head to rest on. (Or fashion a better pillow by rolling up a down vest or other soft garment.) Pad the hip-and-shoulder scoop-outs with layers of pine needles, dry grass, mounds of leaves and, when possible, the skins of animals. One of the better things in life is a caribou hide or two under the sleeping bag. I have used them in the arctic and subarctic, and still use them when I can get 'em legally. The hair is thick, resilient and hollow; it holds a lot of air, and air acts as insulation. During my formative years when I was right-

Foam pad makes good mattress under sleeping bag and rolls up compactly for stowage or carrying inside its own cover; some campers also pack or improvise pillows.

hand man and finally road manager for Captain Earl F. Hammond's Arctic-African shows, one of the big animal-carrying rigs was a truck and trailer in which I customarily slept to keep an eye on the priceless equipment. For a mattress I'd fold an immense Kodiak bear hide into multiple layers, and cover up with a single layer of polar-bear hide. Talk about a bug being snug! I gained 35 pounds of muscle and two inches of height during those wonderful years.

However, the coldest I've ever slept afield was on an elk hunt in Wyoming's Two-Ocean and Buffalo Plateau region when I foolishly tried to emulate my hero Jim Bridger by sleeping with two smallish cow buffalo robes.

Regardless of howls from well-meaning but uninformed elements of the ecology-buff true believers, I'm going to describe how to make the genuine "bouncy balsam" bed. Speaking of environmental purists, in an ill-advised moment I attended a university lecture by a visiting guru of such matters. He got so carried away he advised the audience to press for eliminating all trespass in wilderness areas. *Everyone!* No people whatever, was his credo.

"Bouncy balsam" is springy and resilient by nature. If you're in true wilderness where it is not illegal to harvest a bit of browse, firewood, tent poles and so forth in order to live properly, a correctly constructed bough bed is a joy and an unforgettable out-of-doors experience. Only the tender, springy tips of the boughs are used, the stems no larger than can be handily broken off. (This will *not* hurt the tree.)

First, level the sleeping area. Take away stones, roots and so forth. Cut four pieces of log about a foot thick—two of them as long as you want the bed (six and a half to seven feet) and two as wide (two and a half to three feet). Stake them in place. Lay the pinched-off tender balsam (hemlock, spruce, etc., will also do) bough tips, about a foot in length, butt toward the ground, starting at the head. Pack tiers of them tightly, row upon row, like shingling a cabin. The tighter, the better. Over this cloud-fluffy, heavenly aromatic mattress, lay your ground sheet and bedroll. Recline the weary torso. It's a great experience!

One of the first *portable* camping mattresses invented and still widely used is the "tick"—a large sack made of mattress ticking, about six and a half feet long by two and a half feet wide, weighing a pound and a half or so. Folded empty, it is lightweight and highly portable. At the campsite fill it with dried leaves, grass, and/or balsam or hemlock bough tips—anything soft and insulating. In certain circumstances, this is a practical mattress.

The various foam mattresses are justifiably popular. They vary greatly from thin "war surplus" foam sheets for gung-ho young backpacking enthusiasts to sophisticated models that are bulkier and heavier but are said to be as comfortable as a good air mattress. They may well be for the svelte and sylphlike; personally, I sink and hit bottom like an anvil. Advantages are they do not require inflating or deflating and they never spring a leak. A disadvantage is the bulk of the thicker ones. For general use the foam type is probably the second most efficient camp mattress.

The king of comfort afield, the peer of all portable field mattresses, is a good air mattress. Inflated properly, it not only equals but often surpasses the most expensive home-type coil spring. It is comparatively lightweight, folds compactly, and makes a useful raft and life-preserver (if you have time to inflate it). It should be inflated to about half-capacity for maximum comfort. A top-quality one is quite tough, but it is wise to pamper it to the extent of laying it on a thick tarp, underneath which all sharp or bulgy objects have been removed. Carry a good patching kit and a little pump. If you blow it up with your breath, you put a lot of moisture inside that may harm the fabric.

Some people prefer to sleep off the ground and there is no reason why they shouldn't. Once I took a pack trip with a friend who was crippled (at times) by arthritis. He had a tough time lowering himself to ground level, and it was impossible for him to arise in the morning without help. I noticed his difficulty the first morning and my heart went out to this brave man who loved the wilds so much he'd suffer excruciating pain and embarrassment. "Didn't I see a folding cot in your gear, back at jump-off?" I asked. "Well, yes," he admitted shamefacedly, "but our outfitter ridiculed it and said it

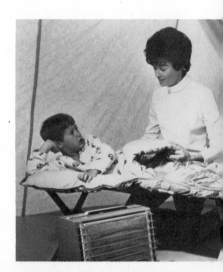

If transport is no problem and tent is large, folding cot can add to camping comfort, as at right. Air mattress (below, next to tent) is supremely comfortable if properly inflated and guarded from puncture. Though author is not fond of hammock arrangements like that on facing page, some campers enjoy them. Man in photo has hung tarp over hammock to form simple shelter from sun or sudden rain.

weighed too much." I approached the outfitter and diplomatically pointed out that his packhorses could carry 150 pounds, that army cots weigh about 13 pounds, and that he had committed a grievous breach of outfitting strategy. Because of his fetish about not packing a cot, he had to extract a new tarp from his supplies, cut it into a rectangular shape and sew four wide hems on it. The wrangler and guides at every stop had to cut four poles, insert them in the hems, and mount the whole on four "Y" legs shaped for the purpose. In other words, new cot legs were fashioned at each camp for my companion's well-being.

Cots can be had with goose-down insulation affixed underneath, offering the maximum in portable insulation, as the down will not compress. Many of the most expert campers swear by these beds.

I am not fond of military-type cots—or hammocks—except perhaps for very warm weather. Over and above the fact that cots are relatively bulky to haul around, they are cold. It is vexatious to insulate them properly for cold-weather camping if weight is a consideration. Any bag-filling compresses under the hips and shoulders, and the common garden variety of cots will do nothing to alleviate this condition, believe me. Better are the low, metal-frame, folding cots. A conventional cot is not at all suitable for a large person, as he will be sleeping on the hard sides as much as in the center.

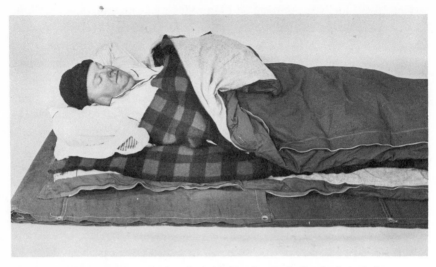

Here's cozy demonstration of Jobson's Cold Weather Bedroll, which includes down-filled bag, wool blanket, pillow case, mattress and heavy tarp.

Bedrolls

It may be worthwhile to describe the ideal true-wilderness bedroll. (The term "bedroll" includes all items necessary for comfortable sleeping, including the sleeping bag.) This information will be of particular benefit to those who are contemplating their first big-time wilderness pack trip. A proper bedroll is the ticket for mountain country from the heights of the rugged Sierra Madres of Mexico to the subarctic and arctic of Alaska, the Yukon and the Northwest Territories. It is nearly impossible to get cold in it—yet the way it is rigged makes it extremely versatile, with an impressive range of temperature-accommodation (75° above to 30° below). My own is typical of those used by a majority of informed sportsmen who frequent the wildest and most inaccessible regions on this continent.

The main item in my bedroll is a top-quality 90-inch-by-90-inch arctic-weight bag, insulated with 100 percent prime Northern waterfowl down. This bag will leave you about 250 smackers or so poorer, but it will amortize out to less than $15 a year with any kind of care. Next item is a good full-length air mattress, a long-nap virgin wool blanket, an empty pillow case, a rather heavy tarpaulin eight feet by ten feet, and two stout, wide, web straps with buckles. The purpose of the heavy tarp and straps is mainly for bag protection. I roll my bag, mattress, and the other items in several layers of the canvas, with the ends tucked in; the whole roll is firmly secured with the web straps. This protects the valuable bag from getting wet or snagged and torn while on packhorse, in a boat, canoe, aircraft, or any other form of transportation. In camp, the tarp is useful for placing on damp ground or tundra under the bag. (Most wilderness A-wall tents have no floor.) If you get caught without a tent, you can rig a nice shelter, indeed, with the tarp, or you can even sleep on half of it with the other half folded over you, which I have done many times in rain and snow.

The primary reason for the blanket is that it can be folded several times, making a thick layer of wool to place under the hips and kidney region where the down compresses and is least warm. A second reason for a blanket is that in comparatively mild weather you can rest on top of your bag with the blanket for a cover.

To accommodate varying mountain temperatures (which can be as changeable as a movie star making an epic in Italy), you can sleep with the down bag fully unzipped, partially zipped, or fully zipped. In the North, I have been warm and cozy with one and a half inches of hoar frost on my bag. I fold my down jacket into the empty pillow slip, and that is my head rest.

Tarpaulins come in many types and sizes. They should be waterproof, durable, and equipped with grommets so they can be rigged for many purposes.

With umbrella tent already pitched, outdoorsman finishes preparing campsite while his wife shakes out sleeping bag. Regardless of insulation, any sleeping bag should be aired often, fluffed and kept as clean as possible.

A final word on this subject: Not generally known these days is the old-time cowboy bedroll cover, known by various appellations. Made of heavy duck, it's an ingenious affair of straps and buckles or rings and snaps that, with blankets and comforter or sleeping bag, will make a nearly indestructible heavy-duty bedroll for the most arduous use. Such bedroll covers can still be obtained from Colorado Tent and Awning, 3333 E. 52nd St., Denver, Colo. 80216.

5

Cooking

Starting Fires

I've always questioned the value of printed advice on which campfire woods are best. For instance, what good is it to tell a new camper in Shinbone, Mont., that hickory makes the best coals for broiling? He will make do with what he has: willow, spruce, fir, alder, pine and cottonwood, say. A guy has to adapt himself to his surroundings. If he's invited to a dinner dance in Atlanta, he does not request the orchestra to play "While We Were Marching Through Georgia." Same thing with firewood. While some woods are all-round better than others, my feeling is that most of them have their good fire-wood points, if we learn how to use them. Let's discuss getting a fire started, irregardless of the wood used.

For the past hundred years, give or take a few, more fires have been started with kitchen or wooden matches than any other way, and this is still the best means of conventional fire-starting. For any city dwellers who aren't acquainted with the common farm "kitchen" match, they're inexpensive, about two and a half inches in length and can be struck "anywhere." They can be ignited with a thumbnail, or on the seat of your pants. There is no question that these are the best, day in and day out, for starting a campfire. They have one glaring fault: They're useless if wet. To overcome this some people dip the match head (and about a half-inch of the wood stem) in melted paraffin (which can be hazardous, incidentally) or they paint the head with fingernail polish or some other clear lacquer. Don't paint the whole match or the flame will race toward your fingers, causing you to drop and waste it. There are waterproof matches on the market and they work pretty well. In addition to a supply of wooden matches, always pack along a windproof cigarette lighter, a spare flint and a can of fuel. Recharge the fuel supply each day before leaving camp. Or get three or four cheap throw-away butane lighters, which work wonderfully for me if my wooden match supply fails for some odd reason. In extreme subzero temperatures, a butane lighter will have to be warmed in your armpit before the solid fuel will make gas to burn. Once warmed, it's quite reliable.

I would no more leave camp without kitchen matches in a waterproof match container than I would leave without my hat. I don't like the metal type of container with fine threads because when your hands are stiff with freezing cold, you can't open it. At least, not fast. The best is a plastic one with coarse rapid-opening threads. Mine, called "Kumbak," has a compass on one end, a whistle on the other. Don't pack your matches so tightly they won't come out. Include a small birthday-cake candle in your match container. Light that first, and with its indomitable, faithful flame, light your fire.

About candles—always have plenty of larger ones around camp. A good short but thick candle (on the order of long-lasting religious ones) will have many uses aside from furnishing light. It can keep a pot of coffee hot and can even bubble stew! The wax itself has many uses around camp, such as temporarily repairing leaks in canvas. But the main purpose of a candle is fire-start-

Kindling can be scarce above timberline, but tea will soon be boiling because fire will start quickly with these fuzz-sticks— small, dry sticks with some of their outer wood whittled to curl away in thin strips.

Top: Scouts demonstrate safe, fast firemaking technique.
Note that fire will be small, as it doesn't take high flame to boil
soup or coffee, and most foods cook best over glowing embers
rather than big blaze. Bottom: On safely cleared ground, evening flame
is enlarged for warmth, light and good feeling of "council fire."

ing. Its heat will even dry out and ignite wet kindling. Some candles, incidentally, contain an insect repellent.

Many campers have their pet fire-starters. One fellow soaks sawdust with oil, but my feeling is that if you're in a camp where you can go in with four-wheel-drive or pickup, why not just take a can of safe diesel oil? I do. It's a reliable starter of sheepherder wood stoves or campfires. Incidentally, most guys I know take a few gunnysacks of coal (or bags of charcoal) in their pickup trucks to augment the embers of a nightly council fire. No harm in it, and it saves wood.

I think the best trail fire-starters are the commercial ones that come in cans, tubes or dry. Canned Sterno is excellent except that the can makes a slight bulge in the pocket of a down jacket. However, in a rucksack or in saddlebags this is no problem. The old army heat tabs are preferred by some. I like the commercial dry "BBQ" starter called Fire Stix and the new "Sizzl' Stix." A square of Fire Stix is so light it barely jiggles the pointer on my postal scale. I wrap two of these in wax paper, then in aluminum foil, and carry them in my pocket for emergency use.

Customarily, I whittle fuzz-sticks on the trail: Shave a dry stick repeatedly, making curls but stopping short of separating them from the main stem. Two or three of these are dandy for starting a "far," as the Old Timer called it. If the wood is too full of hard pitch to whittle, just smash the ends with the flat of an axe, or with a rock.

When you can get it, real pitch wood is the absolute best fire-starting substance—so good it once was called "tradin' wood," and still is in the Northwest. Sourdoughs would split pitch wood into half-inch-thick squares about two or three feet long, and load a packhorse with bundles of it. They'd spot a frontier dwelling, and when the lord and master left, they'd move in and trade it to the housewife. For what, I never got clear. Groceries, probably.

Birch bark is an excellent fire-starter if you can find a dead tree (don't try if from a live tree, you might kill it). Ernest Thompson Seton had an evocative little poem I learned as a small boy:

> First a curl of birch bark as dry as it can be,
> Then some twigs of soft wood, dead but on the tree,
> Last of all some pine knots to make the kettle foam,
> And there's a fire to make you think you're
> settin' right at home.

To start a fire in a hurry, lay the wood in a pyramid, or tepee shape, called by some the "flash setting." Have some dry pieces (if it's raining, cut open a dry log) of kindling about a finger thick and piled in the wigwam shape. Under it there should be some sort of tinder, if possible, fuzz sticks, sliced birch bark or small matchstick-width kindling. Light your candle with a kitchen match and ignite the small stuff. Nine hundred ninety-nine times out of a thousand, the pyramid will flare into fierce flame; then add larger pieces of wood.

Remember, a flame is merely gas driven from the wood by heat, combined with oxygen and ignited. If your wood smokes as it's getting started, it is suffocating for oxygen. Hence, the practice of blowing on it, which dispels the smoke and adds oxygen. Remember the bellows that the pioneers used to goose recalcitrant fires? A neat trick is to use a length of surgical tubing to direct air into the fire with precision and élan. The tube has many uses around camp, making a dandy clamp and, heaven forbid, tourniquet.

Starting fires with flint-and-steel and by other primitive means is a stunt. I did it as a kid, with both the bow-drill and the rubbing-stick technique. It's laborious and requires muscle and the finest dry tinder. But when you get right to the heart of the matter, remember the common kitchen match! Songs should be written in its praise. Statues should be erected in its honor. It is the best campfire-starter the world has ever seen.

Cooking without Pans

A bright-looking young man came up to me one day and said, "I surely do envy anybody who can cook afield with no pots and pans." He went on to say that he'd just read a book where members of a wagon train had the opportunity to observe the famous Jim Bridger prepare his lunch. At the noon stop, several of the argonauts invited Jim to eat with them, but the old scout politely declined. Instead, he casually raised a Hawken rifle and adroitly shot an unsuspecting jackrabbit through the head. In a trice he had skinned and dressed the game, using only his fingers and thumbs. He washed it in an icy creek and placed it on a sage bush to drain while he built a small but hot willow fire. Next he cut a green stick about six feet long, sharpened the butt of it, skillfully affixed the rabbit to the other end and shoved the butt into the earth at an angle of about 45 degrees. The weight of the meat bent the wand down to where it got just the right amount of heat, quite near the fire. Then he sat quietly, his half-closed eyes fixed on the snowy peaks, dreaming his dreams of days when he and his brigade of trappers roamed the West and he didn't have to make a living shepherding sodbusters. Surprisingly soon, one side of the rabbit was a crisp, tantalizing brown. Jim turned the stick and the other side soon was likewise. Juicy inside, crusty on the outside, it was perfectly cooked.

Though the meat weighed several pounds, Jim eagerly consumed all of it while bystanders watched with some envy. The entire operation did not take more than three quarters of an hour. No pots or pans—just a green stick.

Sometimes outdoor writers talk about cooking grouse, rabbits or trout with a green stick and open fire, but they fail to tell *how* they do it. There's nothing mysterious or complicated about it. The chances are that you've already done it, many times. Who hasn't roasted wienies and marshmallows over a campfire? On a stick. To this day, in faraway mountain basins, this old technique of green-stick or dingle-stick cooking is in daily use.

On the pack trips I have been on, many of the meal highlights have been things like sheep or moose ribs set up before a fire and held in place with one or two green sticks. I'm not fond of rabbit, but I wish I had a double-sawbuck for every ptarmigan, blue grouse and trout I've savored that was broiled by this method. And, while my salivary glands are running amok at the memory, I might as well include the hundreds of thin slices of game tenderloin and rib steaks I've prepared by holding them over a fire on a green stick. Fish can easily be cooked too fast and too much, but I've had good luck cooking fowl with a hot fire, fairly fast, so they are well-browned outside, done but juicy inside. There are no hard and fast rules about this. I have never seen any 10 top outfitters do it exactly the same way twice. You adapt the green sticks, fire and food to each other, to fit the circumstances.

If the earth is fairly soft, you can do as Jim Bridger did and sharpen the stick, which can be anywhere from six to eight feet in length, and push it into the ground. Your vittles can dangle from it. And don't worry—a proper portion of meat will always cook way before the stick will burn. If the ground is not "pushy" soft, cut a forked branch, vigorously drive it in the ground and rest the green stick in that. To secure the butt end so it remains near the ground, cut a stake with a fork to hook over the green stick. Another method is to rest the cooking stick over a rock, or a log, and place a heavy object such as a rock on the butt end.

For roasting bits of steak, I cut a green stick about six feet long, with a "Y" on the "roaster" end. Sometimes I leave the Y and sometimes I cut one prong off pretty short and impale the steak on the remaining end; the nub keeps the meat from sliding back. For birds, it isn't the worst idea for your green stick to have one longish center tine, with two shorter ones. You can fasten a bird to this; you can also whittle some little wooden skewers to help hold it. Same with fish. You can fasten a trout or grayling to the end of the stick possibly 817 different ways, including skewers and certain plant roots like spruce. You can slit lengthwise tender shoots and actually tie a split lake trout or salmon to a split log and roast it. To plank these larger fish, some fel-

Left: With fire burned down to coals that give steady heat, author's wife starts ribs and steak on forked green stick—a time-honored, simple way to cook meat or fish deliciously. Below: Island camper digs pit in which he will let fire burn until he has bed of coals for old-fashioned barbecue.

lows split them down the back, some conventionally down the belly, and open them like a book, before the fire. For bread, thick dough can be spiraled around a somewhat larger green stick and baked. Some experts sort of braid it on, making an interesting pattern.

Pit-cooking, in the manner of the traditional Hawaiian luau, is another time-honored panless method. For a real luau, a hole is dug, white-hot rocks are pushed in, and layers of pig, maybe goat, all sorts of fish and shellfish, roots, vegetables and fruits are covered with great broad leaves; the whole pit is then dirt-covered. Done right, it is hard to beat this cooking.

Our traditional Western pit barbecue in theory is much like the luau: The hole is heated with a large fire, some of the coals are removed, the steer (or whatever) is put in, coals replaced, and the whole covered with soil. Many barbecues are faked today, though.

As for clambakes, many people now use some sort of metal steamer, but I vividly recall that when my bride and I were consorting around on the East Coast, from Massachusetts to Florida, we often dug a hole and laid a big fire in it. Then we'd steam fish, clams, shellfish, corn, yams and all the usual, liberally covered with wet seaweed.

Primitive peoples do superb baking with nothing but a long hole dug in a clay bank. I've seen this in Africa, and in Mexico, too. Which reminds me that some gourmets roll game birds or other fowl in mud, and roast it. I have tried it and it did not work for me—so I am not the one to encourage my readers to try it. At the same time, I know it works well for some people, and I'm sure a lot depends on being where the right kind of clay is available. The clay should hold together well, and as it heats it should form a hard, brittle, not very porous shell.

Basic Campfire Cookery

Basic cooking with an open fire is not at all difficult to learn. Besides the romance of it, fuel is mostly free, need not be packed along, and is a rewarding and dependable heat source. All you need is the wood, plus a legal, safe place to make the fire.

The best way to cook over a wilderness fire is with a metal open grill. Some call it grate, or grid. If you are cozily ensconced in a modern, organized, conventional public campground, there is little doubt that your space will be equipped with a permanent grill, or barbecue-type open fireplace upon which you can make do. But every serious camper should own his personal portable grill.

Professionals often have legged grills made of iron-steel, round stock from ⅜-inch to ¾-inch depending upon overall size. Past ¾-inch they aren't so portable any longer or useful for family cooking, but they are fine in a big elk camp, say. To make one of these, the welder or blacksmith heats and bends two pieces of stock into a squared "U." The U's are inverted so that the open ends form legs, and lengths of rod are welded in place to form a grill on top. The whole thing is shaped like a miniature table. The legs do not fold so how do you carry it? It's made to fit inside a stout grub box. You can either place it in upside down and then load up the box, or, if careful, load the box and tenderly ease it in right side up. I like the latter method.

All sorts of grills are easy to contrive. I've seen a good many—from oven shelves filched from a kitchen range to home-grown lengths of steel concrete-reinforcing rod bent into a long "U" or a long "S." These little brainchildren are placed over the cookfire and held in place by rocks or green logs. Their one glaring fault is that they do not have legs, and often are wobbly.

For general or medium-weight camping, an extremely useful type of cooking grid is sold by most any dealer in camping gear. These have folding legs, and you can use them with the legs extended or, if you prefer, leave the legs folded and place the grill over the aforementioned rocks or green logs. A variation in technique is to place one end on a rock or green log (giving back-heat) and have the end facing you supported with legs. I like the big pro job (which I recommend if you have a suitable grub box to carry it, and if you do much heavy-weight camping) from a foot to a foot and a half off the ground. The leg-ends should be sharpened, so minor adjustments can be made by pushing in or pulling out of the earth. A medium-size grid should be set up so it's about eight inches off the ground. These grids are so useful, there are models of stainless steel tubing for backpackers, but those I have require rocks for support. A useful variation employs a steel stake which is driven in the ground next to the campfire. On this is a swinging grill. Works nicely for smaller portions, particularly.

A select group seems to prefer a solid grill with no legs. Claims are made that bacon, eggs, hotcakes and such can be cooked on it without pans—and that pots do not get black. Some are made lightweight—but I don't like them, myself, preferring the portable open grill. With it I can see, enjoy and control my fire, and yet have a foolproof means of supporting my cooking vessels.

The best *cooking* fire is small. Many wilderness experts build a large fire only as a continuing source of hot coals. The coals are carried to the cooking area in a shovel—and now is as good a time as any to mention that no open-fire cook can do his best without a shovel and an axe at hand. This should be part of the kitchen gear. Almost as useful is an old rake of some sort with half

Top: Camping angler prospects water while two foil-wrapped trout bake on legged grill—a highly recommended cooking tool. Other valuable cooking aids include oversized steel fry pan, reflector oven, Dutch oven, kettle and old-fashioned coffee pot, all shown on these pages. Near right: At some public campsites, stone or masonry fireplace is provided, complete with grill to provide level, sufficiently large heating surface.

the handle sawed off. And have some water handy just in case your fire ever gets out of hand.

For most purposes most of the time you'll do best with a fire burned down to coals and carefully fed to maintain it with a minimum of smoke and flame. The secret to being a master at campfire cooking is the knowledge of how to control your cooking heat. It is not nearly as hard to learn as it might seem. A fellow simply must try it a few times. Remember the all-important shovel. This is a must. You can manipulate the fire with it. Move coals here and there as needed. Pile a little dirt on some, if needed. Or you can emulate the best North American open-fire cooks of all time—the old Montana roundup cooks who operated out of a wagon. The best of them dug long, narrow trenches in the sod and placed grates over that. The coals were judiciously shoveled into the trench from a continuing larger fire. There was little heat loss or danger in a wind. It is a trick I still use when camping on the Plains, or anyplace else where the technique is suitable.

Your gear should include some steel restaurant-type egg pans, a giant-size steel skillet, an iron skillet (if you haven't the big ranch steel one), a nested cooking kit. A reflector oven is often useful, but it requires a relatively big, hot fire. I think the most important item of open-fire cooking equipment is a genuine cast-iron camp Dutch oven. The 12-quart size is about right for your first one. (More about dutch ovens in the next section.)

For the coffee fan, a wonderful utensil is an outsize coffee pot with bail and handle near the rear base.

Dutch Ovens and Kafir Pots

Many advanced amateur and professional open-campfire cooks consider the Dutch oven an indispensable piece of equipment. There are a couple of Dutch-oven designs, so let's define and classify them. There is the "home" Dutch oven made for kitchen cooking. It's a flat-bottom ironware vessel with a rounded, self-basting cover. While it's ideal for pot roasts, stews, soups, brazing, etc., in the home, it's not meant for camping. The camp Dutch oven is a heavy cast-iron vessel, also known as a Western Dutch oven or country oven. It's not difficult to recognize. Look for three stout iron legs on the bottom, cast or molded as an integral part of the oven. The tight-fitting recessed cover has a deep flange around the outside diameter. That is so hot, glowing coals can be heaped upon it, thus cooking the contents from above as well as from below. And it's furnished with a stout wire bail. Though made in a variety of sizes, the most popular model by far is the 12-inch, six-quart size—weighing about 18 pounds.

The great majority of these are sold in the West where they are practically a way of life. However, I fail to see why they should not be just as useful and popular in the Midwest and East for those who like to cook over an open campfire. Of course, they can also be used atop a gasoline or bottle-gas camp stove, or even in the home.

It would be prodigiously foolhardy to attempt to give exact recipes and cooking time (too many variables involved), but I can head you in the right direction. Take the matter of hot biscuits. The first thing to do is let a fairly generous campfire burn down to coals. Before adding the liquid to your dry biscuit mix, the Dutch oven must be heated over the coals. Heat the cover separately, to make certain it's good and hot. When the dough is ready, using the camp shovel, make a pile of coals away from the campfire and set the previously heated oven on it. At this stage, grease the inside of the oven and place the shaped biscuit dough in it. Put the cover on the oven and, with the camp shovel, heap glowing coals on it. After 10 minutes or so, lift the cover for a peek to see if your biscuits are getting brown and crisp on top. Chances are they will be; if not, dump the old coals from the cover and add new ones. Our own particular cooking time for biscuits averages about 20 minutes.

How do you handle that hot cover? I have a ⅜-inch square steel poker, 34 inches long, with one end bent to a right angle of about three inches. Since the poker is square, I can balance the lid while lifting it without tilting ashes into the oven and all over the contents. A blacksmith made mine for $2.50, and he rigged it to come apart in the middle (that is, when I want it to) for easy packing. With this, a guy can stand to one side of the hot oven, rather

than directly over it. It's useful for tending the campfire, too. Some expert
Dutch-oven cooks use a piece of round wire or rod stock, but I don't like that
quite as well.

The biscuit-cooking technique also works for small-loaf bread, pies (use a
pie pan), cakes, three-inch-thick steaks; all kinds of fish, cut-up fowl, and
many other like delicacies.

For something more substantial in weight and mass, like pot roasts, thick
stews, baked beans or large-loaf bread (the finished, cooked loaf should nearly
fill the Dutch oven) dig a hole big enough to accommodate the oven with
room to spare—about two feet deep or so. Build a roaring fire in the hole,
fueled right to the top. Prepare the food to be baked the same as you'd do for
baking at home, using perhaps a bit more water than normally. When the fire
has burned to coals, shovel out a portion (I take out about two-thirds). Care-

For certain types of camping,
Dutch oven is neither too heavy
nor too bulky. To lift
hot lid, author uses long steel
poker with angled end.
For some cooking chores, oven
is nestled on coals (above)
and for others it's buried in
fire pit (right)—often
with coals atop rimmed lid.

fully set the oven on the remaining coals, jiggle it around a bit so the legs take "holt," then shovel coals back into the hole almost to ground level. Top off with a layer of dirt, making certain that the handle, or bail, is a trifle above ground so you can lift out the oven when desired. Bear in mind that the oven may sink a bit.

When my wife and I have baked beans, stews, etc., we often prepare them just after breakfast. Then we go about our business with never a care— and when we return, eventually, weary and ravenous, there is a hot meal ready to eat. No waiting and no preparation. Furthermore, the stews, particularly, are amazingly tender and tasty. The meat and vegetables (use carrots, potatoes and onions for sure) hold their shape but are so tender they practically disintegrate at the touch of a spoon. Care has to be taken to get them intact from the oven to the plate. Dutch ovens can also be used for boiling, suspended over the open campfire. They can be used for frying and brazing. They are mighty versatile. About the only method of camping that I can think of where they would not be practical is on backpack trips.

Ironware is porous, so a new Dutch oven generally has to be "seasoned." Manufacturers use a preservative coating, something like wax. All you have

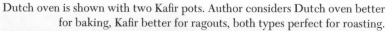

Dutch oven is shown with two Kafir pots. Author considers Dutch oven better for baking, Kafir better for ragouts, both types perfect for roasting.

to do is wash the oven in hot sudsy water, rinse, dry, then heat (without burning) and thoroughly grease it. After washing a new oven, my wife nearly fills it with cooking oil, then deep-fries chicken and French-fried potatoes. The utensil is then well on the way to being seasoned.

When cooking something where an excess amount of water or steam is formed, it's wise to dry and then lightly re-grease, using paper towels. Detergents and soap should be avoided. A well-broken-in dutch oven seldom needs more than rinsing (food does not stick to it) and wiping. Which is, indeed, another of the many nice things about it!

The Kafir pot—an African vessel used by the Bantus, of which the Kafirs are a branch—is catching on in other sections of the world. Its origin goes way into antiquity. In my library is a mint copy *Jock of the Bushveld*, by Sir Percy Fitzpatrick (1907), which I was fortunate to read at the age of eight. The margins are rife with excellent drawings of Kafir pots in use, including natives transporting them atop their heads. This type of pot has several advantages and at least one minor disadvantage as compared to our own camping model of Dutch oven, which it resembles. Both have a flanged lid and short, integral cast legs. To my notion the two are equal for roasting, the Kafir a bit better

Here are two excellent methods of cooking with Kafir pot. Both fires are safe because grass is green and soaking-wet—too wet to burn.

for ragouts, the Dutch a trifle better for baking (breads, etc.). The Kafir is best for conserving fuel. With its long legs, it readily adapts to a small fire beneath, using a minimum of wood. Feed the wood in Indian-fashion with smaller lengths of uncut dead wood radiating like spokes of a wagon wheel; as the spokes burn, you simply push them in.

The overall shape of the Kafir is cunningly devised and it has certain advantages peculiar to no other. For one thing, flames from the smallest cooking fire lick around its sides, utilizing most every BTU of heat. A big Dutch oven lends itself to emergency cooking of fried eggs, bacon, etc., as its bottom is flat, and also you can fry in the inside of the lid, turned upside down. Both the bottom of a Kafir and the inside of the lid are a bit too rounded for easy frying. The Kafir pots made in Africa are quite rough on the surface as compared to our Dutch oven. Apparently they are cast in grainier sand and so look more porous. But then all cast-iron vessels are very porous. Some say this adds flavor to the food.

A good cast-iron pot should never, ever have soap on it. Soap will absorb right into the pores and cause all sorts of malversations including ruination. If food residue has stuck (which is seldom with a well-seasoned pot) soak it a bit, then wipe it out with paper. Never scour, or use any cleaning chemical.

Stoves

You should have at least one portable camp stove that utilizes some form of petroleum fuel. Alcohol stoves are best aboard boats, for wayward fires can be extinguished by water (not the case with gasoline). For the ultimate in heavy camp cooking, a chap should sooner or later latch onto a folding (or collapsible) wood-burning sheepherder stove. It's a highly useful piece of equipment where wood is plentiful. Fairly plentiful, that is—it uses less wood than an open campfire. Fuel is free and you don't have to pack it around. A good wood stove is a joy inside an A-wall tent (or any large tent with an asbestos-ringed stovepipe hole), exuding healthful, warm, dry, cozy heat. You can dry clothing and be snug in cold, wet weather. Also, a wood-burning sheepherder stove emits only an infinitesimal amount of the dreaded carbon monoxide. You can button up the tent for short periods because the pores of the fabric afford sufficient ventilation. (As I hope most of you don't have to be told, *no* stove or anything else that emits dangerous fumes or might start a fire should ever be used inside small tents such as the backpacking models.)

Fumes from petroleum-fueled stoves are toxic, so when used inside a tent be sure you have plenty of ventilation. The girls readily take to these stoves.

Above: Collapsible woodburning stove is the ultimate for those who can manage relatively heavy camping equipment. Another excellent item is grub box that opens both on one side and top, so that side wall drops down as counter while top gives access to foods or cooking accessories.

Left: For long camping session, gasoline stove is very convenient, as is cooler chest with large capacity.

The comforting blue flame of the somewhat dated pump-up pressure camp stove is as familiar as a kitchen range. Adjustments are about the same, though you may find the flame from the camping stoves a mite hotter. Older family camping stoves can use either commercial fuel (akin to naphtha) or "white" (unleaded) gasoline. There are models that burn leaded gasoline, if need be, though I used to use unleaded fuel in all my pressurized camp stoves. Here is how these stoves operate: There is a little fuel tank which must be properly filled; then, with a built-in air pump, the operator pumps in air pressure as needed. And that's it. There are several adapters on the market that economically convert a gasoline pressure stove to LP gas. I'll cover LP stoves in detail about a paragraph from now.

Finally, I have long felt that Sterno Canned Heat is not sufficiently appreciated. I always carry a few cans, with their tiny stove. As an extra burner when there's no more room on your larger stove, and as a food and coffee warmer, it is as handy as any general camp item I know of.

Cooking with Bottle Gas

It's a pleasure, cooking with bulk refillable-bottle gas. Mind you, I'm not putting down other stoves—gasoline, alcohol, or those fueled with the little *disposable* propane containers. All have their places, and do certain chores afield best. But for a lot of cooking afield, the camper ought to recognize the worth of the refillable setup. Advantages are that it's easier and safer. There's no pumping, no filling a hot stove with raw gas in the middle of a meal, no flame going up and down (or out). The stoves are small, light, neat, compact.

A disadvantage remarked upon by a few is that the heavy tanks take up room in a car trunk and, when they finally run out, they have to be taken to an LP dealer for refilling. Particularly when a lantern is hooked into the stove-tank system, hoses dangle and people can trip over them, upsetting the whole shebang. I may be obtuse, but I can't see any of this as a real disadvantage. About the dangling hoses: When the rig is set up, it's easy to use marking tape and secure them snug and out of the way. Incidentally, besides a gas lantern, you can tie in a gas refrigerator.

I'm a great believer in pleasing the ladies. If I can fix it so my wife can prepare meals in a conventional public campsite with a bright, blue, uniform gas flame—which does not "run out" during a two-week campout and is practically nonpolluting—I don't mind packing along a 25-pound tank. Manufacturers were quick to recognize the need for a tank both refillable and smaller than the RV type.

Top: Refillable propane tank feeds camp lantern plus
two-burner stove. Compartmentalized grub box
has swing-down side for counter. Atop box is tiny but
useful backpacker's single-burner with propane
cylinder. Bottom: Side-wings shield propane stove from
wind, then fold in flat when not in use.

"LP" does not mean "long-playing" (though in a sense it is). It is the standard abbreviation for "liquified petroleum" gas. Some is butane and some is propane. LP is a true gas, compressed into a liquid and pumped in that form into your refillable tank(s). What you burn is the gaseous vapor that "boils" (evaporates or converts) off the liquid inside the tank. Boiling is a loose term, here meaning that at a temperature above minus 44° F., it gives off under pressure (hence no pumping on the part of the camper) the dry vapor that burns. A gallon of LP gas contains about 90,000 British thermal units and produces 36 cubic feet of vapor (dry) fuel. If your particular tank carries five gallons, you have a bit of leeway afield and are not likely to run out under ordinary circumstances. Leaking propane, by the way, has a strong smell somewhat like garlic. Burning properly, it is exceedingly clean and odorless.

Be sure your tank is never tilted. Have it straight up, and this almost always means with the controls and valves and hose connections on top. This kind of tank is not supposed to be filled more than 80 percent of capacity, as you should have a 20 percent space for vapor to form. That's why on most tanks there is a little device known as a 10 percent valve, a 20 percent liquid-level gauge, and other terms. You will notice when the dealer is filling he lets this blow like a wildcat oil well in a movie epic. He isn't wasting gas—he's filling the tank properly.

Like gasoline stoves, the LP models are to be used outside—ideally under a tarp (fly). However, if you have a large enough tent—a family type or an A-wall—you can use a bottle-gas stove in it as long as you observe sensible safety precautions. Have the flaps and windows fully open. If you smell "garlic," indicating a leak (which is rare with these outfits) locate it with soapy water (which makes bubbles)—*not* with a match. Brass fittings on the hoses sometimes work loose under temperature changes or vibration in transit. Brass can eventually fatigue and crack with age-stress, but it's uncommon with this sort of equipment.

Cooking with Foil

I would give long odds that in the U. S. there is not a man, woman, or child above the age of three and a half who has not heard of cooking with aluminum foil. There are a great many people who have tried it, liked it, and then for some reason let it go by the board. There are others who have never tried it for themselves—perhaps being a bit cautious about experimenting with expensive victuals.

It's an easy way to cook, and the food is delightful (and tastes a bit different), and you can nearly eliminate dishwashing. Foil lends itself to practically any variety of grub: red meat, fish, fowl, vegetables. When the meal is cooked you can, if you like, unfold the aluminum into a "dish," and when you're finished eating toss it away.

Perhaps the best heat source is a good big fire burned down to glowing coals. It is customary to scoop a hole in the embers, and with a green stick or some such, bury the foil-wrapped items to be cooked.

Prepare vegetables exactly as you wish them served. For example, before cooking diced carrots and peas, the peas should be shelled, the carrots scraped and diced or sliced, and the whole washed just prior to wrapping. It doesn't hurt to add a small amount of water for steam, a dab of butter and

Two- or three-burner petroleum-fueled stove is excellent
for outdoor cooking, and some campers also pack small single-burner
for boiling coffee or whatever while larger stove is in use.

seasoning. Corn on the cob, whole baked potatoes or yams require little preparation, other than washing. Any raw food should be prepared, generally, just
as you'd do at home for baking, roasting, grilling or steaming.

Allow a generous square of foil for each portion so that when it's folded
once over the food there is sufficient material to close off the package with
three or four tightly-pressed crimps. A lot of astute cooks then wrap the package again, reversing the open sides, with plenty of foil for another crimping.
This double layer makes the package a veritable pressure cooker, sealing in
the heat and steam, the flavor and aroma.

Another nice feature is that the aluminum molds around the food, and
when you are cooking several items you generally can tell which is what. Often at home, when preparing baked potatoes or corn on the cob, my wife for-
sakes her electric range for the foil-wrapped version cooked in our fireplace.

About the amount of cooking time involved: Foil is faster. Remember
that fires vary in heat (as do coals and the depth to which each individual bur-
ies the food). The weight and mass of food—let alone the type—make a difference. For a rule-of-thumb, though, average-size baked potatoes take 20 to 30
minutes. In our home oven, baked potatoes take an hour at 425°.

Grilling is something the camper shouldn't overlook. Fish, particularly,
seems unusually good to me when wrapped in foil and cooked in this manner.

With heavy-gauge foil you can also make disposable cooking utensils,
utilizing heavy wire, like coat hangers, or forked sticks. It works wonderfully.

Sourdough

I have known a few guys who were virtuosos with a sourdough crock. One
was a research chemist in the film-processing lab of a Hollywood studio.
Some innocuous but evidently challenging remark of mine had gotten him involved, and after a while there was little he didn't know about making
sourdough bread and hotcakes. At one time he had four large crocks "working" and it got so that about 11 percent of the studio personnel used to check
in daily to view his efforts, much as horse lovers might visit the foaling barn
of a $25,000 mare about to give birth. May pal analyzed the emitted gas, the
acids, the bacteria culture—and he ran charts on a time-temperature study.
He weighed the ingredients with the precise care he used to mix chemicals
for gamma tests on film used in shooting five-million-dollar epics. I still recall
him, rubber-aproned, with a graduated beaker poised, about to add water to
one of the crocks. He wrote the formulas, which I had for years until a flood
destroyed them.

Another sourdough expert was a charming old fellow with two dogs, more wolf than dog, who lived in a squalid tent some miles south of Dawson City, Yukon. His sourdough bread and biscuits were so delicious, the thought of them makes my mouth water to this day. He didn't go at the art at all like my Hollywood friend. Around the edge, his ancient crock was encrusted with decades of cruddy-looking dry sourdough "starter." Apparently, he thought measuring was for sissified city-slickers. He'd absently grope into a tin of flour, take a few handfuls and carelessly toss them in the crock. He added water from a warm teakettle with a superb grace and bored nonchalance beautiful to behold. Half the time he did not look at what he was doing. He added baking soda by pinching a dab between thumb and finger. His bread was the equal of, if not superior to, that made under laboratory conditions.

There is an unnecessary amount of secretiveness connected with sourdough. It is merely a simple chemical process that can be learned by any earnest taxpayer. Many recipes are bewildering because of brevity. An example: "Mix a pail of batter from plain flour and water, and hang it up in a warm place until the batter sours. Then add salt and soda (not baking powder), thicken with flour to a stiff dough, knead thoroughly, work into small loaves, and place before the fire to rise. Then bake." This brief recipe (from Horace Kephart's classic, *The Book of Camping and Woodcraft,* published in 1906 by the Outing Publishing Company) will work, no doubt of that. However, I am skeptical of having batter working in a metal pail, as the mixture forms acid; a great many people do it, but an earthenware crock is better.

Few experts will be overwhelmed with the notion of "kneading thoroughly." A lot of bread dough requires kneading, all right, but the less you push and pound sourdough, the lighter the bread and biscuits will be. Bubbles of gas are what makes bread "light." It is easy to rudely push most of them out of the average sourdough. With bakery-type bread dough, the gas-inducing ingredients are more hardy and vigorous and the dough must be well kneaded, lest great gas pockets form. But I have made a loaf or two of backwoods sourdough in my time, and with my versions of raw sourdough, I've found I can virtually flatten it unless I take care. Your own sourdough crock may, of course, develop a strain of sourdough which dictates otherwise!

In the above recipe no specific time is mentioned. Kephart had his reasons. It is futile to list exact times, as too many variables enter. Temperature is a big factor. The warmer it is, within reason, the faster a mixture works. Note Kephart's advice to let it work "until the batter sours." This is tricky, getting a vigorously live sourdough starter. I have never had a sourdough starter function at its best in less than a week, and sometimes it has even required two weeks.

A point to remember is that sourdough mix can burn out and become useless unless nourished with additional flour and water, after it is bubbling. Matter of fact, this is a good test: If it bubbles and raises overnight after adding fresh flour and water, it's live and ready for use.

If sourdough mixtures aren't used regularly (and thus replenished) they must be refrigerated. If you like, you can dispose of most of it and let the residue dry; the little scrapings will function as a new starter when the time comes.

Here's a recipe that works for me: In a gallon crock put four cups of flour, two tablespoons of sugar (optional), two teaspoons of salt (many experts like to add the salt later, to the actual dough), a tablespoon of vinegar and enough water to make a light, syrupy batter.

Cover the crock loosely and keep it warm. Depending upon the temperature (and perhaps other factors), the mixture can be ready for use within three days or as long as two weeks. If too much clear yellow liquid forms on top, pour off and add more flour and water, and wait some more. When it's working properly, the mixture will give off a sour odor, will bubble and froth a bit and increase in volume.

Into a pan or mixing bowl pour all but about a cup (which is left in the crock to serve as a fresh starter). Add a tablespoon or so of liquefied cooking fat. For bread, add more flour into which *a small amount of baking soda* has been well mixed. (Try one teaspoon. Do not overdo the baking soda. Add too little rather than too much. A wee pinch is required.) Keep adding flour until you have a resilient, thick dough. Work *fast*. Don't knead it much past the stage of being well mixed.

Cut chunks which will fill one-third to half a greased bread pan. Set the pans aside in a warm place until the dough at least doubles in size. Bake until the crust is toasty brown and the sides of the loaf shrink from the pan. Simple though this bread recipe may seem, you'll find the result delicious. There may be a mystique to sourdough but no big mystery.

Much the same procedure can be followed with biscuits, except they must be quickly rolled and cut. Hotcakes get the same routine, but keep the batter at a looser consistency by adding less flour, and include some sugar and an egg or two.

When you want another batch, add flour and tepid water to the cup of sourdough culture left in the crock, bringing it to its original amount. If kept warm it will be ready for use well within 24 hours. Most old-timers, by the way, were under the rock-firm impression that the longer a sourdough culture had been working, the better it was. Something akin to aged wine being better than raw new wine. There may have been differences of opinion as to when the flavor reached its peak, but it was not uncommon to have a crock's contents stay alive for decades, and the old-timers took pride in the feat.

I'd be doing you a disservice if I failed to mention that some recipes call for adding "store-boughten" yeast to force the initial starter. Do what you will about this, but many sourdough experts consider it unnecessary and there's a certain satisfaction in being a purist.

In passing, when making your first sourdough always scald the crock and don't use heavily treated water—this kills the necessary bacteria.

Some of the best sourdough I ever came by was not under the happiest circumstances. We were making a tour for Metro Goldwyn Mayer, ballyhooing a film about the arctic. "Eskimo," I think it was. We had dog sleds, around 30 huskies, and all the paraphernalia that we could pinch from the studio—our noble motive being to travel the key cities where the film was opening and entice paying customers past the ticket taker by displaying this wealth of Eskimo curiosa. We stopped for petrol, as they say, in some little burg in Washington and after a local inspected our giant rig and dogs, he told us about the recent death of an old Alaskan ex-prospector who had retired to a little cabin on the edge of town. The old fellow had owned a dog sled, a beautiful big Eskimo dog, and much other gear from the North—and his "junk" could be had for a song.

Well, naturally I sought out the place. The dog, chained to a tree (with a log chain) was the best specimen I had seen to that time. We bought the dog, the sled, some harness and snowshoes. I looked around the cabin. By the stove was a sourdough pot encrusted with old, dried dough. I felt sad at that mute reminder of the old chap's last days on earth.

"Want anything else?" the authority said with one hand on the door.

"I'd like that jug if you don't mind."

"*That?*" His lip curled. "Take it."

You'll be pleased to know I added water and flour to the jug and when it came alive from those old scrapings, I bought some bread pans and prepared several loaves. In a local restaurant an obliging waitress (cute, too, I remember) had the chef bake them for me and everyone in the place had a slice of steaming, oven-hot bread. The chef was so taken with this delicacy he tried to do me out of my pot—and I presented it to him with the understanding he would not let the strain die, for of all things not needed on an exploitation tour, a sourdough pot has to be in the vanguard.

An interesting little how-to-booklet on sourdough cookery which delights all aspiring *Cordon Bleus* of the camping world is sold at a nominal fee by the popular old camping-supply firm of L. L. Bean, 259 Main St., Freeport, Maine 04032.

Bannock

"Ain't nothin' to making bannock," Johnnie Johns explained. "Nothin' atall. Any fool can do it. In fact"—he looked around for a kitchen spoon as I waited anxiously—"it'll help a feller learn if he ain't overly bright." He gave me a swift, speculative look, assessing my capabilities as a potential bannock expert.

"One time I had a client from New York who was so smart he bought all his pencils without erasers on the ends, and he never did make a decent bannock. We got six-year-old kids around here that never miss with bannock."

We were fixing supper that first day of a lengthy Yukon hunt, starting off with Dall sheep. Luckily for me, I had Johnnie for my outfitter and personal guide, and I was taking full advantage of his wilderness wisdom. There was never a better Northern guide than Johns. If he had a peer, it was the late Red Higgins. When Prince Philip of England asked Johnnie where he was born, his reply was "under a spruce tree." To actor Robert Taylor, Johns replied, "In a grizzlie's den." Either or both quite possibly might be true.

What Johnnie meant about fools lucking out on bannock the first try is that an imaginative person cannot believe it actually is so simple and uncomplicated as it is. The secret of making bannock is to follow the basic recipe *exactly*. Don't experiment or attempt to improve it if you want to eat good bannock. Obviously, bannock isn't at all like the breads that require yeast (or like sourdough breads, for that matter). There's nothing tricky about making it, as there is with all yeast-rising breads until you learn to control the variables.

I haven't learned all that my doting parents hoped I'd learn, by far, but I have managed to follow (unwaveringly) directions from an expert. I never brag to a guide. For any city man to brag to a real "bush" man of his alleged wilderness skills is the height of folly. For one thing, the bushman despises this. For another, if you play ignorant, with modest manner, the outfitter is inclined to take you under his wing and educate you. Also, you get out of a lot of work, but that's another story.

When I asked Johnnie Johns how to make bannock, I had been making good bannock since I was a Tenderfoot Scout or had grown as high as my dad's belt buckle, whichever came first. But my notebook was ready when he explained the recipe for his superb, toasty, crunchy, delicious hot bannock, and here it is:

> 1 level cup white flour
> 1 level teaspoon *fresh* baking powder
> ¼ teaspoon salt

That's all. No more, no less. The basic ingredients for one serving. Double it for two people, and so on. Mix very thoroughly so all the baking powder and salt gets in with all the flour. Warm a frying pan, then grease it. Add enough ice-cold water to the dry mixture to make a thick dough and don't delay getting it into the pan, as the split second the liquid hits the baking powder, the gas bubbles (carbon dioxide, if memory serves) are created and they dissipate quickly. These tiny bubbles are what puts the minute air pockets into your bannock to make it light. Clap the dough into the pan, and sort of shape it like a giant hotcake, an inch or so thick. Crust-fanciers make a hole in the center, like an outsize doughnut. Cook it until a crust forms on the bottom—the loaf will slide about when you jiggle and rotate the pan. If you've seen a short-order cook wiggle his two-egg pan from side to side, to free them, just before he flips them over—that's the technique. At this point, the loaf has enough form and rigidity so that you can either flip it, turn it over with a pancake turner or (what all better campfire cooks do) stand the pan on edge quite near the glowing coals (depending on the size and heat of your fire) and brown the top crust by broiling or toasting, rather than frying the top side. This imparts superior flavor and texture.

Johnnie Johns stressed fresh baking powder because old stuff is not as potent, so you must use more for the same raising effect. Baking powder will weaken if you leave the cover off the can. There are different types of baking powder, so read the label.

You can use liquids other than water. Milk, say. A pal of mine used sparkling water (packed along for his evening scotch and soda) and it worked great. A neighbor uses 7-Up. Cold water, though, is best.

Along the trail Johnnie used to gather low-bush blueberries or other berries to mix with the dry ingredients for a tasty variation. And you can mince dried fruits, like apricots, and mix in.

In a permanent camp, a good cook will eventually make yeast bread. But on the trail that toasty-crust, steaming hot chunk of bannock eaten with hot stew (or practically anything!) or dunked in scalding, sweetened tea, is the true staff of life.

Game Meat

Flesh from a fat big-game animal (one not too far into the rut) can be as tasty and as nourishing as any domestic meat—but it needs to be handled with the same care and skill that a packing house uses in butchering and processing prime beef.

Care begins the moment the animal is defunct. You cannot get the insides out too quickly, for at this stage body heat and the various glands, juices and bacteria inside the beast begin to work. The longer the "dressing out" is delayed, the "gamier" the carcass is going to become. Do not bother to cut the animal's throat. In these days of high-velocity bullets, the trophy is already bled, inside.

Some chaps like to remove the musk glands on deer. These can be found inside the hind legs—two oval-like patches of wild hair. Now cut off the scrotum. If you like, you can tie a length of cord tightly around the end of the penis so that the bladder content will not leak onto the job at hand. Some purists likewise tie a cord around the anus (first cutting around it with a sharp knife, being very careful not to damage the colon). Others feel this step is gilding the lily. In any case, the anus and the end of the colon must be cut free of the body, cord or no.

Run two fingers of one hand under the abdominal skin, and work it and pull on it so that it comes free from the abdominal sac (the intestines—we do not want to slice into *them*). Now, with the tip of a very keen knife between your two fingers, slit the skin from anus to breast bone—a good long incision which will give you plenty of room to work. If the head is to be mounted as a trophy, don't cut so far that you slice into the cape or scalp.

At this stage it may be comforting to remember that dressing out a large game animal is not much different in principle from eviscerating a squirrel or rabbit. The only thing is, there is so much more of it.

After making certain that the anus has been cut free by careful cutting around it, reach up into the beast's throat and sever the esophagus, windpipe and all that business. It is amazing how quickly a gullet will sour (particularly on elk, for some reason). You will see approximately midway down the animal's insides a diaphragm, or "wall," separating the portion containing the lungs, heart, and other vital organs (called by the Indians "where-the-animal-lives") from the digestive section. The entire viscera can now be removed.

On an animal the size of an antelope or a small deer, a fellow can usually get behind the beast and by grasping each of the front legs in the vicinity of the "elbow" hold the carcass forward and shake vigorously. Quite often the whole mass will drop free. If it doesn't, check to see if the diaphragm is clinging to the cavity wall.

If the animal is a large mule deer, bighorn ram, or small elk, two fellows working from either side can generally accomplish the above. On something the size of moose, bull elk, or bull caribou, you will simply have to roll up your sleeves and tug the viscera out of the animal. If parts of it are recalcitrant, again, check the diaphragm. Sometimes, fatty organs can "grow" against the cavity wall, but generally they are easily freed with the fingers or hunting knife.

Once the cavity is empty, a stick should be inserted crosswise in the opening, keeping it wide apart for maximum cooling. The carcass should be placed on a slant in some manner, head up, so it will drain. The inside of the beast should be wiped clean of clotting blood, hair, pine needles, etc. If you don't have a clean cloth in the field, a few tufts of sweet grass will do the job. Almost immediately a glaze will form on the surface—greatly resembling a plastic coating.

The legs should be severed at the "knee" joint, and the head should be removed. If the animal has been gut-shot, dressing out is messy, and the cavity should be thoroughly washed with cold water. Cut away all the bloodshot meat caused by the bullet wound, and make your cuts generous. The carcass should be raised off the ground and into the shade as fast as possible. The quicker this is done, the better the meat will be.

In the case of large deer, elk, moose, caribou, or even a big ram, the animal should be quartered then and there so it isn't too heavy to handle. This is accomplished by chopping (with a sharp hand axe or a folding meat saw) lengthwise through the spine to give you two pieces. Each of these is cut in half crosswise, giving you the four quarters of meat. If the animal is not particularly huge, it is, of course, possible to pack it back to camp as a whole carcass or half-carcass.

There are nearly as many variations of dressing-out as there are guides and experienced hunters. On the very largest animals, it might be necessary sometimes to butcher a carcass from topside. The Plains Indians used this technique with heavy buffalo. They got the animal spine up, skinned the hide free so it fell around the animal as a kind of clean work table, and skillfully cut the carcass into its component parts. I have seen Northern Indians (and others) do this with very large bull moose too heavy to handle any other way.

At camp your sections of meat should be hung promptly and as far off the ground as is feasible. The hide should be removed (if it hasn't been), the meat should be carefully inspected for "blown" spots (eggs and maggots) in the event some enterprising flies have sneaked in for a guerrilla attack. If you find patches of this, cut it all away ruthlessly. Wash away any loose hairs you may discover, and likewise inspect the wound channel again, for bloodshot meat.

Now the meat should be placed in cotton deer bags, or wrapped securely in cheesecloth. Hung overnight in the sharp mountain air, the meat should cool clear through. This is exceedingly important. Never attempt to transport home meat that hasn't had a chance to cool all the way through, not merely on the surface. Three or four days and nights of hanging in a cool spot will not hurt the meat. In fact, it will improve it. Once these relatively large masses of meat have been chilled, it is astonishing how long it will keep "sweet."

Wrap the pieces loosely in canvas tarps and pile some newspapers, sleeping bags, or whatever is handy on top of the meat, and you can drive for two or three days with the unrefrigerated meat in an automobile or pickup. My pals and I for many years carried elk meat in this fashion over 1,200 miles—a good part of the journey over the Mojave Desert—and we never lost an ounce. If your journey is very long, it may pay you to stop along the way at some public freezer and have it cooled again (not frozen). I believe that the best place to have the carcass processed and frozen is at homebase. Once it is cut and packaged and frozen, it should stay frozen until used. It isn't necessary to freeze game immediately, and it isn't practical if you can't keep the meat frozen while you're on the road. Game birds and fish can be brought home on ice, normally, but if the trip is lengthy they should be packed in dry ice. It doesn't usually take much (for birds or fish, that is; it would take plenty for big game).

If you get an old bull or buck whose flesh isn't exactly tender, bear in mind that a butcher can make hamburger from it or delicious sausage, salamis and other cold cuts. It all makes powerful good eating.

Roadside Repasts

For the tent camper who travels with a conventional automobile, there are enormous advantages to be gained enroute by preparing uncomplicated but tasty and energy-giving food at highway rest stops.

Equipment required is compact, low-cost, long-lasting and nicely supplements regular tent-camping gear. The heart of roadside cooking equipment is a one-burner stove. One of two that we use and know to be excellent is a one-burner which is packed and carried in its own metal case, the bottom of which makes a saucepan, the top a fry pan with detachable handle. It's indispensable in camp as a third or fourth burner, and we use it for such odd jobs as heating five-gallon tins of bath water. A few ounces heavy for purist backpacking gear, it is ideal for the family auto-tent vacationer. It's powered with unleaded liquid fuel, and has a hot, intense blue flame.

The second one-burner we're fond of is powered with convenient disposable propane cylinders. There are other one-burner stoves powered with solid tabs, jellied alcohol, and such. (There are many one-burner backpack stoves—but we've never used them for this purpose.)

Top: For backpacking trips when you want to travel light, you can buy single-burner
gasoline stove that's hardly bigger than a soup can, weighs only a pound
and has detachable-handled cover that acts as cup or pot. Bottom: Some propane
single-burners, like this one, can be adjusted for use as heaters.

The second main item is a camp cooler. For roadside meals you should
have it handily available. For station wagons (using the tailgate for a table) a
good cooler design is that with a swinging upright door. There are extraordinary times when you'll prefer a *disposable* camping cooler; for instance, if

Just off many roads are well-maintained picnic sites that make fine
mid-day rest stops during long drives, and some spots are close to lakes or streams.
Father and son in this photo are preparing to fish for their lunch.

you go rockhounding, driftwood catching, or bushels-of-apples-getting from the farm and need a cooler *going*, but coming home you need the space it takes. You can make one with a couple of corrugated paper cartons, the top and bottom nesting, the insulating airspaces filled with wadded newspapers. It will leak otherwise, so cool it with something frozen (a sealed tin of plain water is good) in your home freezer. For years we've used a syrup pail of ice cubes. With the entire contents pre-chilled, you have a surprisingly effective disposable cooler.

Another useful gadget is a little heating element that plugs into the cigarette-lighter receptacle. It rapidly boils water for instant freeze-dried coffee or soup. We use disposable heat-retaining plastic or paper cups and tumblers, and glazed-paper plates, both of which are much superior to the old-fashioned soggy paper cups and plates. A cutting board is also handy for roadside meal preparation.

You can generally find a pretty spot off the road for a brief stop. The conventional roadside stops are the best, though. Many states are loaded with them and they have shade, trash barrels, toilet facilities, picnic tables, grates, and often some scenic or historical significance. Having a couple of meals a day off-the-cuff saves time and money. While traveling in a car, you don't get much exercise so you don't burn bushels of calories. You do not need big meals. We draw heavily on our cooler for cold meats, fruit, juices, carrot and celery sticks, olives, chilled canned tuna, etc. Icy milk is a favored noon beverage. Before leaving home we freeze quarts of milk, tea and coffee, and some drinking water. These help to keep the cooler cool. For the one-burner there are tasty canned goods like soup, stew, pork and beans, spaghetti-meatballs. The freeze-dried camper meals are relatively expensive and are better used while actually in camp, or where weight is a problem. Fresh fruits are great for road eating and so are dried fruits. And peanut butter is all-around useful.

When I was a boy working summers on a ranch, during infrequent visits to town we lads would get to starving. Not having cafe-type funds, we'd chip in for a hunk of yellow bulk cheese, soda crackers, and cans of tomatoes. This is a tasty, satisfying lunch, although it lacks flair.

I have a well-heeled pal who indulges at roadside in such exotics as Beluga caviar and French pickled mushrooms, stuffed with anchovies. But what gets me, is that the first thing he does is light a little charcoal hibachi. When that's going, he slices wafer-thin pieces of tenderloin steak and as quickly as one is browned on either side, he pops the morsel into his gob with a self-satisfied smirk. He douses the coals from a waterbag, dumps them into a trash barrel and is ready to go when we are. He also has a beach umbrella that he pitches over a reclining beach chair!

Freeze-Dried Foods

My first encounter with freeze-dried foods for sportsmen was way back in 1962, when I witnessed a demonstration at the National Sporting Goods Association show in Chicago. I was (along with about everyone else) quite impressed.

The excellence and practicality of this type of food can be strongly emphasized. I used it in quantity, for months, on two lengthy wilderness trips to the north-central Yukon Territory and the coastal grizzly country of British Columbia, not to mention many forays into the mountains near my home. I have never eaten better lightweight foods in the field. I did not, by the way, experience any stomach or bowel distress from eating too much of it, as some people claim to.

In the Yukon, with shrieking subarctic gales assaulting the tents during a spell of lousy weather, my companions and I lallygagged around a cherry-red sheepherder stove and consumed such exotica as fresh shrimp cocktails, fresh

Snacks are valuable energy-boosters during rest stops on hikes. Dried
fruits, cheeses and nuts are recommended, and there are even a few freeze-dried
foods that require no preparation and can be eaten right out of the packet.

boneless pork chops, the most aromatic and wholesome of chicken stews, superb shrimp Creole, choice beefsteaks, and other goodies. I use the word
"fresh" advisedly—for that is exactly how freeze-dried food tastes when prepared according to directions. Take the matter of beefsteaks. As they come
from the package they are rather small, undistinguished-looking objects. You
get the impression of little substance and less weight. But add water and an
amazing transformation occurs. As the cells fill, the hemoglobin unites with
the water and blood is formed. The steak swells and soon is a juicy piece of
meat ready to be broiled or pan-fried.

As far as preservation is concerned, one doctor exclaimed that this
method is the greatest invention since the metal can. Even though these foods
are incredibly light, more than 90 percent of the fresh flavor remains. I, for
one, can scarcely differentiate between them and the best victuals straight
from the supermarket. Full meals are available as well as individual dishes.
Examples are the ranch breakfast of sausage, fried potatoes and scrambled
eggs; and swiss steak with gravy, whipped potatoes and peas.

Some sportsmen seem to have an aversion to certain of the older dehydrated foods—but comparing the freeze-dry technique to simple dehydration
would be analogous to saying Herman's Greasy Spoon down the road serves
the same food as Chasen's.

Freeze-drying combines the best features of quick-frozen foods with dehydration. The food does not change a whole lot in character; it retains essen-
tial nutritive elements; it rehydrates readily and rapidly, absorbing a volume
of water approximately equal to the amount removed in drying; and it is
stable without refrigeration. Combine all this with space-saving light weight
and ease of preparation—no trimming, peeling or long waiting—and you can
see that this deal deserves a long, interested look from all outdoorsmen. The
first time my wife prepared a freeze-dried beef-and-vegetable stew near the
Arctic Circle in the Yukon, our outfitter looked on with concern, as if we'd
gone daft. He muttered, "I don't care for dehydrated food." In a short time
the stew was simmering and tantalizingly fragrant. It looked beautiful.

"Have a sip," we coaxed.

To be polite, he took a tentative spoonful, then another. He beamed.
"This is *good!*" He called the guides and wranglers and, before all of us were
finished, we consumed three chicken stews, two chicken-with-rice dinners
and two more beef-and-vegetable stews (some of these designed for four serv-
ings). As we patted our outraged belt buckles, the outfitter wiggled his fore-
finger at me and solemnly declared, "Next year I am bringing in *plenty* of *this*
stuff." I don't blame him a bit.

Some firms now specialize in "trail" foods with menus so varied, nour-

Both food and garbage should be kept in sealed containers or odors may attract anything from skunks to bears. At commercial or public campgrounds like this one, covered trash cans are usually provided for garbage disposal.

ishing, tasty, condensed, light and easy to prepare, it would boggle the mind of yesterday's outdoorsman. (Many of these meals are a form of dehydration other than freeze-dry. I still like freeze-dry though.)

Garbage

Packing out the trash is a noble notion when it will work, and that includes a majority of situations. But experienced campers know there are valid exceptions to most every field rule. A Wyoming outfitter was here recently and I told him I thought I'd write a short piece on garbage techniques afield. He nodded (with a patient but weary expression) and confided that of late, on some of his pack-horse big-game hunting trips, he's had ecology purists who request that he load his pack horses with garbage and rubbish for the trip out. After all, "The horses carried it in!"

He tells them, "The horses have to carry out elk, deer, and bear, plus the rocks, driftwood and pine cones you chaps have gathered as souvenirs. Which do you want, the garbage or the elk horns?"

He told me, "We aim to please, and if it makes the dudes feel uplifted, we can pack out all the garbage, whenever there are spare pack horses, in good shape. When I do pack it back, I just bury it at the ranch as soon as they're gone."

"How do you get rid of camp rubbish normally?" I asked.

"Same as you do, I'll bet," he laughed. "Burn everything. Cans are stomped on and then buried—burned can oxidizes quickly. Glass is unbelievably durable, but cleaned and buried it has never caused me grief. I predict that before glass becomes a *wilderness* problem we'll have a substitute that will burn or self-destruct. In our back country, and there's still lots of it, a well-maintained camp garbage pit pollutes the wilderness about like a belch contaminates a cyclone."

It's all the rage now to advise people never, ever to take anything in glass to camp. But that is just not practical. No packer *likes* glass. It sometimes breaks, and if left unburied the sun's rays can start a forest or grass fire. And then there's the outside possibility of someone getting cut. But if glass containers are cleaned and scalded to remove odors which attract bear and rodents, then buried five or six feet, there's no present or foreseeable problem.

I think the best rule is to take out the trash whenever it is possible and *reasonable* to do so. And don't take glass or plastic if you can use a practical substitute. There are ways to be comfortable and healthful, with excellent meals in camp, without sullying the pristine wilderness.

6

Clothing

Once when I knew we were going to hunt in Africa in June I told my wife to order herself a new prime goose-down jacket and down-insulated underwear jacket; also, some of those fetching little lady's type two-layer ski underwear with the fleecy cotton inside, virgin wool outside, and the frills. She looked at me in amazement.

"But we're going to Africa, way below the equator," she said. "I should think what we'd need would be cottons and those Stewart Granger-style bush jackets."

We took those, too. Having been indoctrinated by Tarzan and Jungle Jim films, which depicted vapor rising from Congo swamps, great lurking pythons gimlet-eyeing the unwary trekker from lush vines and creepers, outsized aspidistras and man-eating plants—why, it is understandable that people assume the correct African wardrobe consists of a bush jacket, English riding britches or shorts and a Frank Buck pith helmet. The fact is the Dark Continent has lofty plateaus as much like eastern Montana as anything else. And being below the equator, it was winter in June. Our down jackets were exactly correct, mornings and evenings.

By the same token, a fellow would logically think that an autumn trip in the Yukon Territory would require down and wool. It does. But it can get hot enough to prostrate a sheik, too. Which brings us to the point: The foremost feature of astute dress afield is the right clothing *at the right time.*

If you are going to a place you know well, where the average mean temperatures are predictable, there's no problem. When you head for Phoenix in August or Hawaii most any time, you know lightweight duds are about all you need. Though I once hunted feral goats on a big volcano in Hawaii and zipped up my down jacket every frosty morning. And there was a July 4th in Jackson Hole, Wyo., when the motor of my car froze so solid that it cracked the block.

For general camping trips in North America it is best to plan for a wide range of temperatures and varied weather conditions, particularly in our

Construction worker's hard hat may seem odd as item of camping equipment but it affords excellent protection and is especially practical for mountaineering.

mountain states. Concentrate on comfort rather than style; make certain clothing is cut full and a little larger than you would normally wear.

Head Gear

Through the ages, mankind has evolved some wondrous creations to adorn his noggin. Head gear has been fashioned from a staggering array of substances: animal hide, wood, processed fur, vegetable fibers, various wools, metal, etc. I have a pal who wears his construction worker's hat for deer hunting. He has painted it a violent, blazing red and swears it's the best danged outdoor hat he has ever used.

Head gear fills two purposes. The major reason for having something on your head is for protection against the elements; secondary reason is custom or adornment. The latter is more important than most of us consciously realize. Look at the popularity of African safari hats bought by sportsmen who know they will never go to Africa. A safari hat greatly resembles in principle our own "ten-gallon" Western or cowboy hat, and fulfills the same function. Many experienced sportsmen are convinced that the cowboy hat is the all-round best for the Rocky Mountains. It keeps the rain off the neck and eyes, it shades the eyes, a good one sheds water, in hot weather it is cool, and conversely in cold weather it is warm. A horse or dog can drink from the crown. It's a durable, attractive hat, an excellent value for the money. And a good one is very comfortable.

Here are several kinds of useful and popular head gear for campers. Wide-brimmed safari hat gives shade plus protection from rain or snow. Western straw is perfect in hot weather. On cool days, soft tweed is comfortable, and it can be stowed in small space.

For hot weather, the common old straw hat which in shape resembles the ten-gallon hat is a treasure. Straw hats are sold at nearly give-away prices, and I know a lot of fellows who wouldn't be caught outdoors without one. Strangely, they are mostly overlooked in the vast array of outdoor hats available today.

For the Rockies, even if you have a cowboy hat, you need a cap with earflaps. In bitter cold that's the ticket, and it's also handy for open-country stalking of animals.

Another great piece of head protection is a good inexpensive rain hat. The kind called a Southeaster, which is generally pictured on certain bottles of cod liver oil, is okay but my own preference is for the flat-crowned, broad-brimmed type. Both have ear flaps and a chin strap. A rain hat is an absolute must for regions like the northern Pacific Coast, where it sometimes rains interminably.

For the past four or five years I've been using a little hat I find (for general use) better than any. It is a British tweed hat—generally considered a dress hat—with a narrow brim which resembles the Tyrolean hat. I started wearing one of these more or less by accident and I've worn one on most of my trips in the mountains since. They're wonderful little hats. The brim is just wide enough to keep rain from pouring down the back of my neck, it shades my eyes, is utterly comfortable, and can be folded—or rather, crushed—for convenient packing.

Another excellent type of head gear for the outdoors is the navy wool watch cap. These are generally available at war surplus stores and I wouldn't be without one. They are superb for wearing under a parka hood and sleeping in extremely cold weather.

For warm weather, if you prefer a light cap with a bill there are dozens of types available, usually made of cotton twill, inexpensive and practical. It's hard to go wrong with any of them.

I should mention that another excellent hat for all-round outdoor use is the common felt street hat of good quality. It's enormously versatile. And versatile is what head gear should be. It ought to perform its No. 1 chore superbly, yet offer a bonus or two. Take the World War II GI helmet. Its primary purpose was to deflect hits. GIs bathed from their helmets, cooked with them, even used them as a scoop shovel. Last time I was in Italy's boondocks I saw several suspended from a balcony and overflowing with geraniums.

There are specialized headcovers, such as the poplin-drill cap with greatly extended visor affected by many charter-boat skippers. They shade the eyes dead ahead, keep the sun's rays off the head and brow, but not much else. They're light, cool, inexpensive, expendable.

Ann Jobson wears foldable brimmed cap and guide Johnnie Johns wears ordinary felt hat, both good outdoor styles. Folded across her pommel are leather chaps and hanging from his are canvas chaps; either type is useful on pack trips.

A misunderstood hat is the European beret. I've never had the nerve to use one, but I recognize their desirable features. The felt is warm in cold weather and cool in hot; it stays put, and keeps hair and perspiration out of the eyes. Some years ago a genius added a little visor, which makes it one of the world's great caps, equally good for black-tie occasions or under a fur parka. Few designs have such versatility. And in this general category add heavy-knit tams (like Cowichan), increasingly popular for fishing, skiing, etc. Another excellent field hat suffering from prejudice is the high-quality Scot tweed Sherlock Holmes "deerstalker" type, which has a bill fore and aft plus full-sized earlaps.

European beret, excellent for high-country hiking, is warm in cold weather and cool in hot weather. It won't blow off, and it keeps hair and sweat out of eyes.

The "balaclava," another with a select following, is a knit device continuing past the point where the Navy watch cap leaves off. It covers the head (except for eyes and nostrils), neck, and some even cover the shoulders or extend clear past the kidney and umbilical regions. No doubt, a conventional balaclava is great for rapid movement through frigid air, as when snowmobiling, for example.

A tidy little emergency hat can quickly be fashioned by tying a knot in each corner of a handkerchief—a ubiquitous sight in Mediterranean countries.

Worth trying is the old-fashioned duck hunter's cap of brown lightweight canvas, usually turned up in back, down in front, making a bill. Older ones invariably had parsimonious fold-in ear flaps only protecting a third of my poor ears.

A good (but homely) cold-weather cap is the Down East "Havelock" with flat top, wide visor, generous ear muffs tied in front. Old lithographs show them worn by Vermonters harvesting maple syrup or hauling Yule logs with a horse sleigh. I still see them in backwoods stores. They're good hats.

Probably the best all-round hat for woods use is the genuine Maine-Michigan visored cap with outside earflaps (tied atop when not in use). A boon to mankind! If you get one of ample size, I predict you'll look upon it as you do the comforting nudge of an old setter's silky nose reminding you he's there. The design is widespread, and quality and materials vary but it is often made of blanketing.

Some campers prefer "Trooper" caps, with ⸱⸱⸱ or pile earflaps and visor that "snap" up. Those insulated with down are great, my friends tell me. The "X-large" I have ordered twice were too small. I presume listing sizes this way (S, M, L, XL) works for mail-order houses, but saying an item is "large" is akin to saying a man is "tall." One should be able to buy a hat marked 7⅝ or a coat 48.

An exceptionally fine head-garment, which I wore for years until they "improved" it, is the *old* (not new!) capote made of a Hudson's Bay blanket, with an attached hood like the monk's cowls shown in Robin Hood films. You

Last girl in this line of hiking Girl Scouts is wearing fur-felt Western hat and light but insulated quilted jacket —good clothing for fall days outdoors. She also has on insulated rubber boots, which are fine for riding or staying in one place in cold weather but are not good for long hikes.

could wear it elegantly tossed back, or fully forward. Even in a vicious Montana-plains crosswind it was cozy.

But for me, the queen of all hats for open and semi-open lands unquestionably is a top-quality, fur-felt wide-brim generous-crown model. It cannot be excelled, whether the style is cowboy ten-gallon, Smokey Bear, India *terai*, African white hunter, Australian army (a goodie), or whatever. It'll fan a fire to life, water your horse and dog, and make a splendid rifle rest.

The Western style with the sides exaggeratedly flared up is attractive at rodeos (and I wear one on occasion) but I don't believe it's the most practical afield. Ultimate efficiency is mostly achieved with brim down all around, as worn by professional white hunters. Have your wife add two eyelets on the brim for a chin thong. Buy the hat large and put lamp wicks in the sweat band. Eventually, it should shrink in. Cheap felt hats, like cheap binoculars, seldom are a bargain.

Once at Red Higgins' Wallawa elk camp I saw a wrangler frying a tremendous skillet of pork chops. They caught fire and, after recoiling, the wrangler with inventive forthrightness whipped off his cheapie cowboy hat and clapped it firmly atop the roaring conflagration. It smothered the flames, but there must have been a considerable eruption of hot grease plus steam. As the wrangler's triumphant expression dissolved to one of hynotic horror, the hat shrunk with a slide-whistle rapidity . . . down, down until (actually) it was the size of a play hat that toddlers keep on their heads with a rubber band!

Down Jacket

Back in the 1940's I was hunting pronghorn antelope out of the famous old John Kirk Ranch south of Lander, Wyo., and there on the lofty Red Desert it was unseasonably cold. Before daylight my pal Scott Claytor, Kirk's son-in-law, brought around to the kitchen door his 1938 Ford pickup with stock rack. As my hunting companion was a preeminent film star who could ill afford a head cold, I grandly gestured him into the warm cab and climbed aboard the open bed of the truck with the guide. We looked at each other with the doleful air of two buddies about to face a firing squad. It was bitterly cold just parked in the ranch yard. When we began moving, the high-altitude temperature made the breeze cut like a razor—and as Scott turned onto hardtop and hit 60 mph the awful cold instantly was unbearable to any exposed skin surface. The poor guide, though used to adverse weather and attired in longies, wool shirt, blue-denim cowboy jacket and heavy wool mackinaw, dived to the floor behind the cab, frantically motioned me to join him, and

Down-insulated jacket or vest designed for wear under coat is warmest, yet lightest of camping garments, and good ones will outwear leather or heavy wool.

covered up with an ancient, odoriferous tarpaulin. Earflaps securely tied, hands in my pockets, I lolled against the wooden stock rack, back turned to the vicious wind, and was utterly comfortable. I was wearing my first down jacket, which, by the way, I used for over 15 years and finally gave to a Yukon guide. For all I know, it is yet in service.

Like most school kids, I had seen textbook illustrations of surly-looking Mongol tribesmen on the frigid rooftop of Asia, attired in thick, padded clothing which to me, at least, looked as if the garments were fashioned from grandmother's batting-insulated comforters. And I was not unaware of ladies' stitched, padded housecoats. But if my pals and I thought about it at all, the absurd notion of ever wearing a quilted coat afield was in the realm of fantasy, like Buck Rogers going to the moon. When, with some trepidation, I purchased that initial down-insulated jacket of mine, I was leery that my ole buddies might make snide remarks and they didn't disappoint me. Also, I was fearful the jacket might suddenly disintegrate in a blizzard of loose feathers the first time I scraped against a twig. I cautiously took along as spares a leather jacket and a stag shirt—one of the most useless precautions I've ever indulged in.

Without qualification, a top-grade jacket, insulated with 100 percent new premium-quality prime goose down from dry, mature birds, is the warmest yet lightest sportsmen's coat on earth, and is incredibly dependable and versatile. It is among the toughest, most durable of field clothing. It will outwear the average leather jacket or heavy wool coat.

Good goose down has loft, resilience and great buoyancy. It breathes, which is to say it efficiently expels body moisture, and keeps you warmly dry. Down maintains your normal body temperature so well you will not believe it until you experience it. There are many varieties of waterfowl down—just as there are grades of wool. You can get horribly gypped on down that is wet-plucked and allowed to remain damp for several hours. This deteriorates it terribly. Watch out for second-hand, mixed, baby-gosling, unclean, and certain summertime down. Your best bet is to buy from a national advertiser who guarantees he is selling you virgin prime Northern goose down. There are regulations regarding labeling practices so you can feel reasonably safe if you make a point of carefully reading all the labels attached to this type of garment.

Eiderdown is not better than goose down. We've been brainwashed about the alleged superiority of down from the eider duck. Experts tell me they can obtain all the eiderdown they want, but that for clothing and sleeping bags it is inferior, though expensive. Eiderdown is proper for stuffing high-quality furniture, and ladies like to use it for homemade comforters, as it has a tendency to mat. This is exactly what you do *not* want for jackets and sleeping bags. Eiderdown is unclean in its natural state (robbed from the nest) and must be laboriously cleaned and sanitized.

In the beginning, sportsmen were a bit apprehensive about the quilting because it did look fragile. A few fellows I knew bought the type that is smooth on the outside, with the quilting hidden. These are good jackets, too, but I prefer the other.

With a down jacket you should carry a light slipover rain-jacket that folds to pocket-size, as a thoroughly soaked down jacket can be miserable.

Chaps

When I brood deeply on unappetizing subjects (an exceedingly rare occurrence) tears of self-pity cascade down my weathered cheeks until I'm fearful of erosion, and I mutter undying oaths never again to recall the many times when in abject stupidity and irresolute planning I have allowed my gnarled, abused legs to endure wet, freezing weather, impalings by tree snags, cacti, sharp rocks, thorns and the multitudinous other shin hazards which the unwary and the preoccupied encounter afield. At last maybe I've learned.

A guy's legs are particularly vulnerable while big-game hunting, fishing or camping by packtrain in the high mountains or Far North. On horseback, a great many undesirable situations can confront the rider, chief among them the distinct possibility of snow and a cutting, vicious wind seemingly off the Polar ice cap. While astride, a fellow's legs don't have the same circulation they do when trudging on foot. Reading about it, this may appear as a trifling nuisance—but take it from one who knows, it can grow past the annoyance stage. On horseback 10 or 12 years ago at a lofty plateau in the Yukon Territory, my legs got soaking wet from rain, then sleet and, finally, a hurricane-type wind so bloody cold it would make a polar bear seek cover. I damned near froze to death, literally. When we had left base camp at lower altitudes, the day had been sunny, even balmy, so I carelessly left my leg protection in camp. Never again. Whither goeth my horse, likewise goeth chaps of some kind, from here on out.

Chaparejos, which is the long way of saying chaps, probably are Mexican in origin (at least in North America) and were, 'tis said, designed to protect vaqueros from chaparral and cactus (perhaps even from surly range-cattle horns). They can be had in a great many varieties, including the angora-wool type. It is generally agreed that the all-round best working chaps for sportsmen are the cowboy batwing type of lightweight top-grain elk or chrome-tanned leather. Good chaps should be relatively thin, pliable and not inclined to stiffen in bitter weather.

I prefer my leather chaps to ride a bit low, so I get a shorter inseam measurement than do most. Chaps are best suited for sportsmen's use if secured to the leg with the customary three conchos and snap-rings. That way, if you have to pile off your horse in a hurry for a trophy stalk, you can shed them in a hurry. They are also made with zippers instead of snaps.

New chaps can be purchased for around $30 to $60 if you like the plain, unadorned pattern. In the West, if you should by chance wander into a saddle shop, occasionally you can pick up a good used pair for about half that amount. Cowpokes sometimes hock or sell their gear during periods of stress,

Batwing chaps of good, pliable leather (left) are Jobson's preference for
horseback camping trips. Also useful are light, inexpensive rain chaps (right).

like being out of work or having tried to fill an inside straight. You can make
chaps. Borrow a pair that fit you, and make a tracing on heavy manila paper
or muslin.

One thing about chaps for sporting use: Your first cost is your last, because a leather pair will never wear out during your lifetime. Teddy Roosevelt, who knew a thing or three about wilderness matters, wore a pair of seal-
skin chaps. I've seen them in a museum in New York.

Another type, not commonly seen, is the legging version which stems
from the leggings of the Plains Indian. The old mountain men wore these,
with the addition of a breech clout. We scarcely would venture into the untrammeled wilds attired in a breech clout, but the modern counterpart of
plains leggings, known as "rain chaps," are highly useful. They are light,
weighing mere ounces, and are made of waterproof nylon; they are big
enough to go on or off over hunting boots. They sell for about five bucks.

One time under duress I tried a pair of lambing chaps, likewise inexpensive, but they were of heavy duck and were an abomination (at least, to
me they were) on horseback. When it comes right down to it, the trousers
from your rain suit are 100 percent better than no chaps at all.

Footgear

Without proper footwear—suited for the type of country, terrain and weather encountered—you can be miserable. If you slip or slide, if your feet are too cold or too hot, wet, or chafed or cramped and aching, it is impossible to enjoy any endeavor afield for very long.

Furthermore, a couple of very nasty things can happen to you with ill-fitting or unsuitable footgear. If blisters form, and especially if those blisters become infected, you are not only out of business as far as that trip is concerned—you may be in danger if you are isolated and far from medical attention. The second appalling danger concerns a sheath of tendon called the Achilles heel, or Achilles tendon, on the rear of the heel. This can become bruised from poorly fitting boots. The pain sneaks up on you. You don't notice much at first. From cumulative effect it can become badly bruised. In which case you've had it as far as that particular trip is concerned. The bruising of that tendon is excruciatingly painful and is not one of those deals cured by a couple of days' rest. I have known cases where it hung on for weeks.

So blisters, stone bruises, heel bruising and chronic cramping of the feet

For various camping activities, it's hard to beat these
six types of footgear: A) rubber hip boot; B) Vibram-soled mountain
boot; C) low, moccasin-toed upland boot; D) leather-topped,
rubber-bottomed shoe-pac boot; E) camp lounging moccasin; and
F) insulated rubber boot for walking in extreme cold.

must be avoided. The first precaution is to select the correct footgear as to type and size, and make certain it is tested and broken in before leaving home. A busy breadwinner is fortunate if he finds the time to remember to buy new boots for that cherished wilderness trip, let alone to wear them a few days. Thus, he arrives at camp with new, untried footgear. Chances are that he has purchased them of the same size as his street shoes. He is a prime prospect for foot trouble.

Now, as to the right size: *Always* purchase boots a little longer and a lot *wider* than your street shoes. You 'will be wearing heavier socks, perhaps insoles, and your feet will swell nearly a full size during a tough day afield. An added advantage of getting roomy boots is that the extra space around your foot will cushion it from stone bruises (common in the mountains).

Ideally, breaking in leather footgear is done gradually, starting with brief use (half an hour or so) and increasing the hours until you are able to wear your boots comfortably all day. At this point they are fairly well broken in— perhaps enough to take a chance on (though you *are* taking a chance). The perfect situation is to continue wearing them while walking over rough terrain for longer and longer periods, so that all stresses have given way to accommodate your particular foot. A lot of chaps do not realize that while the leather is being "worked" by your foot, the fibers in the leather are being softened and broken down, and they begin to conform to your foot. The dampening action from the sweat helps this process, while your feet become toughened up.

A shortcut is often used by some woodsmen, especially lumberjacks whose boots are made of heavier-grade leather than those generally used by sportsmen: If you have a really good, high-quality pair of oil-tanned leather boots, some weekend put them on over the socks (wool) you will be wearing afield and stand in a tub of water until they are good and wet. Say 15 or 20 minutes. (Do *not* do this with alcohol!) It is best to do it in privacy, lest the neighbors think you have suddenly gone off your gagoot. Now walk until they are dry. Then give them a good dubbing and you are a long way toward having a pair of broken-in boots. But don't try this little dido with cheap boots.

One way to ruin good leather boots is to dry them with direct heat. Always air-dry (in the shade) any leather boot that has been watersoaked—stuff the boots into shape with some dry material while they are drying.

I have long been convinced that I can get by nicely at least 98 percent of the time with six pairs of outdoor footwear. For mountain use, nothing beats a boot called (strangely enough) the mountain boot. Total height should be low (merely high enough to protect the ankles and to enable you to wade shallow mountain rivulets), say eight to ten inches of oil-tanned leather. Years ago the soles of such boots were studded with blunt hobnails. The modern Vibram lug

These fine-quality
mountain boots feature
scree-proof tops,
speed lacing, Vibram
soles and protective
reinforcements.
Such boots need to be no
higher than 10 inches.

soles of tempered rubber (or synthetic rubber) are much better. Don't make
the mistake of confusing these soles with any lug sole. These are scientifically
designed for *mountain use* and they cling to steep places like the hoof of a
mountain goat. There are other lug soles possibly as good for other uses (see
next section), but here we are discussing the true mountain boot.

For the deep woods and timberland where the snowfall is heavy, it's
tough to beat the leather-top, rubber-bottom shoe-pac type of boot. I like a
10-inch height. It is standard operating procedure to have at least two pairs
of good insulating, absorbent innersoles so that one pair can dry while the
other is being worn. These boots are equally useful in swampy terrain like
some of the woods in Maine or Michigan.

Possibly the most useful boot for general wear is the upland bird-shoot-
ing type which generally has a moccasin toe and a low profile. Its usefulness is
by no means confined to upland hunting but it is not a boot to be worn by
most of us on steep, rocky slopes, as the construction is too soft to give adequate protection and support under these trying conditions.

Extremely useful, even necessary for the keen sportsman, is a pair of
good rubber high-top insulated boots. There are leather ones which are not
only insulated but, the makers claim, waterproof. Be that as it may, my own
happen to be of rubber. I use them when I know I'm going to walk a little
and probably sit a lot, in cold weather. I use them, too, on horseback in frigid
temperatures, under my chaps, so that my feet and legs are cozy and warm.
Removable innersoles are a necessary accessory, the same as with the rubber-
bottom, leather-top shoe pacs. Don't put these boots on when they are icy
cold—some of them are so insulated your feet stay cold for an abysmally long
time. Becoming enormously popular ("discovered" by snowmobilers) are the

old-fashioned heavy felt booties slipped inside rubber footgear. These go back to 1880 or so, when all Northern farmers had a pair. They are delightful if you don't have to walk too much on bare ground. As I get older and smarter, I've taken a great liking to them.

Sooner or later, an item of every sportsman's equipment should be a pair of rubber hip boots. These are enormously useful for stream fishing, waterfowl hunting, even bear hunting on the coastal belt of Alaska and British Columbia. They are likewise handy if you have to negotiate low-growing thorns. Insoles are a must with these, too.

One of the most important items of footwear (though often overlooked) is a comfortable pair of lounging slippers for camp. These are as vital as a hat or a pair of trousers. In dry cabins, good old felt carpet slippers are excellent. So are moosehide moccasins, of which I am so inordinately fond that I get them by the half-dozen every time I hit the Yukon. These, alas, aren't worth a hoot for extended tent camping because they are not at their best when damp. There are many easy-on, easy-off slippers which thoroughly rest the feet and allow them to recuperate from a strenuous day afield. Among these is the Navajo-inspired (or possibly Apache) paleface version of ankle-high loungers, usually of chrome-tanned "elk" leather with sponge or foam-rubber soles. I have found the ones that work best are comfortable medium-weight-leather slipper-moccasins, both oil-tanned and chrome-tanned versions, with a composition or rubber sole. Once broken in, mine always feel about as comfortable and truly restful as anything I've ever had on my feet. And I can sashay around on wet ground for a reasonable distance without them getting soaked through. Indeed, there have been many occasions when I've hiked all day in them.

These few designs make up my own basic foot "wardrobe" and, I might add, they are the choice of many of my friends. There are variations on the theme, of course. Some will observe that I have omitted canvas-rubber sneakers, for instance, which are practically a way of life with many good fellows, especially on our sea coasts.

Soft-soled moccasin isn't
best footgear for hiking or
climbing, but it's hard
to beat for lounging about camp
or wearing in car or canoe.

Soles

The soles (including heels) of field boots or shoes aren't accorded the prestigious billing they deserve. I sympathize with boot pundits as they manfully strive to formulate rules to deal with a subject as rife with intricate variables as poker hands. For decades a colorful guide and shooting expert counseled that boots for all mountain use should have outlandishly high, undershot heels. These, he wrote "dig in" on precipitous slopes and insure the trusting tyro will not catapult derriere over tea-cozy, hurtling to a gruesome demise in some chasm. A pal, Terry Stone, tried these in the Yukon and nearly killed himself on talus slides. He fell so often he was black and blue, and the heels forced his toes forward until they ached. A light dawned when I met the expert. He was short, and fancied these elevated heels as an aid to height. More important, perhaps, he'd grown up in Western high heels, so maybe he couldn't walk or climb properly in anything else. So they suited *him*, in his unique locale.

I used to hunt the Yukon with a world-famous outfitter of Indian descent who was small and light and who'd grown up in soft-sole moosehide moccasins. He was agile as a chipmunk and tippy-toed over slithery shale slopes with the grace of Pavlova. For the heck of it, I treated him to a Utah deer and cougar hunt one time, and the first thing he did was shed his store leather oxfords and purchase canvas sneakers. He took that Wasatch Range like a praying mantis does an ailing June bug. For him the sneakers are correct, but they'd be just about the worst possible thing I could wear in the mountains. Once, I innocently took as gospel word that these no-heel flat-soles were murder because several highly respected outfitter cronies told me there ought to be a law against them. They had me accepting it. One Christmas I was sent a pair, and wore them about the property. They just suited my feet! For level country (unless it's slippery) they're so super that mine have taken me on two lengthy African safaris—the only shoes I wear there. Good as they are for flat walking, they're worthless to me in the mountains. The smooth soles with no heel to aid traction slither on dewy-grassed or snowy inclines or rocks.

Mountain and all rough-terrain soles must not slip. Traditionally traction was accomplished by soft-iron Hungarian hobnails affixed to rather thick leather soles. Some out-of-date books and die-hard authorities still mention them. I used to swear by them. The thick soles and sturdy heels dug in and the hobs and Swiss edging nails would catch on rock fissures and irregularities. But they did (rarely) slip, were noisy afield, tough on canvas and wood floors, and when the soles were wet the hobs pulled out. Came the day, as mentioned a ways back, when an ingenious, scientific lug sole called Vibram was invented in Europe. Mountain climbers fell upon this revolutionary development with glee. It's not just another lug sole. The pattern is cunningly conceived to guard your life and limb. The rubber composition is tempered in some way, to *hold*. Believe me, your first consideration and the primary function of good mountain boots *is to keep you on your feet, erect, in dangerous places*. Vibram soles on proper boots do this best.

There is an old wives' tale that lug soles are no good on flat ground because (get this) they "grip the sod" and your feet "slip inside the boots." In other words, the boots are anchored, but your feet slide about. Nonsense. Any baseball, football or golf expert will tell you it is not criminal for shoe soles to grip flat terrain. They *should* grip. You don't have to have soles bristling with fearsome spikes like lumberjacks who must walk on wet, rolling, mossy logs, but soles are not supposed to "slip a little," either. Prizefighters do not shuffle in that rosin box because it's stylish.

I'm aware of other soles-and-heels, from the leather cowboy "packer" to cord, plastic moulded like chain, or cleats—or with circles, arrows and other artistic creations. You may have your local, regional favorite which does well. In that case, I urge you not to tamper with success. One of the best *regional* soles I've ever seen is that used by African natives who cut sandles out of old truck tires. Splendid for the purpose.

Hiking on *dry* "flat" undulating terrain, nothing will beat the upland bird boot with low heel and composition sole. Preferred by some is the same type of boot with crepe, ripple or checkered "wedge" bottom. For snow, many like rubber-bottom leather-top pacs with a chain or cleat pattern.

Rain Gear

Thank heaven the old days of heavy, sticky, unwieldy oilskins are gone. You still see them occasionally, but most sportsmen are glad to be rid of them. In cold weather they turned stiff, and in hot weather they became soft and tacky and exuded an aroma not pleasing to everyone's nostrils.

There are many excellent heavyweight sets of rain gear that not only keep you dry but are so ruddy tough it is nearly impossible to snag and tear them in ordinary use. The best are those that consist of pants resembling big overalls, topped off by a roomy jacket. They are fine for a duck blind or steelhead angling where you won't have to walk much. In short, they are most useful for rugged, long-lasting wear. They are, however, heavy and a trifle unwieldy.

For most outdoor use, the full-length slicker is not so suitable. It's noisy,

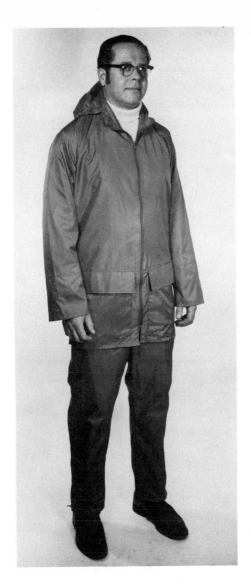

Good modern rain suit
is waterproof, extremely
durable, astonishingly
light. This one
features hooded, zippered
jacket with roomy
pockets. Pants have
elasticized waist and
fly front, plus
side zippers at leg
bottoms for easing on
or off over boots.

apt to become tangled in the legs, and the constant flapping and rustling has no place in nature. Saddle slickers, still preferred by many old-timers in the West, are longer than ordinary and have a slit up the back. This commodious rig protects not only you but the saddle, saddle bags, rifle scabbard and the whole upper mid-section of the horse. This is fine if you are going to stay in the saddle, but if you have to dismount and walk frequently, an oversized slicker is an absolute abomination.

Much better are the space-age lightweight rain suits. These are reasonably tough and durable, yet astonishingly light in weight. For some years now I have been using a lightweight rain suit consisting of roomy pants and jacket, and it is so light I can carry the pants in one pocket and the jacket in the other. The suit has other uses. The trousers double as chaps to protect the wearer's legs.

To look at this suit, you'd think it was a fragile thing. I suppose they can be torn, but I have worn my own on several pack trips in the Yukon, a couple in our Rockies, one jaunt in British Columbia—plus all the wear it gets in regular use at home—and I have had it for 21 years. Another advantage of this suit is that it makes an excellent windbreak garment, worn over other clothing. It has turned any wind I've ever encountered. The thing weighs a lot less than two pounds, total. It is an exceptionally tough nylon, coated with a modern plastic.

Since most waterproof fabrics don't breathe, one of the main problems encountered with rain gear is that of excess perspiration. Often a fellow finds himself as wet and uncomfortable as if he'd worn no rain gear at all. I try to avoid this by having the proper amount of clothing on under the rain suit, so as not to get overheated. Also, my rain suits are cut full. They are loose at every point—even the sleeves and legs are loose, allowing some moisture to dissipate. This suit, sold in better sporting-goods stores, is usually called a "golfer's rain suit."

I recently acquired a rain suit that is lightweight and indeed embodies all the qualities I feel a rain suit should have. It is close-weave nylon, tough, roomy, waterproof (as well as water-repellent, which is something else again)—and the fabric *breathes*. This is accomplished by a microporous coating that allows body vapor to escape through the fabric.

A rain suit, to be perfect for use afield, should always be cut very roomy, and I cannot stress this point too often. The suit should be cut so full it can be taken off or put on instantly. The pants should easily and quickly go on over the biggest boots—like mountain boots or rubber hip boots. There are times, as in a canoe or boat, when it is advisable to get rid of the suit in a hurry. Or conversely, to put it on without delay. You should never get "hung up" while doing either of these things. It could be dangerous as well as irritating. On horseback, in the mountains, donning or doffing rain gear easily is particularly appreciated because weather is as changeable as a pampered courtesan. I have, by the way, taken mine off or put it on while on horseback, but I don't suggest you try it unless you're an old hand with a steed. Some of those mountain horses may not take kindly to the procedure and will pile you alongside the trail. In any case, it isn't much trouble to dismount, quickly do the chore and remount.

7

Accessories

Packframes

No single type of pack or packframe is ideally suited for every backpacking purpose. Modern packs can be loosely categorized as three basic types. There is the little frameless day pack which is merely a canvas bag with two straps attached. Second, there's the ruck pack utilizing an "A"-shape metal frame. These packs are low-riding and concentrate the load low—great for negotiating dense undergrowth, for rock climbing, skiing or any situations where a high, heavy load on one's back is not to be courted. Third, under the normal conditions likely to be encountered by the average camper, certainly no other rig known to man can equal in comfort and efficiency the modern alloy *rigid-frame* backpack.

The frames are engineered to keep the load from contacting your back and to provide a bit of air circulation between the pack and your body. Properly loaded and adjusted, they project above the shoulders with part of the total weight not only high, but forward. Such a frame gives a minimum amount of back pull, thus enabling a hiker to travel in an upright, comfortable posture. The best rectangular alloy packframes not only are high, they have enough lower frame length to permit use of a sturdy, wide, hip belt which transfers an appreciable amount of the weight usually endured by the shoulders alone to the hip region.

In making your choice of a packframe, if you discover all other considerations and features are equal, check the weight. Some are lighter than others. All else being equal, it may behoove you to choose the lighter frame for your purpose. Ounces are as important to the backpacking enthusiast as to the gold prospector. The neophyte generally carries too much.

Most manufacturers of packframes sell a fine bag which is a fitted companion for a particular frame. While you may not actually need the bag, I advise getting one as it's so much more convenient. I wouldn't be without it. A modern Helio-welded packframe weighs from a bit less than three pounds to

With well-designed, rigid-framed backpack like Kelty model shown here, weight is distributed to reduce fatigue, and air circulates between pack and your body.

around four pounds. Many veteran outdoorsmen make exceedingly successful weekend backpacking trips without toting as much as 18 pounds. Or they have a full week of fun in the wilderness by carrying a total weight of less than 25 pounds! The secret of course is (1) proper planning, (2) lightweight equipment and (3) modern freeze-dried and dehydrated foods.

Backpack camping is a truly wonderful sport. Young people quickly, routinely fall under its spell. And while a doctor's advice should be asked, a good many senior citizens enjoy it. I have one neighbor in his 70's with a history of heart disease who regularly packs high into the Wind River Range out of Pinedale, Wyo. His obsession is taking color photographs with a heavy 4x5 Speed Graphic, and he goes *alone*. Age is no barrier, if one is in reasonable health and has medical sanction.

My favored day bag is the Eddie Bauer model; my pet *ruck*sack is the marvelous North Face "Wrap-around"; my favorite packframe is a Kelty.

The Alaska Packboard

There is continuing interest in the old-fashioned packboard. I do not know of an outfitter, guide, trapper, prospector or other sourdough in the North who does not have a packboard for his personal use. It may be custom or habit—but whatever the reason these men depend on the rig for their very lives and are staunch defenders of the design's admirable qualities.

Up North the general design (which may vary slightly in trifling details,

Top: on Crest Trail in
New Mexico, young backpacker
leading trio is using
padded hip belt to minimize
load on shoulders.
Bottom: Modern day pack
holds surprisingly
large cargo but is light,
comfortable, and
designed to permit full
freedom of movement.

but actually most of them are alike as two peas) is known as the Alaska or Alaskan packboard. It's easy to construct at home, once you've had a gander at one and make a couple of rough sketches; and ready-made packboards are still available through some camping-supply dealers. I have seen them listed under such sobriquets as "Indian," "Yukon," "Trapper Nelson" and "Guide Association." Some are made of aluminum, but the genuine unadulterated old Northern bush packboard is a frame of clear spruce. Spruce is light and strong, though other woods can be used.

The frame of an Alaska packboard consists of four or five pieces of wood—two uprights always, and two or sometimes three cross-pieces. Around the frame, a cover of 12-ounce canvas is *tightly* laced. Two adjustable shoulder straps of leather or webbing are affixed and you're in business.

The canvas runs around the frame, creating an air space between your back and the load. This keeps your poor back from being chafed by the load. With a packboard you can transport such items as large outboard motors, chain saws or other tools, moose antlers, odd-shaped (and some are odd, indeed) containers of grub, and so on.

In other words, the packboard lends itself to professional backpacking as well as casual jobs. It is magnificently versatile. The load is simply lashed to the frame (eyes or hooks being provided for the purpose). For a backpack trip you can just roll all your gear into a canvas shelter, lash it to the board and take off.

With the commercial models you can purchase a companion canvas bag which is instantly on or off by means of a couple of light steel rods securing the grommets in the canvas to the eyes on the packboard. Thus you have, in effect, a light framed rucksack—one which can quickly be adapted for heavy, bulky loads.

A good packboard is light—the largest size weighing three pounds. The canvas bag that came with mine weighs 1¾ pounds. The Army, by the way, had its own versions of the packboard. They aren't bad. Of course, the military made a passel of different backpack rigs. I heard that the packboards were made of plastic so I bought one and sawed a chunk off. This particular one was of molded plywood. I am not enthralled at the thought of using it. For one thing, I am leery about the fact that on mine the lacing (which should face out, away from the packer) is on the inside, next to the spine. And there are two rows of lacing, not a single row as on the genuine Indian-inspired packboard.

The old-fashioned (to some, outmoded) packboard may not win any beauty prizes. But it would be a mistake to sell it short for general wilderness use, whether in the North or elsewhere.

Jobson is shown here
using traditional
Alaska packboard, fitted
with canvas bag that
can be attached
or removed instantly.
When bag is off,
large, odd-shaped loads—
from tools to outboards
to grub containers—
can be lashed on securely
for easy carrying.

The Wilderness Knife

This particular little essay is not about war souvenirs, stilettos, Bowies or any other such collector's delights. Let's define a true wilderness knife: It's a high-quality cutting *tool* easily carried on the person, which will perform, away from civilization, any reasonable chore it is called upon to do. And it should do so for a period of years.

Good wilderness or bush knives fall into two basic categories—the sheath and the folding pocket knife. They must be well made, preferably with blades of high-carbon cutlery-type tempered steel. You often hear about "Sheffield" and "Solingen" steel. It saddens me to reveal that these names mean little as a guide to good steel. Sheffield is a city in Britain and Solingen a district in Germany, both long noted for the manufacture of cutlery. Using the terms without further elaboration would be akin to our saying Pennsylvania or Ohio steel. Some excellent knives come from both of these sources, and from others in England, Sweden, Germany, Japan, Italy, Spain, the United States, etc. Metallurgists and mechanical engineers of my acquaintance confide that our own steel is second to none, in all classes and grades.

There are laminated steel knives (quite highly touted), chrome and/or stainless steel (several varieties of stainless steel), and so on. Most of us do not have in our basement the means of determining if knife-blade steel is the kind designated #1040, #1095, or whatever. Nor do we have a Rockwell instrument to see if the blade runs 54 on the "C" scale. And we don't need it. The difference, afield, between (say) a custom $100 belt knife of top steel and a production knife costing about $10, made of high-carbon cutlery steel, is about the difference between 97¢ and a dollar. In fact, the high-carbon cutlery-steel blade may be better for chores afield. I find it so. The advantage of the high-grade custom knife is pride of ownership, and its relative scarcity. I will guarantee you it works very little, if any, better.

Whether you choose a pocket or a sheath knife is largely a matter of individual preference. If your inclination is for the pocket knife, for true wilderness use by all means get one designed for North Americans—for North

One-, two- or three-bladed folding pocket knife is among most versatile and useful camping accessories. Note simple, reliable, strong construction—without scissors, pliers or other such gimmicks.

Main blade of author's pocket knife is slightly over three inches long, and
after years of hard use all blades are "tight"—with no play or wiggle when open.

American use. That is the most practical. I do not know of a single top outfitter, guide or experienced rancher habitually carrying a European design of
knife unless it happens to coincide with our own time-proven types. Be especially skeptical of the ones that have (besides a blade, which is what we really
need) screwdrivers, files, scissors, magnifying glasses, bottle openers, pliers
and, as a medico pal of mine observed, "enough instruments to perform a
frontal lobotomy." These intricate and bulky examples of Old World skill undoubtedly have their place—but that place is either in the Swiss Army or on
certain specialized expeditions such as climbing mountain peaks. You are carrying a miniature tool kit.

The best all-round outdoor pocket knife is the design somewhat loosely
referred to as the stockman's knife. The main blade should be no less than
three inches long. It should, preferably, have a serrated edge on top for the
thumb. The rivet setup acting as a fulcrum or hinge for the blade must be of
the very best. The blade, when opened, should be tight (no play or wiggle)
and it should stay that way under years of ordinary use. The back spring holding the blade open (or closed) should function slick as a whistle. When the
blade is opened, there should be a smooth click or snap.

A stockman's knife is usually multibladed, but another excellent folding
pocket knife for the outdoorsman is the 3½-inch *single* blade. On this one, the

blade is working from the centerline of the handle and some experts like this feature. Another time-proven goodie is the two-bladed "Trapper's Model."

It is truly amazing what a good pocket knife can accomplish. My old hunting friend Johnnie Johns lived, hunted, fished and trapped in the Yukon bush for nearly 60 years: since around 1925 he carried a pocket knife with a single 3½-inch blade. He used it through 1960 when he gave it to me. It's on my desk right now where it serves me as a letter opener. What makes this knife a remarkable souvenir is that it has skinned out well over 100 grizzlies plus scores of other animals like Dall sheep, caribou, moose and beaver.

I have seen Johnnie fashion a very effective cold-weather woodburning tent stove with this knife and two 5-gallon oil tins. As anyone knows who has tried to cut them, the metal is pretty tough. With this same knife, Johnnie cut an end out of each can and then fitted together with force. Next he cut a door, a draft and a stovepipe hole. Without sharpening the knife he cut fine wood shavings and built a roaring fire. This sturdy little knife has a blade of high-carbon steel.

A large percentage of fellows prefer sheath knives—and, again, you can't go wrong with a good one. The ideal sheath knife has a blade no more than 4½ or 4¾ inches, 5 if you *must*. It should be at least 8/32-inch thick at the top near the hilt. It should have a generously wide blade with a sweeping, curved point for skinning, cutting meat and a thousand and one other outdoor uses. The top of this blade should be serrated so your thumb won't slip when covered with blood or grease or when your hands are numb. The sheath at the bottom should have a metal guard riveted on. If it doesn't come with this feature, lace the sheath with copper wire, so the sharp blade cannot come through the leather.

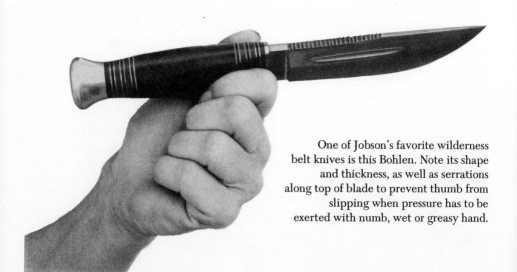

One of Jobson's favorite wilderness belt knives is this Bohlen. Note its shape and thickness, as well as serrations along top of blade to prevent thumb from slipping when pressure has to be exerted with numb, wet or greasy hand.

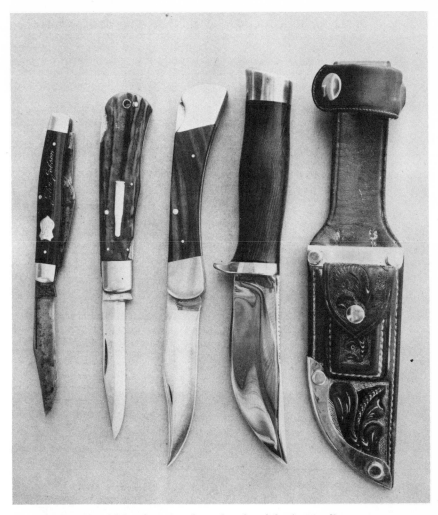

Here are three fine folding knives and one fine sheath knife. Handles are
shaped to provide firm hold and constructed for durability. Blades are shaped to
perform variety of tasks and made to hold edge and withstand abuse. Note
that blades are rather short; novice woodsmen tend to buy cumbersomely big knives.

If you wear your sheath knife on your belt, have it hang over one hip pocket, never in front. I carry my own sheath knife in the rucksack, and keep a folding stockman's knife in my pocket.

Here's a tip about the folding pocket knife; it is very important to apply an occasional drop of oil (with a pin) at the point where the blades hinge. Many good pocket knives are utterly ruined by failure to keep a little oil on the joints. Without lubrication, constant opening and closing quickly wears away the spring end, and the tip of the blade rises. It also develops side play.

"Why in the world do you suppose," I once asked several wilderness guides, "so many custom knife makers advise their customers to sharpen their blades with a stiff, rather blunt 30° or 35° chisel edge?" They shrugged. "It's no way to sharpen a field knife," one of them said.

They claim that a cold-chisel, blunt-wedge edge is best, because it lasts longer, and the knife doesn't need sharpening so often. But that's no great virtue. A blunt edge undoubtedly will "last" longer because it was never sharp to begin with. Amateurs fail to realize that in the woods you're constantly touching up a knife in use. A sharp edge simply cuts best. A pro works with a *cutting* edge.

Knife is pictured with cased honing stone in heavy, non-slip mount. Fine knives like this one deserve fine sharpening equipment and gentle, patient honing.

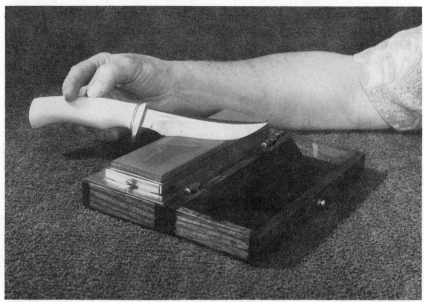

Any skilled outdoorsman uses a knife to *cut* with. It's an instrument for skinning, butchering, trimming fingernails, making dingle sticks, fuzz-sticks, cutting packs off a downed pack horse, and so forth. It must have a *razor-sharp* edge. It is not a machete, a hand axe or a cleaver, and it's not meant for hacking ten-penny nails in half.

For home or base-camp honing, manufacturers generally recommend using a bench-mounted soft Washita stone moistened with cutting oil (so far, so good) and tell you to patiently draw the blade over the stone, edge forward, as if the stone had grown hair and you were shaving it. Alternating sides, you proceed until the blade is sharp. If you want the most durable edge, hold it at approximately 30°, as they tell you to. A compromise edge is held at 20°, and the keen, sharp edge (which I recommend) is 10° or a mite less. A sincere old-time guide may tell you not to use that edge-forward technique except as a finisher to eliminate any wire edge. Well, I say *never* do it with a pocket stone. Afield, use a circular motion, and/or a barber's figure-8—probably the best. Don't be rough. Let the knife do the work and don't push or force it. In the bush you seldom have honing oil, so use kerosene if there's some on hand; next best is saliva, but water will do. In camp I have an eight-inch Washita soft bench stone and a four-inch Washita hard. On the trail, in my pocket, always, there's a double-surface stone of pressed bonded grit. Finish off the sharpening by stropping the blade on the heel of your hand if it's calloused, or on your boot. At this writing, there may be a new breakthrough in methods of sharpening. Much is claimed, but so far unproven.

The Camper's Axe

If you asked a Brooklyn Scout Master what is the best of all camping axes, one will get you three his choice is a belt axe. For the general use to which the average young Scout's axe is put, a belt tool is ideal. Besides, it looks jaunty and feels great, riding along on his hip. If you inquire of a logger in the State of Washington which is the best axe for camping, he may tell you he uses his big professional double-bit. He pounds in tent stakes with the flat of it, cuts with one side of it, and splits kindling with the other. He may, in a spirit of devilment, lovingly hone the keener side and shave with it. For him, this axe is correct. It is not best for most of us, though. Pin down a Wyoming rancher (among the most expert of all campers) and odds are he will tell you that the best axe for professional pack-train camping is the old barnyard single-bit chopping-block hardware-store axe—a heavy, practical, general-purpose axe.

Small belt axe, or hatchet, is light and easy to wear at hip, and it's perfect for light chopping or pounding jobs. But typical models like those pictured are too short for serious two-handed work.

Before leaving for the high country, the rancher may touch up the edge on a water-cooled abrasive wheel and make a handy, temporary sheath from a flattened tin can, to protect the edge. Then he'll possibly wrap the head in a gunny sack and tie it all up with binder twine. This rides on a pack horse and with it the rancher can, if he wishes, cut trees all day and he can use the blunt side for a hammer or even a maul. For him this is the perfect camp axe. But if he's hunting elk and moose he may tie on a *belt* axe to a saddle string. It's a good tool for splitting the carcass.

It is not difficult to figure out, from the foregoing, that the best camping axe for most of us is a compromise of various types. Fortunately, there are several beauties around, specifically designed for pleasure-camping.

The ideal axe for general camping is easy to carry, yet it must be able to perform in an emergency the duties of a full-sized axe. It must be light enough so it can be easily backpacked, and compact so it is no nuisance in any method of camping, including canoeing. Above all, the handle should be short enough to use one-handed, as a hatchet, and long enough to use two-handed, for serious axe work.

The steel in the head should be of the highest quality, and tempered to stand up under possibly grueling, brutal work. If the handle is wood, it must be of properly laid-out straight grain, tough, resilient and dense, such as hickory. There are other types used, like ash, and there are metal-handled camp

Top: Lumberman gives youngsters instruction in safe, efficient chopping of firewood. Right: Best" axe depends on chores it will most often perform. Here, from left, are full-sized utility farm axe, double-bitted logger's axe, camp axe of the Hudson's Bay style and all-round camping axe that Jobson helped to design. That last axe is light enough for easy backpacking, short enough for light work and long enough for two-handed use.

axes. It should come with a good leather sheath, and it should weigh approximately three pounds—2½ pounds of steel and half a pound of wood.

Such an axe is amazingly versatile! In fairly capable hands it can build a cabin. It will ride gracefully in your rucksack or tied on your packboard, ready to aid you in any situation from blazing trails in true wilderness to opening recalcitrant cans in camp.

You have a choice of three types of axe heads. There is a cunningly designed straight-handle double-bit camping axe. Another is the fairly ancient but romantic-looking and still popular "Hudson Bay" canoe cruiser axe. It's light, with a dogleg or sheepsfoot handle, a narrow shank and wide blade, giving the vague appearance of a Mohawk tomahawk. It's useful—if you overlook the thin, narrow portion of the head where the handle is inserted. To me the best of the lot is one that looks like the Hudson Bay but has a bone-hard hickory *straight* handle and a wide shank to hold that handle tight under extraordinary field use. I prefer the straight handle to the dogleg because I use it a lot one-handed, sometimes from horseback, blazing or clearing branches from trails. Its balance is simply perfect for me, whereas a curved handle is an abomination.

Power Saws

We are not concerned here with the big professional chain saws such as those used in lumber camps. They are too heavy, too expensive, and are not designed for camp use. A camp chain saw usually has direct drive with an automatic clutch. One feature of the automatic clutch is that when the motor is idling the chain does not turn, or at least if it should turn, it goes very slowly so as not to be dangerous. When ready to cut, you advance the throttle and the chain simply whirs.

There is another type of gasoline portable saw which isn't a chain saw but rather has a blade that goes rapidly back and forth in a reciprocating manner. This type makes cleaner cuts than a chain saw and is very light, but from what I've seen it cannot begin to put out the amount of general work a chain saw does.

A small chain saw is good for many things. It's wonderful for clearing old trails. By carrying a few spikes and a hand axe in your gear, you can build a picnic table in the wilderness. Some fellows use a chain saw for cutting holes in the ice for fishing!

Some of the better features of a good contemporary camp chain saw include roller bearings throughout, all-position carburetor, fuel-resistant air fil-

Gasoline-powered chain saws now come in very light, compact models like this one, which has innumerable base-camp uses and can be handled as safely as an axe.

ter, self-energizing centrifugal clutch, hard chrome-lined cylinder, forged steel crankshaft.

A chain saw is no more dangerous than an axe. We shouldn't daydream and woolgather while using either. Never use a chain saw in an unventilated enclosure, and keep away from the moving chain. Never touch the chain when it is moving. Don't spill fuel on a hot motor and (needless to say) be careful of smoking around fuel. Read the manual of operating instructions that comes with your saw; it will inform you how to maintain and operate it. Some show you the basic cuts to make when "logging" and trimming.

Chain saws are at their best away from conventional organized family campgrounds. They are more for the serious outdoorsman—the wilderness camper. There are laws in some sections restricting the use of "internal-combustion engines" and these laws are interpreted differently by different officials. If in doubt, check with your regional forester, ranger or other local authority. Ownership of a chain saw does not give one license to promiscuously cut standing timber. It seldom gives you the right to fell live trees. If you have a compelling reason to do so, again, check with the local authorities in charge of such matters.

The Versatile Tarpaulin

One of the all-time greatest boons to healthful and enjoyable outdoor living is a common square of fabric so unpretentious it rarely gets a second look. Called *"tar*paulin" (from windjammer days when canvas sheets sheltering hatches and gear were tarred to withstand heavy weather), it quite possibly is a camper's most versatile piece of gear.

There are all kinds of tarps. Big ones called "covers" top haystacks, leaky barn roofs and gridiron turf. In earlier times, smaller ones called "wagon-sheets" safeguarded the precious cargo of prairie schooners. Today tarp covers still enclose the payloads of farm trucks. In wilderness base camps, little ones dot the area like dandelions, covering supplies, saddles and such. They're used as shelters, sails, covers, beds, water reservoirs, canopies, and in emergency are fashioned into chaps and functional clothing.

When a tarp is rigged over a tent to insulate it from the sun's heat (lowering the temperature 15 degrees) or to aid in fending off heavy downpours, it's called a fly. It's likewise a fly when improvised as a shelter to sleep or cook under. Fly shelters are erected snug or airy, high or low, taut or loose, peaked or flat. An excellent emergency canoe is made afield by constructing a wooden framework and covering it with a tarp. When loading a conventional canoe, store the gear on an opened tarp laid on the bottom, then fold over the rest of the tarp. To make a cozy nook for sleeping, lay the canoe (high and dry) on its side, staking and stretching a tarp over it. California campers pack tarps for windbreaks to keep the flying desert sand and grit out of food and hair and eyes.

Most tarpaulins offered for sale are rectangular, but all-round bests are square. I prefer a 10-foot-by-10-foot tarp of 10-ounce, top-grade, high count cotton fabric (not plastic!), made water-repellent with a tent-type treatment, not "oil tempering." Your all-round tarp is better without the traditional rope sewn in the hem but, depending upon which tentmaker is doing it, the edge should *at least* be lap-felled and double double-stitched with heavy thread. The corners (ideally) should be reinforced with grommets set in sewn-on leather. Extra grommets lend versatility. My 10-by-10 tarps have eight to each side.

Have your personal tarp *always* with your bedroll. Don't lend it. It doesn't hurt to have several tarpaulins. Another useful square of canvas (particularly to backpackers), usually made of 5½-ounce fabric about 11½ feet by 11½ feet, weighing 6½ pounds, is the so-called "tarp tent." In addition to grommets, it has about nine strategically paced tie-tapes sewn to the square. This doesn't take the place of a conventional sportsmen's tarpaulin—nor does

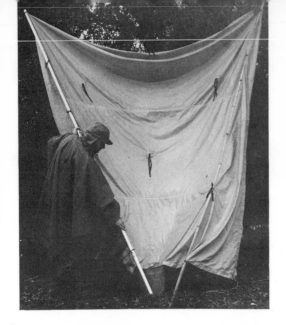

Your tarp's uses are limited only by your own needs and ingenuity. Photos
show one being used to catch rain water (top), as simple wilderness tent (above,
left) and as temporary fly (above, right) when showers threaten during
lunch break. Author recommends 10-by-10-foot tarp made of 10-ounce water-repellent cotton. He likes plenty of strong grommets and no rope sewn into hem.

Here are some additional clever uses for large, square tarps,
including quickly pitched one-man shelter (top left),
"porch-style" lean-to that will accommodate two or even three
sleepers (top right), insulating and moisture-stopping
wrap for sleeping bag (above) and temporary roofing over
campground picnic table (right). Note that guy line
holding tarp roofing in place is doing double
duty as clothesline. And garments hanging there serve as
warning flags so that no one will inadvertently
bring Adam's apple into painful contact with taut rope.

a sheet of inexpensive plastic, which has camp uses but can never substitute for a real tarp.

Basic Compass Points

The average camper doesn't need a course in abstract navigation. All we want is to be able to find our way back to camp after an adventurous day afield. A reliable pocket compass and rudimentary know-how should do it every time.

We are here discussing the *low-price* pocket compass. I know there are such revolutionary instruments around as pocket transits—and, indeed, a whole line of more expensive (and more reliable and accurate) portable compasses. I own and use them. But I likewise own and use inexpensive, expendable, light pocket compasses. I have "reckoned" with them since pre-Tenderfoot Scout days with complete satisfaction. Like old Dan'l Boone, I never truly got myself lost, but a few times I have become real confused. A compass would have saved me much annoyance. Incidentally, do not *ever* consider yourself hopelessly "lost" in a permanent sense. "Lost" is a state of mind. Ignore it. Recall the yarn about the Indian who was never lost. It was the camp that rudely got lost. The same applies to sportsmen.

The thing to do is to remain calm. Occupy yourself. Build a fire if fuel is available. Don't be in a hurry. Construct some sort of shelter. Have some green material handy to throw on the fire for an eye-catching smudge. You may miss a meal or two and have to awaken several times during the night to feed the fire, but these are not catastrophes of lasting import.

In selecting an inexpensive, featherweight pocket compass for ordinary use, bear in mind that the functions required of it are not elaborate. You seldom hike more than 15 or 20 miles, and you do it at a *slow rate of speed which enormously lessens risk of error.* If you're looking for a fishing spot, hunting or taking photos, you'll be wandering and sometimes more or less circling, so you'll be closer to your camp or other point of origin than the miles walked. You may not walk over four or five miles and often, therefore, are within a mere rifle shot of camp.

I should caution that there is one hazard in continued use of *inexpensive* compasses: The needle bearing on some wears rapidly; they are not to be used with confidence for too extended a period—say, five or six seasons. But for casual, uncomplicated "charting" and navigating a few miles at walking speed, all that's required of a compass is to indicate the four main points. Other degrees can be reasonably estimated from these four alone.

Some compasses, like this one, have adjustable marker to indicate declination—that is, deviation of magnetic north from True North. This is convenient, but you can compensate for lack of such features by following instructions in text.

Physically, the simple pocket compass is quite small. It has a needle (sometimes a floating dial). The needle on the proper end should be plainly marked "N" or "north." Do not ever consider any compass lacking this feature. Some compasses have the needle tip and key directions artistically dabbed with luminous paint—which, if you've managed to find yourself far from camp after dark, could be a convenience in extricating your person from shintangle in pitch blackness—but that situation is to be avoided if possible.

The *only* function of the inexpensive compass is to indicate key directions by showing where North is, nothing more. It has no magic qualities to lead you to and from camp by itself. When you know where North is, you calculate the rest.

Obviously, a compass is enormously more beneficial if used with a detailed map. Compasses and maps should be inseparable companions. If you are near major rivers, roads, and highways, an ordinary road map will often keep you out of extreme difficulty. But in unfamiliar wilderness, a detailed topographic map of the area is advisable. On this, you should plainly mark your campsite.

Take compass readings as you leave camp—orient yourself on the map with the camp—and at regular intervals throughout the day as you change direction, note the time (as closely as 15-minute quadrants; later as you grow more expert, you extend this to hourly readings). At each new compass reading, lightly mark your present position on the topographic map. After the lunch break (customarily about midway through your day afield), if you've been going straight out from camp, start heading back. If you've been circling the camp area, sometime during mid-afternoon head for camp. Adopt the strict habit of not cutting your time too fine. If for no other reason, there are camp chores which are best done in daylight.

In addition to the geographical north pole, which is north of wherever you may be, there is the very important magnetic pole, which is where your compass needles should point without outside interference. Sometimes the magnetic pole is dead north of you; more often it is not. In the United States the true-north line proceeds diagonally from several leagues off the east coast of Florida to where it crosses the Canadian border north of Lake Superior. Which indicates that if you live in Ohio, for instance, chances are your compass needle points true north, or so close as to be of slight consequence for compensation purposes. The farther we travel in this land east or west of this line, the greater the error with which we have to cope, especially in the Northwest (such as Washington, Oregon, Idaho and western Montana).

The solution is astonishingly simple: find the approximate number of degrees by which True North deviates from magnetic north (where the needle points). If the map you are using doesn't have this difference (called declination) marked on it, do it yourself. Suppose you're camping somewhere in our West; the declination from magnetic north to True North would be rather a substantial pie-wedge portion of the compass dial. Place the identifying "N" on the compass dial to coincide with where the "N" end of the needle tells magnetic north is. Then rotate the compass body or housing slightly to line up with True North on the map, and you'll see the angle of difference. You can simply mark this declination on your map. You can see (accurately enough for hiking purposes) where True North is—and can take it from there. A number of compasses have some method of compensating for deviation of magnetic azimuth—in other words, they can be set for the declination.

Those wishing to know the correct east and west declinations in this country can send 50¢ to the Coast and Geodetic Survey, Washington, D.C. 20025, requesting a copy of the 1960 Isogonic Map. As the various lines on this map "waver" slightly, I assume that not only is magnetic north indicated but also local disturbances such as ferrous and other mineral deposits. Which reminds me that local interference such as high-voltage cables, guns, knives, metal buttons, belt buckles, proximity of automobiles, outboard motors, etc., can lead to erroneous compass readings. My general procedure is to see if the compass deviates when I'm holding a rifle. If there is any deviation at all I find a flat spot, lay down the topographic map with four rocks (or whatever)

The late Red Higgins, well-known guide and outfitter, sights his Army compass on landmark. Good compasses usually have simple sighting devices that help you check direction fast and accurately.

holding the corners, place the level compass on the map and step back a trifle for the final accurate reading.

Many cheap compasses have no means of "sighting," i.e., holding it at eye level and looking through it or its mirror to line yourself up accurately with terrain or landmarks in your chosen direction. The solution is that when you wish to choose a specific direction, get your compass reading, select an unmistakable, immovable landmark such as a distinctive hill or whatever and walk directly toward that. I mention immovable because I once had a buddy who took a dead reckoning on a heifer and didn't make it back to our Colorado camp for 82 hours. He finally arrived disheveled, tawdry, red-nosed, with horrible bags under his eyes and vague references to passing through Taos, N.M. He also muttered something unintelligible about two cantinas and three senoritas.

Binoculars

A good, standard-weight binocular is among the most important and useful items of outdoor equipment a camper can own. Put it to your eyes, properly focused, and your eyesight takes wing. Where before you may have merely been looking at a mountain or a canyon wall, with the binocular you are there. Instead of mass and color, you see individual rocks, twigs and wildlife. In terms of clarity and detail, with a binocular your eyesight equals that of any mammal alive, including even sheep and antelope.

It is a waste of money to purchase a cheap binocular. Generally the cheap ones lack definition—the ability to resolve detail. If you are looking at a moose, you see it magnified, all right, but it is a magnified blur. With a good binocular you see the hair on his coat and the gleam in his eye. Cheap binoculars more often than not aren't properly collimated (or if they are, they do not maintain collimation very long). That is to say, the images you see through the "monocular" at each eye do not exactly fuse, or mesh. There is some slight bleeding or overlap of the two images. Buying a binocular is one of those things in life where it pays to get the best.

Binoculars are designated as 6x30, 9x35, 8x32 and so forth. The first number is the magnifying power and the second is the diameter in millimeters of the front, or objective, lens. Generally, the bigger the objective lens in relation to power, the brighter the glass. Six power is probably the best for timbered country; for the mountains and plains, 8, 9 or 10 power. The 7x35 is conceded to be the best *all-around* glass for most people. The 7x50 binocular is a good marine or night glass but most campers feel it is too bulky to be worn suspended from the neck.

Obtaining a good binocular and becoming educated in its use are two separate endeavors. You can always spot an amateur at the game. He will stride purposefully and confidently to some excellent vantage point, adjust his glass, and make several casual, sweeping panoramic gestures hither, thither, and around and about the horizon and mutter, "Nope. Nothing there." He then replaces the glass in the case or inside his shirt front.

Not the expert. If he is looking for game, the first thing he does (if he can) is to be inconspicuous. Whatever he's looking for, he assumes a position where his glasses are rock-steady. He makes no grand sweeps. He blocks off (in his mind) the areas he wishes to search, and then painstakingly scrutinizes each little chunk of topography. He is patient. Is that a twig? Or a portion of an antler? Was that a movement? Let's watch that for awhile. Is that little patch of white a bit of snow, frost, a rock—or is it a portion of a ram's rump?

Good binocular is among most valuable items of camping gear, and spotting scope is also very useful. Best general-purpose binocular is 7x35mm.

An experienced outdoorsman will study an area as a dedicated scientist will study a rare culture of bacteria or virus under a powerful microscope.

Let me mention three other kinds of glasses a camper might carry. If big-game hunting is the purpose of some of your camping trips, you should have a good 20-, 25- or 30-power spotting scope. Its field of view is too small for effective scanning and locating of game—the binocular does that—but the spotting scope's greater power tells you whether you're looking at a good trophy. Without a time-consuming, laborious stalk, it really provides a close look at an elk's antlers or a sheep's curl. The other two optical accessories I have in mind aren't for hunting but for all kinds of camping trips. Whatever you're doing and wherever in the wilderness you happen to be, they can enhance your enjoyment. One is a low-power pocket microscope, with which you can closely examine insect life, tiny plants and the tiniest parts of plants. The other is a good magnifying glass, which can do the same sort of thing to a slight extent and—besides enhancing your enjoyment—can add to your comfort and safety. It's excellent on trips for many things, from taking out splinters to even starting a fire if you have good tinder and the sun is out. By the way, in picking a binocular, do not overlook the value of the small "pocket" models. These days they are excellent.

Plastic Containers

Through the years, I diligently sought the ideal wilderness container, and about a decade ago I found it. I took a long canoe trip on that chain of mighty inland mountain lakes in the southern Yukon Territory. It was impossible on a journey such as this to avoid moisture. Not only moisture, but pure drenchings. At times it rained the way it does in Pago Pago, and in two emergency beachings we hit the breakers and swamped. But not one item of food got the least bit damp. My film and optics remained bone-dry. Our first-aid kit remained as it came from the pharmacist. Our ample supply of bakery bread remained fresh until used. Eggs came through perfectly. Lettuce, celery, bell peppers remained crisp and delectable. Likewise some grapes. Our dehydrated and freeze-dried foods were the same as when shipped from the plant. No mice or insects got into our food.

And so we come to the wilderness containers themselves: common plastic household and refrigerator boxes with watertight lids. Before that Northern trip, my wife introduced me to them. They're the semi-rigid, durable plastic type whose covers seal with such tenacity they could be termed her-

Grub box at left has folding legs. Its compartments hold portable camping
stove, plenty of freeze-dried meals, large pot and other utensils, plus foods in
tight-lidded plastic containers. Lantern sitting on top is mantle type
powered by LP gas. Another good grub box is double-opening kind, shown above.

metic. Or perfectly airtight. They are dustproof, waterproof, verminproof.

Before leaving for the Far North, I filled a nine-quart one with water, installed the lid according to directions, and tossed it off my front porch. It did
not spill a drop, nor was it damaged in any way. It would hold that water indefinitely. These containers are obtainable in a formidable variety of shapes
and sizes. By judicious contemplation it is possible to find the correct size and
shape for most any item with little wasted space. Another dandy feature of
these plastic containers is that they impart no odor to the contents, and they
are easily cleaned. But they will not stand boiling grease nor should they be
placed too close to the campfire.

Boxes

For some reason, all kinds of boxes appeal to campers. We are pushovers for
them and if our wives didn't surreptitiously adopt some sort of inventory control, heaven alone knows where it would end.

For a good many years we had a couple of wooden boxes with mortised corners in which shotgun ammunition was shipped. These had been painted, many times, and I'd hinged the covers and installed a rope handle on each end. They were exceedingly useful to us until they wore out. I still miss them.

Older box aficionados had a field day after World War II as the military has a necessary fondness for boxes and containers; a cornucopia of surplus poured into civilian hands, and you can still find a few goodies. There comes that time, all the same, when a fellow takes tools in hand and builds himself his heart's desire.

An instance when it could be astute to do it yourself is the decision to acquire a set of panniers or pack boxes. These are for sale—but necessarily rather expensive—so many chaps build their own. Of all the box-type equipment I can visualize offhand, these are the most practical if a guy takes pack trips—that is, travels by horse and uses pack horses.

Another exceedingly practical box is what we usually call a food box. A well-planned one carries food as well as the tools and utensils used for preparing and serving outdoor meals. Generally there's space for your camp stove and other necessities such as soap, towels, spices, condiments, dry foods, matches. Usually these boxes are built so that the front drops down as a (shelf) work area or outdoor kitchen table.

An excellent feature is that it is pretty tough to forget any food item. The nested cooking kit, cutlery, spices, etc., can be stored in the box at home. We have freeze-dried meals, canned butter, tomato paste, dry soups, canned bacon, etc., along with other gear, in the box, so whether it sits in the garage for three days or three weeks matters little. When we're ready to go we place it in the pickup or station wagon and take off.

Some fellows customarily set their food boxes on a stump, rock, or opened tailgate; others like a folding stand or legs on the bottom of the box. We have both types and use them both, depending upon which kind of camp we're making. The type with legs is most versatile.

It's no great feat to build a food box from exterior plywood, fastened together with marine glue and either bronze anchor nails or screws. It should have a hinged front cover which (open) suspended on chains serves as a work table. Dimensions are not at all critical: a food box is larger than a foot locker but not so big as a large trunk. The main thing is to have it handily accommodate food and cooking equipment. One of my food boxes measures 30 inches long, 20 wide and 18 high. The other is 36 long, 16 wide, and 17 high. All manner of compartments, hooks, rods, didos and curlicues can be built in to safely hold your little goodies.

Cold Cache

"Cache" is a term used by old-timers in the North to mean most any kind of storehouse. Specifically though, a Northern cache is a platform atop three or four tall poles to store food and gear above the reach of bears, wolverines, mice and other marauders.

If the cache is a more or less permanent one, quite often a little cabin is built on the platform. If the builder is lucky, he is able to select a spot where he can utilize two or more living trees for the uprights. This will save him digging post-holes, often through permafrost. In an outfitter's wilderness base camp, the boys find three trees growing suitably close together; they trim the branches and cut the trees off at a height that will discourage the most enterprising grizzly. Around the poles they nail slick tin or aluminum sheeting so that no beast can get a claw hold. Horizontal poles are placed between the cut off trees making a triangular platform-base. Across this they lay smaller poles to make an adequate floor upon which to place supplies. Over the supplies they generally secure a tarp, lashed down firmly enough so no storm can whip it awry.

The ladder for reaching the platform is made of two stout poles with smaller branch lengths for the rungs; it is kept away from the structure when not in use. A cache is a most necessary item where a grizzly or wolverine can quickly find access into an ordinary cabin (and a tent presents no problem to them). Often they will destroy everything in the way of food they seek, and they will tear to shreds anything made of leather or fabric. It's wise to keep the bulk of the food out of the dwelling and safe atop a cache.

Making Leather Straps and Accessories

Leather straps are fun to make and some prefer them to web straps. Leather can be obtained in bulk from a leather supply house in many of the larger cities. To cut straps accurately, in one continuous length, nail a small block of wood to some flat surface like a plank, then measure on the block the exact width you wish your straps to be. At this point drive in a knife with an extremely keen blade. Carefully and slowly feed the edge of your "squared off" bulk leather between the block and the blade, and *voila!* Soon you have a length of strap leather. Woodsmen use this same idea for cutting thongs—except that instead of using a piece of hide with one squared off edge, they begin with a round piece of leather.

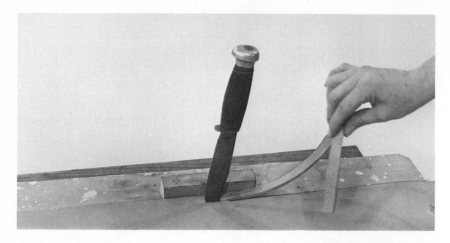

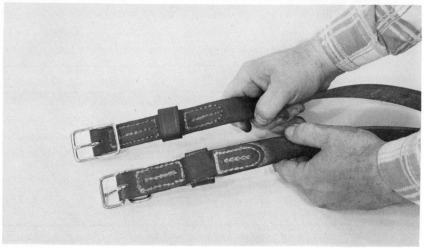

Top: Using small wood block as guide, it's easy to cut leather straight for straps. Bottom: Heavy, durable stitching, done with awl, harness-maker's needle and beeswaxed harness thread, makes well-buckled straps and belts for camp use.

A more accurate way to cut straps is with a tool known oddly enough as an adjustable strap cutter, likewise obtained at leather-supply establishments and large hardware stores. I've had one for many decades and I imagine I paid something like $3.75 for it; possibly now they cost seven or eight bucks. It has cut hundreds of straps and is good for cutting thousands more.

It's best to have a leather hole punch—either the type hit with a mallet or the pliers type which has a little rowel with several different-sized punches

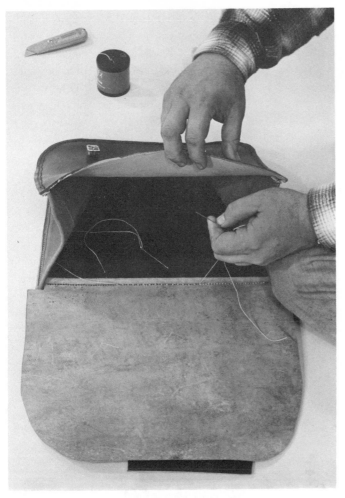

Jobson likes to make his own saddle bags for pack trips.
They hold so many items so conveniently and look
so good that they often end up as gifts to admiring friends.

on it. I like to sew buckles and keepers on, rather than riveting. The projects go smoother if you have a few harness-maker's needles, an awl (though a sharpened ice pick will do for this) and a supply of harness thread and beeswax for lubricating it. As you progress in leather-working, a few more tools can be added that will give the finished work a more professional look. All the tools are inexpensive.

We like to make our own saddle bags. Mine have a habit of ending up in my pal's outdoor gear. Some fellows like ornately tooled leather work. I am one who doesn't, particularly if I am the guy who has to do it. I like to tell myself I enjoy the pristine sheen of well-kept English saddle-tanned leather; that the texture of good leather pleases my eye, but then it could be that I couldn't do a real job of tooling leather anyway, if I tried. I'll never know.

A lot of fun for campers, this leather work! Fun and worthwhile. Straps are a good place to begin. If you like working with leather you'll discover it when making straps—and conversely if you aren't wild about it you'll discover that also. In either case you aren't out of pocket a heck of a lot.

I do not like to fasten together *any* leather article with rivets. I'd rather sew it. Sewing is easy. Experienced harness makers may scoff at my technique, but I learned it from old-timers on ranches when I was a boy, and I've never changed my method. First you clamp or cement together the parts to be sewn. Next, punch the holes with an awl. Thread two harness needles, one on each end of a length of harness thread, and go through the holes from each side, making a double stitch. Pull up tightly. When finished, place on a hard flat surface and tap with a hammer, sinking the stitches. This works for me. I have never had any of this kind of leather stitching come apart—and I am still using certain items made as a boy.

Some campers who often go by horse prefer to have their own saddles. Author feels this one has good cantle for mountain riding but not enough pommel swell. Scabbard is vital accessory if hunting is purpose of camping trip. Homemade saddle bag and scabbard show here are excellent.

Petroleum jelly has many camping uses, including rust prevention. If axe head begins to work loose, author coats metal with jelly, then soaks it in water to make wood swell.

Petroleum Jelly

Petroleum jelly is a handy item to include in your camp gear. Besides its more common and general uses, it is an excellent means of painlessly removing ticks which have submerged their dratted heads in your tender epidermis. Put a glob over the tick. This cuts off his air, or something—in any case he backs out, head and all, and you then can properly stomp the little s.o.b.

If you run out of regular grease and oil, you can coat a thin layer on axe heads and other gear liable to rust. On the subject of axes—if the head is working loose, coat the *metal* portion with petroleum jelly and then soak the whole head in water. The wood will swell and tighten in the axe head.

While petroleum jelly will not exactly burn like a magnesium bomb, it does burn and in wet weather it can be smeared on damp twigs for an emergency fire starter.

It makes a pretty good lamp, too. One time in the Rockies I was most eager to catch up on my notes. Many things had happened that day and I was anxious this evening to get something on paper before the inspired flush of memory waned. For me, it's easy to happen. We were long out of candles, and I was down to my last set of flashlight "D" batteries, which were too valuable to use for extended periods. It was raining pitchforks outside the tent, so a fire was out of the question. I grumbled a bit and the ever-considerate outfitter got two tin can lids. One was flat, having been cut from the top of a can of tomatoes—and the other was a screw-top from a pound tobacco tin. In the center of the flat lid, he fashioned a small hole with his pocket knife, then he cut a short length of cord (he said a strip of rolled rag would work just as well) and smeared it with petroleum jelly. He put part of it through the hole in the flat lid, leaving a "tail" dangling. This was the "wick." He put a liberal amount of jelly in the dish-like lid, placed the other atop, and touched a match to the wick. It sputtered and then worked perfectly.

Especially when the grass and undergrowth is wet with dew, or in rainy weather, some archers like to put a thin layer of this substance on the feathers of their arrows. It's good, too, for recalcitrant ferrules on fishing rods. If leather items in your gear start to weather and crack in the wilderness (and you are fresh out of leather-dressing), a judicious amount of petroleum jelly will fix things nicely. I never put gun oil on leather, by the way. It soaks in too deeply, darkens, and generally just ruins good leather.

If enamel or paint is chipped from camping equipment (lanterns, outboard motors, etc.), coat the spots with petroleum jelly to prevent rust—until you can sand and repaint the unprotected areas. If small patches of canvas (like a tent roof) start capillary leaking, smear the offending area with jelly. Often this stops the water from coming through most effectively.

One time on a hunting trip in British Columbia, I found myself in the excruciatingly sad position of being completely out of gun oil. We had flown into the area by bush plane and the rapid changes in altitude had leaked every last drop of oil out of the metal container. It rained like a blind cow and I noticed with agitation that specks of rust were forming on my two gorgeous custom sporting rifles. I was teary over the whole thing, of course, but was especially concerned with the bores.

After some brooding, I went to the outfitter's medicinal chest and rummaged about. There was his supply of Vaseline, which I promptly confiscated. I smeared a trifle on a patch and warmed it over the sheepherder stove. Also, I warmed the metal portions of the rifles. Then I pushed the patch through the barrels and finished the job by wiping all exposed metal on the pieces. The guns arrived home in perfect condition. A word, though: Never shoot a gun that has any kind of grease in the barrel without first wiping it out with a dry patch.

Camper's Fishing Rod

Some of the best natural stream and lake angling anywhere is found when a camper is packed way in back of beyond. I know dozens of trout- and grayling-filled streams that are fished no more than a couple of days a year by two

Light flyrod can be camper's delight. Conventional type, like rod that took this rainbow, is practical around many camps, but backpackers may prefer four-section takedown model.

or three sportsmen at most. There is no book of etiquette or pamphlet on State Department protocol I know of which says it is either gauche or unlawful for a man to take his favorite two-section fishing rod on a Rocky Mountain pack trip. However, I would not do it. The average case for these, made of aluminum, fiber, or fiberglass, is rather long and just a bit awkward; and it's not the easiest item to secure to a pack horse.

So it's an astute maneuver to include some other means of angling those unfished waters. Of course, a fresh-cut willow or birch pole will put meat on the table, but it's not considered angling by most. There's a better answer. I have had fine success with a "backpacker's" four-section, 4½ ounce, seven-foot fiberglass flyrod which fits into a sturdy aluminum case only 23 inches long. It's a breeze to pack. In fact, I often carry it in my saddle bag. There are even lighter and stronger rods on the market.

Archery for Campers

One of the best side sports for family campers is archery. My own bow-shooting background goes clear back to kindergarten days, and at one time I earned coffee and Danish by means of exhibition archery. I used the old-fashioned English long bow, which has not changed since the battle at Crecy in 1346. In comparison, the new recurved fiber bows cast a shaft like a bullet.

I haven't read an archery book in 20 years, but I doubt if the following basic games have changed a great deal. Before leaving home as a lad to seek adventure, my pals and I played the game of "roving"—shooting to varied "targets" or marks at unknown distances. You select a mark in the direction you're hiking. If not in precise line then zag a little. Just so you get back to camp in the end. We'd select a mark like a certain tuft of field grass, a clod on a bank, a big weed, most anything that stood out, was harmless to shoot at and easy on arrows. We'd try to vary the distances and it taught us to judge range accurately and to gauge wind. There is no harm in this, if reasonable safety rules and good judgment are adhered to. There are all sorts of variations of roving and if natural targets don't grab you, good ones are quickly made of old wire coat hangers, tape and cardboard.

One or two of my old cronies were golf fans—so we'd lay out a nine-"hole" course on some cooperative farmer's back forty. The cup was an upright circle of paperboard. We made markers of little rag flags tied to sharpened laths. Our "drivers" as they were known then were flight arrows—made mainly for distance. Our "putters" were flu-flu bird arrows.

Flight shooting for maximum distance is worthwhile sport, particularly if you like a lot of fast walking or jogging to get into prime condition, and so is what we called "butt shooting." This may be the traditional name for an ancient game they played in "Merrie Olde," but our game was to try and hit marks on the ground at greatly extended ranges.

If archery games have any disadvantage for the camper, it is that usually they cannot be played in parks or at most conventional public campgrounds. These days it is mandatory to obtain permission from landowners before trespassing to camp or to rove or play archery golf. But that is not generally as irksome as it sounds. I have yet to be turned down by a rancher or farmer.

Newcomers should find a sporting-goods store with a salesman who knows about archery tackle and is himself an archery enthusiast. It is just about vital to have the tackle fit each member of the family—size, weight of pull, length of arrows. There are times when small youngsters with toy archery sets can have a world of fun in camp, shooting rubber-tipped play arrows at animal cutouts and pictures pinned to a woolen blanket backstop. The

Jobson teaches a camping friend, Maynard Lambert, rudiments of archery. Bow and arrows offer enjoyable diversion for campers.

This archery target was improvised from cardboard, tape and wire coat hanger. If reasonable safety rules are followed, good camp sport is long-distance bow shooting at marks on ground—a challenging test of range estimation and wind judgment.

backstop should not be hung where arrows can cross a campground road, path, or adjoining campsite.

Another fine archery game is balloon breaking. Multihued balloons dancing across the grass make a colorful, harmless target and will train youngsters in the art of estimating trajectory and lead. Balloons can be pinned to the aforementioned expendable heavy wool blanket, or they can be tied to a string and staked. In a breeze, they dance about enticingly, making the game more tricky.

Another interesting game, in a safe place, is shooting at targets tossed in the air. A suggestion here is to use flu-flu arrows. Flu-flus are made to slow down by various devices such as employing large untrimmed feathers, greatly lowering the sectional density of a shaft, using large concave heads, etc. They can be purchased or made. This not only is safer, but you lose about 92 percent less arrows. Toss aloft soft articles, like old balls (from tennis to soccer). Never anything hard, especially glass.

Snowshoes

Snowshoes conjure up visions of the frozen, silent North, red-tunic Mounties, and the awesome splendor of the aurora borealis. The North American snowshoe is a pretty romantic item of gear. If you have wanted to take up snowshoeing and have refrained because it looks hard, set your mind at ease. A snowshoe is just a device attached to your feet that greatly distributes your weight and thus enables you to walk over snow into which you'd otherwise sink to your knees or crotch.

The Indian snowshoe is traditional and effective, but it is not the only way to keep going atop snow. For instance, in our town, when I was a lad, there was a high proportion of emigrated Scandinavians, and it was quite an ordinary sight to see elderly ladies, their long skirts flapping about their ankles, going marketing and such on skis. *Homemade* skis, mind—just long slats of ash or hickory with the end steamed up. So a ski could be called a snowshoe in the broad definition.

Emergency snowshoes are quite easy to contrive. For each, get two one-inch to 1½-inch curved branches or little trees, about four feet in length. Tie the big ends together with strips of rawhide. Place in two cross-members (use your hunting knife) in the front third, and bend and tie together the front. Now just fill the entire web with strips and lacings of wet rawhide and bind and tie with damp rawhide every place that looks like it will take. Dry by the fire. Lo! You have snowshoes!

This well-provided, well-organized campsite has everything camper may need, whether he wants to stay where he is and fish, or snowshoe across nearby glaciers.

But to conventional snowshoes: There are only three basic types—each best in its own general region. They could be described as (1) long and skinny, (2) average and (3) short and fat.

Because I dote upon the Far North and have spent much time there, my favorite snowshoe is the number one, the long and skinny. This is a fast-traveling shoe for open country and trails. It is not the best for steep terrain. It's called by such names as Pickerel, Siwash, Yukon, Trail Runner, Alaska and Eskimo. Mine are 10 inches wide by 59 inches long. As with most snowshoes, the ends are moderately turned up so they can't catch under a snow crust or buried root or branch. If your thing, like mine, is open country, I recommend this type.

Far and away the most popular of all snowshoe designs has been the number two, or "average." It's lovingly called the Trapper, Maine, Michigan and so forth. An effective version is about 14 inches wide by 48 inches long. Snowshoes of this sort are best for all-around use.

In times past, the number-three type—a short, roundish snowshoe known as Bearpaw—was only considered good in heavy timber, along creeks, etc., but I've seen Bearpaws used effectively elsewhere. They are useful in the brush, and handy for people who have to get close to objects (like timbermen marking a tree, or maple syrup gatherers). But the Maine type is good for that, too. The average Bearpaw shoe runs around 14 inches by 32 inches, but these measurements can vary.

An increasingly popular design is known as the crosscountry, or the racing. It's best described as a sort of connubial cross between number one and number two. The one I've used is 10 inches wide by 46 inches long. The webbing is heavy compared to the true Northern trail model.

Good snowshoe frames are still second-growth white ash, the webs of processed rawhide or treated steerhide (which does not sag). You'll get many arguments as to the best harness, binding, rigging, boot cups, or whatever. I've had good luck with three-buckle rigging.

When do you need snowshoes? When you want them for fun, or when you wish to travel on snow and cannot because you sink in. It's easier to learn than skiing. Just step high at first and take steps long enough so you don't step on the other shoe. As you gain skill, you'll shorten the high step and length of stride until it suits you.

Snowshoes take a minimum of care. Keep them clean and dry when not in use. I hang mine, rather than toss them in a corner. Replace broken rawhide (or whatever is used for webbing on yours), and coat the wood every year or so with a liquid of the manufacturer's recommendation (it may be old-fashioned varnish and it may be some new plastic).

Incidentally, if you own a snowmobile you ought to have a pair of webs strapped aboard, so you can get out in case of a breakdown. I personally do not care at all for cheap plastic snowshoes, but some snowmobile enthusiasts find them better than nothing.

Photography

Along with your health, your home (mortgage and all), a loyal wife with a (mostly) sunny and loving disposition, one of the most priceless possessions any man can own is often taken for granted. It's your collection of outing photography.

Personal photographs are a source of pleasure the instant they are taken and processed. With the passing of years, your photographic record of glorious days afield assumes such staggering value to you that it's truly beyond price. Most of us take far too few photographs on trips. The more you shoot, the more outstanding pictures you are going to have.

Don't think photography afield takes a lot of study. In bygone days there were some failures due most often to improper exposures, but now there are beautifully easy-to-operate cameras. Some have built-in light meters, and some even set the exposure automatically. There are great values in all price ranges.

If you wish to pursue photography to the advanced-amateur stage (or even beyond) visit your local library. But here are a few potent points to remember. Unless you *must,* try to avoid shooting in the high-noon range, say from 11 a.m. to 1 p.m. If you must shoot then, use a flash on faces. The best outdoor action pictures generally are taken with the sun at three-quarters, or lower, and scenics with the sun even lower.

If you use a meter, decide what it is you want the most detail in—the highlights or the shadows. Unless you do your own processing, I take a dreary view of splitting the difference and trying to get a little of each. That is what you generally get—little of each. I go for one or the other and most often it is the shadows.

You learn as you shoot. For example, if you get pools of inky blackness where a set of eyes should be, from then on you'll say, "Hey! Lift your hat brim or take off your hat." Or you'll learn that flashbulbs are worth their weight in black pearls, even outdoors. Try to get your subjects in action. In other words, show them performing something significant. Action will tell a little story. There are exceptions. The old trophy pictures, proudly holding aloft that great bass or trout, have their place.

Electronic Gear

A couple of the newer camping activities have grabbed us old apple-knockers out here in the West with a grasp of iron. Each concerns modern electronics. One is the wonderful pastime of camping in lonely lands and packing along a metal detector to go over old battle, fort, mining and Indian encampment sites, ghost towns, long-forgotten steamboat landings (in Montana, particularly) and places where old trappers' cabins have long turned to dust. It's fascinating and remunerative.

By no means do I claim this to be a brand new game—it's been coming along for many years, beginning when the first ex-GI latched on to a war-surplus mine detector and began digging up treasures. (Also, incidentally, gold nuggets from streambeds and such.) Word spread, and commercial metal detectors appeared on the market. Some were rather primitive, heavy, clumsy, and not wholly reliable. I have one "feather"-light, simple to use and so reliable I have followed chaps with older, bulky models who passed over goodies without their instrument registering, while I got a potent signal on my own up-to-date little jewel.

Camper in Montana uses metal detector to hunt for pioneer and Indian relics. Electronic gear is becoming increasingly popular among America's camping vacationers.

Another fine hobby booming out here with campers is calling up wild predators for an eyeball-to-eyeball look. It's every man to his own taste, but I like to call them right on in (literally to our laps, sometimes) and merely photograph 'em. I do not care to shoot called varmints except with camera, but then I have long fancied myself as being a purist long-range varminter.

You can fetch up predators inexpensively, indeed, with a hand-held call, and have a whale of a time. But we get enormous fun and greater satisfaction utilizing an electronic call, which is a portable but high-class record player and amplifier. With that baby we get action and no foolin' around about it. We have records that bring coyotes, foxes and bobcats on the run. And we can bring crows, magpies, owls, *et al.* We have a new mountain-lion record for which we have high hopes.

It's best to invest in camouflage clothing for calling up predators. Have your back against something and keep your face concealed. The camera should be covered so the sun won't glint on it. We've found that windless days are most productive.

If you have not yet tried a metal detector or an electronic predator caller as part of your camp gear, you may be missing a bet. Most who try either gadget are enthusiastic.

Name Tags

Sportsmen benefit if they have some means of quickly and positively identifying their cherished belongings. This sometimes helps prevent it from going astray and is a fairly strong deterrent to the odd sneak thief. But the main idea of having quick and positive identification on your equipment is that often it is less confusing for you. I recall the time I got off a plane in Salt Lake City and nine bags exactly like my own came in view on one of those endless belts. When the first one hove into sight nine of us dashed over. Then eight of us, and so on. I learned my lesson right there.

It used to be fashionable to have little bitty name plates and/or discreet initials or monograms on luggage. Those are about as useful as ivory-handled button hooks. You should have the identification large enough so you can see it at a reasonable distance. This usually requires some form of sign painting or stencil.

All gear should be marked, one way or another. It is fairly common practice to have one's name or initials in gold on a pet firearm. Axe handles can be initialed with a burning tool sold at hobby shops. Plastic name plates can be put on pressure lanterns, binocular cases, and so on.

8

Pack Trips

Sooner or later those who love camping in wild places will inevitably progress upward to the nonpareil of all North American camping: the packtrain. A packtrain is a string of hard-working, sure-footed mountain-bred horses that resolutely wend their way deep into unspoiled lands, carrying everything you require for comfortable living afield. Packtrains go where no other mode of transportation can follow. No backpacker can follow a packtrain, for he'd soon run out of energy and supplies.

With muscle and wind enough to pack what amounts to a little settlement, a packtrain permits the camper to be unbelievably free, yet secure. If you wish, you can have such luxuries as the makings for high tea. Your home each night is a clean, white A-wall tent with a woodburning stove, a down-insulated "bed" and all your familiar goodies and necessaries at your fingertips. On most well-run pack trips a wrangler will start a cozy blaze while you're awakening. The packtrain can have a ton and a half or more of gear and supplies, yet it can cover a lot of wild country.

Ideally, it travels at a leisurely pace; but mountain country being what it is, it can go a bit faster or it can go a whole lot slower. Among its unforgettable attractions are the leisurely days on the trail, astride a well-mannered saddle pony. You relax and enjoy the keen coniferous air, the soft clop of horse hoofs, the startle of exploding grouse. There are comforting sounds of muted horse bells, your steed contentedly blowing his nostrils, the creak of saddle leather, the splashing as rivulets are forded.

The origins of packtrain travel are lost, but the practice as we know it stems from man's domestication of the donkey. North American packing came to us from North Africa via Spain to Mexico—thence north. Mexican nationals are burro-packers born to the art. I've seen them cargo up unbelievable loads, including (hold on to your beanie) respectable stacks of *loose* hay. Seeing a haystack meandering up the road with four dainty hoofs barely peeking out the bottom has caused *gringo* motorists to toss out their jugs of pulque. But burros are too slow and too small for the elite mountain pack-

Ann Jobson and outfitter Johnnie Johns ride at head of packtrain that transports everything needed for comfort during long sojourn in remote mountains.

train. For someone walking, like desert-rat prospectors of yore, they're great, and indeed there's a cult of modern hiking campers who use burros to pack the load, or most of it. Mules have some advantages over horses in some dry sections of the Rockies and some disadvantages in wet, muskeg terrain.

The best packer I ever saw, anywhere, was the late Red Higgins of Wallowa Mountains. He'd pack the Rose Bowl if you gave him a free hand. He easily carried lumber, big beams, king-size mattresses, steel fireplace units, shower stalls and once a cast iron cook stove for his upper elk camp.

The oldest and most accepted method of packing a load on a horse is to use a sawbuck pack saddle, called that because it has two wooden "X's" atop, over which you loop the straps of boxlike panniers or canvas *alforjas*. In parts of Idaho, Montana and localized "pockets," an esoteric rig vaguely resembling a World War I Browning machine gun Cavalry saddle (called a "decker") is highly esteemed. Made of leather, with iron loops instead of wood X's, it carries loads both high and low, and of odd shapes and weights if necessary. Its boosters have a touching faith in its merits, but the old sawbuck is more widely used for general packtrain camping.

It's fun to learn to pack. The pack saddle is placed aboard like any saddle, with a folded blanket under it, a commercial pad, or both, and prop-

Here's one traditional method of loading up—hanging canvas container called *alforjas* on each side of wooden sawbuck pack saddle.

erly cinched. There's a chest-strap rigging and a breeching, likewise, around the horse's bottom to keep the load from shifting fore and aft.

Always use the same saddle on the same horse. Two panniers of *equal* weight (from 60 to 70 pounds) are loaded, one to a side, hooking the strap loops over the convenient X's. You now have a platform for the light but often bulky top load. Atop all goes a square of sturdy canvas called a "manty," and the whole is neatly tidied up with an all-encompassing lash-rope often tied in a diamond hitch. (In spite of old wives' tales, they're still popular and not difficult to master.) Your outfitter or guide should show you how, if you request it, although if unimaginative he may feel that your asking to pack horses is comparable to a yard bird requesting latrine duty.

Worthwhile packtrain camping ranges from the costly big-game pack trips in virgin country to a week or so campout from a dude ranch. In between these extremes are all manner of variations, some tailored to the individual. There are packers you can hire to take you and yours into a remote area, leave some saddle horses with you, and return with the pack string on a specified date. It's not advertised, but I have heard of ranchers on the edge of prime country who, if they like you, will for a modest fee rent you dependable horses and the gear to go with it. It's better, though, to go on a professionally operated pack trip (and that's the *only* way to go if you're not experienced).

Taking care to balance load, packer will lash tarps atop boxlike panniers.
In some regions, mules and burros are used at least as much as horses.

On Yukon trip, Jobson displays affection to his favorite mountain horse, Billy. Firm but friendly relationship with horse is important in rough country.

Your Horse

I want to pass along a few tips regarding a good working relationship with your (truly) noble servant and companion. Knowing a few basic rules can make a big difference to the inexperienced. It might save your life. While it is true that your outfitter, dude rancher, stableman, trail guide or whoever bosses the train will, to the best of his ability, furnish you a dependable mount, it is a fact that your horse is a live, warm-blooded animal with all the necessary accouterments such as eyes, ears, brain—and a remarkable degree of sensitivity. This is best mentioned, for many people, particularly some from the cities, actually seem to regard the beast as a different kind of four-wheel-drive vehicle whose fuel is grass instead of gasoline.

While horses are among the most gregarious of animals, their personalities vary quite as much as those of grizzly bears, dogs and people. They are individuals in the strict meaning of the term and are blessed and cursed with eccentricities, foibles, fancies, notions, fixations, cupidities, complexes, yearnings, vague resentments, hostilities and fears, varying amounts of experience and intelligence—even, on occasion, perhaps a neurosis of sorts. They are creatures of habit and of pride. There are strong and weak ones (size is not an infallible indication); and there are wise, foolish, willing and lazy horses. Some are affectionate and loyal; others have a mean tendency or two and could not be less interested in becoming your buddy.

Your horse is extraordinarily gifted in many respects. He can see in the dark like a cat, has the homing instinct of a pigeon, normally has a built-in sixth sense (a kind of equine radar) for secure footing, is endowed with the traction of an Israeli tank, has fine eyesight and a superlative sense of smell. He generally is blessed with great patience.

Yukon guide gives his horse tidbit before morning's ride. Kind treatment won't spoil animal but will make him cooperative.

One of the most astute things you can do on pack trips is to personally saddle and unsaddle your own mount. Even though the wrangler tells you something like, "Oh, please don't bother with that, Mr. Skidmore. You're here for a vacation. We'll take care of it."

The advantages of performing this little chore yourself are: 1) in spite of what some wilderness mentors may claim, your horse has a bit more respect for you; 2) you will know your saddle is placed and cinched properly at all times; and 3) once you're adept at saddling and unsaddling, you aren't helpless if your guide is unavoidably separated from you.

One thing I always do (secretly) is swipe a little handful of oats and surreptitiously give it to my horse each morning. If no oats are available, a piece of apple, carrot, oatmeal, a bit of salt or some tidbit is effective and is not harmful *if not overdone.* The gesture is the thing, not the amount. Incidentally, present these tokens to your horse in the flat palm of your hand, always, so he doesn't accidentally bite you. I must confess I pat and stroke my horse's neck and speak kindly to him. Most of the time, before I finish a trip, my horse follows me like a dog and usually comes when I whistle or call.

Never walk up to any horse from behind without speaking, for otherwise even the most placid old nag may be startled enough to lash out hard with a hind leg.

When riding, check now and then to see if your saddle is canted or slipping to one side. This frequently occurs in the North where there is a preponderance of round-back horses (not bred for the saddle). The weight of items like gun scabbards can work the saddle to one side. It takes but a minute or two to dismount and adjust the saddle properly. Speaking of scabbards, be sure you rig it so it can't possibly chafe the horse.

Cinches loosen during the day because, for one thing, the horse's abdomen expands and contracts; so shift your weight once in a while ("rock" the saddle) and see if it moves appreciably. If it does, you'd better tighten the cinch immediately.

Most horses should be mounted (and dismounted) from the left. However, a few outfitters train their horses so that you can operate from either side, and this has many advantages for the rider—among them being the obvious likelihood that occasionally you will want to dismount on a steep hillside. About half the time, your horse's right side will be the uphill side; making it simple, indeed, to dismount to the right as the slope comes up nearly to your right stirrup. But alas! On the left, as you gracefully leap out of the saddle, you'll unaccountably find yourself 10 to 15 feet down the dratted hill (or even farther). To mount again is even more difficult.

Jobson demonstrates proper riding technique with mountain horse, setting comfortable, steady pace and maintaining his seat, with toes in both stirrups.

Always keep your toes in the stirrups—both stirrups. In other words, maintain your "seat." Do not shift about in the saddle as many expert riders do with one stirrup dangling free and a leg cocked around the pommel. Cowboys do it, but sometimes they get stacked, too. The reason for riding with both stirrups is that no matter how mechanically a horse is plodding and dozing along, he can galvanize into action in a split-second. I had one horse who was inordinately frightened of yellowjackets; the appearance of one would send him out of his mind. I knew another horse who was terrified of cigar butts. If a member of our party tossed one away and my horse smelled it, he immediately rolled his eyes and began to pitch. Yet another was periodically scared nearly to death of a little old piece of discarded facial tissue and I've seen a horse shy at shed moose antlers.

If you have a choice, ask for hooded stirrups. They protect your feet from weather, stumps and rocks, and they're safer than open stirrups. Incidentally, never allow pack horses to ride above you on a hill. If they do (and they will), stop your mount until they've passed. They can dislodge rocks which might hit your horse, knocking it off its feet.

Do not ever, under any circumstances, try to ride a horse where he has shown you he does not want to go. Chances are overwhelming that he knows more about the situation than you do. He feels or sees something you do not. If you have to travel in that direction, dismount at once and gingerly try it on foot, leading the horse. Wise old bush-trained horses rarely make an error of judgment in this respect, though I have seen them do it.

Many sportsmen like to walk a bit during the day, not only to rest their mounts but to stretch themselves, get out the kinks and gain the exercise. A tip here is to walk downhill. This is okay for the horse, for while his powerful hind legs can cope with mild upgrades, his relatively weak front legs will benefit from not having to extend themselves holding back the combined weight of the rider, the saddle and himself while descending. On murderously steep or long grades, a horse should be rested when he requires it.

Most Western horses are trained to stay put while you're briefly away from them if you merely drop the reins on the ground. However, sometimes Dobbin is stricken with a bit of wanderlust for one reason or another. (Then, too, some horses are disconcerted by rifle-fire.) In cases like this it is better to tie them by the halter rope. If it is to a branch or anything else that can sway or give, be sure the knot is high enough and the tether sufficiently short so the animal can't get his legs fouled in it. If it's tied to a solid tree trunk or limb, have the knot at a level about even with the horse's mouth when he is standing normally, leaving about 3½ feet of rope.

Never leave a valuable rifle, camera, or binocular unattended on the horse, as often he will have an overpowering compulsion to roll. When hunting and game is sighted, do not turn loose of your horse's reins until your rifle is out of the scabbard. He may run off with it. If your horse accidentally steps on your foot, don't panic. Simply tap-kick him (not too hard) on or slightly above the hock, and he'll obligingly lift his hoof.

Some horses like to drink lengthily at every confounded creek or other bit of water, no matter how frequently they appear. Don't let them. On the other hand, don't deprive them of water entirely.

It is not necessary to yell "whoa" at a trained saddle horse—that should be reserved for plow horses. A slight, gradual pull (not a jerk) on the reins is standard operating procedure. I have never seen a mountain saddle horse that did not neck-rein. If you want to go to the right, you gently maneuver the left rein so the strap lies on the left side of the horse's neck. Just the opposite to turn left. While riding, hold the reins securely in either hand, with very little

In Western mountains, saddle horses usually have both bridle and halter. Most of them will stand and wait if you drop reins on ground, as in picture. But it's better to tie your mount so he won't wander. Always use halter for this purpose.

pressure. Just enough to let your mount know you are in control of things. Too loose is very poor practice—and too tight will be uncomfortable for the horse and confuse him. One quickly acquires the knack.

When bridling the horse, which again is quite easy to learn, the main thing in cold weather is to remember to warm the bit before inserting it in the animal's mouth. If no fire is handy, put it inside your shirt for awhile.

When mounting or dismounting (and this goes double for hillsides) stand as close to the horse as you can. Leaning "out" increases leverage upon the animal. I have, more than once, seen a heavy man pull a horse off its feet. To mount properly a person (if on the usual left side) should hold the reins in his left hand and stand by the horse's neck, facing back toward its rump. He should then turn the stirrup with his right hand so the opening faces his toe (the left one, naturally). Now, still holding the reins in the left hand, grab a goodly hunk of the horse's mane (keeps the saddle from tilting) and then the saddle horn. At this point, the left hand is grasping the reins, saddle horn, and a bit of the animal's mane. Place the foot firmly in the stirrup with the ball of the foot taking the weight and working as close to the horse as possible, swing aboard. Some fellows like to give themselves an added boost by grabbing the cantle of the saddle with the right hand; there's no law against it.

By the way, never try to shoot from the animal. Most of the horses that have been laboriously trained to stand with cool equanimity at this appalling blast in their sensitive ears are already working in Hollywood.

Now we come to the Dude's Dilemma. It is one of the more frustrating phenomena in nature that a horse with an inexperienced rider positively refuses to set his gait with the other horses. With the most languid slothfulness he indolently dawdles until the pack train, outfitter, guides and so forth are nearly out of sight. Often the poor dude is helpless to cope with this situation. Indeed, if a horse gets away with it through a long succession of tolerant hunters, he will even try to con a fairly experienced rider. The answer is to find something the horse is afraid of. It may be a real gruff voice, the threat of a length of rope, a willow switch, or a certain nudge with your heels.

One time in the Yukon, I had a perfectly wonderful little horse named Two-Bits. Two-Bits was a gentle thing, without a mean bone or thought in its body, and we got along like two retired ladies-of-ill-repute reminiscing in the county home. However, Two-Bits tried this dawdling jazz with me. Neither spurring nor a birch quirt nor a piece of lash rope would cause him to extend himself more than a few quick strides—whereupon he'd lapse into an abysmally torpid shuffle. Finally I discovered his Achilles heel: the sling from my rifle. There was something about it, possibly the sling swivel or the brass fittings that terrified him. When I detected a bit of loafing coming on, I dangled it by his nose. That was enough! I never did tap him with it. But I do not believe I have ever seen a more determined, brisker walk!

In a recent magazine article some pundit proclaimed that saddle bags abuse a horse and you should, therefore, carry all your stuff in a packframe on your back when riding. Nonsense. Sure, you could—conceivably—injure a horse's kidneys if you were idiot enough to burden him with bags too large and heavily loaded. But proper saddle bags properly used won't harm a horse in the least. A packframe might easily harm *you* if you wear it while mounted. For one thing, it can make you top-heavy and perhaps cause an accidental unseating if you're not an expert rider. For another, it can be plain tiring to carry a heavy weight and remain somewhat unbalanced while riding a long way if you're not used to it. And finally, its top is liable to catch on some obstruction, even though you bend low to avoid branches, and can knock you off as forcefully as the bucking of the famous old strawberry roan.

Horse at right has good saddle, properly cinched, with pliable fenders and stirrups hung toward front of seat. Pack horse is carrying Jobson-designed panniers.

Your Saddle

The following bit of saddle guidance is designed for the majority of once-in-awhile trail riders and more experienced pleasure riders who are not too familiar with the Western stock saddle.

First check to see where the stirrups are hung. They should be *forward*, well at the front of the seat—if possible, right below the horn. Stirrups positioned further back have their uses, but pleasure riding is not among them, for most people. Then examine the straps (called fenders) on which the stirrups are suspended. If the leather is not pliable and soft, be skeptical. If it's old and brittle, beware. Even if it's new, yet very stiff, be cautious. One way of curing stiff straps is to take a pail of water and a damp rag and apply moisture to the leather until it *is* pliable, then get on and ride until it's dry. Stiff leather stirrup straps will keep twisting your knee, insidiously, slowly, until you're crippled and the pain is excruciating. A Western saddle with stiff fenders may be fine for a person who has broken in that saddle and rides it exclusively. It can be awful for anyone else. Some riders never loan their saddles.

This is most favored way of mounting rifle scabbard in North Country,
where big-game hunting is generally main purpose of wilderness camping trips.

The next vital adjustment is to have the stirrups hung fairly long (not short!) for trail riding. Never, ever, sit with your knees bent noticeably like a jockey. A rule of thumb is to stand in the stirrups and double your fist—it should snugly fit between the saddle and your crotch. Or have them as long as you can without easily losing a stirrup from your foot. The stirrups should share your weight with the seat. If you don't lay into those stirrups pretty good now and then, you'll think your bones are coming right through the hide on your bottom.

Next, look for a "tree" (seat) that fits you: not too long or too short. The saddle should have an ample (preferably wide) swell on the pommel for most Western pleasure riding, so your thighs can get a "holt" on it. It helps going downhill, in steep mountain country, too, although the stirrups then take much of the weight. The cantle on a saddle serves like the back rest on a chair. If you can, get an old-fashioned "high" one, sort of straight; these are great, provided the saddle also has a substantial pommel. They don't always go together. A high cantle is awkward for some folks to clear with their leg when getting on or off.

The girth-cinch-latigo—that which secures the saddle upon your horse—should also be toward the front, right behind the stirrup strap. This is the one that is tightened and kept that way. Another *cincha* toward the rear, sort of beneath the cantle, is kept loose enough so you can slip your hand in between it and the horse.

These are the main points to look for. After you've ridden some, you may then differ on a detail or two, to suit your own personal requirements, but you will not go wrong with the foregoing. Don't select a flat-top Mexican horn, by the way. The *norteamericano* type (like in most cowboy movies) is best at first.

Panniers

When I went on my first big pack trip I should have been 100 percent happy. I was about 93 percent happy, because my cherished equipment was being manhandled. I'd arrived at road's end with all my necessaries (except bedroll and rifle) contained in a "war bag" (an ample canvas duffle). When I saw two husky young wranglers manty up my precious sack, as part of one top load, I was apprehensive. When next I observed them, one to a side of the horse, tying the diamond hitch, they had put their backs into it, and as the rope tightened on the duffle bag, the effect was sort of as if you'd press into a fresh marshmallow with the back of a knife. I let out a holler that startled all livestock for a mile, and the outfitter himself, at least 300 yards distant, dropped his upper plate. I explained my dilemma and requested a spare set of panniers. He gave me the same expression a guy sees when he is the last man into an overcrowded lifeboat. Then he said wearily, "As you proceed through life, Mr. Jobson, you are going to find out a good many vital, necessary, and illuminating facts. Chief among them is that *no* outfitter or rancher *ever* has spare panniers, being as he is always about three pair short."

So as I sat there on that Alberta log, I swore an oath to obtain my own, personal pair of panniers at the first opportunity. I would, I moodily said, paint mine a highly distinctive color, like yellow. I might even have my name on them. That way, when the packstring was unloaded, I'd quickly sort them from the outfitter's and pack them to my sleeping tent. At home I'd keep them loaded and ready to go at a moment's notice. They'd be stout enough for shipping air freight or truck freight. And they'd protect my frangible gear.

Whether one calls them pack boxes, panniers, kyacks (or names rooted from Moorish, Spanish, or Indian), they basically amount to the same thing. A pair of containers that fit on a horse. They're made of such assorted materials as steer, camel or moose hide (rawhide, at that), metal, scrap wood—and I've heard of (but not seen) high-impact plastic ones.

As to shape, the most common look like an old orange crate; these are widely used by professional outfitters who pack in open country. They stick out most unglamorously, like two open doors on a taxicab, but they provide a nice wide base upon which to install an outsized top load. The main reason for these "square-rectangular" crates is that ranchers used to get oil (in the old days, lantern coal-oil) in 10-gallon units—two five-gallon standard cans to a crate. Those discarded crates made suitable pack boxes. When they wore out, ranchers fashioned new ones to the same dimensions.

For my own, I wanted the classic type with folded corners, the horse-hugger kind contoured to fit a horse properly. I knew that future trips would take me through dense timber, along narrow ledges and through the thick, nearly impenetrable willow-birch brush of the subarctic. Trying to force a horse with spread-out oil-crate pack boxes through this stuff results in ghastly accidents. I have seen them pitched into swift rivers (sometimes drowning) and off narrow game trails, going end over end onto sharp rocks below. Frank

In dry Yukon country (left) Indian guides and wranglers sometimes omit
square canvas cover called manty when loading pack horse. Jobson
(above) checks fittings on his panniers. Three sides of pack boxes are visible
in this photo, so you can see how contours will hug horse's sides. Boxes
are made of white pine, laminated plywood and fiberglass, as explained in text.

Golata, the old-time dean of the Prophet River Stone-sheep outfitters, used
form-fitting panniers quite similar to those I favor and will describe here.

Once settled upon the design I wanted, I confidently took the blueprint
to a manufacturer of luggage. I knew he made those tough, light, fiber-riveted
custom cases for professional motion-picture cameras. When he told me the
price, I had a roaring in my ears, black spots swam before my eyes and I felt
faint. So I built some just as good and perhaps better from clear white pine
(ends and bottom), exterior plywood, waterproof boat-type glue, bronze anchor nails (see your friendly boat yard), a few bolts and plenty of boat-quality
fiberglass.

These are exceedingly, even unbelievably strong. If you can catch a pal
who is fiberglassing a good-sized boat, he'll have enough scraps to do. If not,
boat yards might have some "ends" which with a modicum of resin you can
make do. If not, you can always throw caution to the winds and purchase
enough new fiberglass and resin.

Reproduced herein is a pattern drawing showing how to do it; the sections are laid out and labeled as to materials. And the result to be striven for is shown photographically. If you make your own, and want them shaped like mine, be advised that the dimensions are not extremely critical. A quarter of an inch among friends isn't going to make much difference. But to give a point of departure, here are the measurements on the ones shown:

Bottom: white pine ⅞" thick, 6" wide, 23" long.
    Ends: white pine ⅞" thick, 17" long, 9¾" at widest part, 6⅞" across narrow portion.
   Front: laminated plywood ¼" thick, 23x18¾".
   Back: laminated plywood 23x18".
  Cover: ⅜" plywood 24½x11", with strap hinges.

To stiffen up the box a trifle, I have inside along the top, both front and back, a ¼-inch laminated strip 23 inches by 2⅝ inches. Suitable cutouts in the ends will have to be made to accommodate these stiffeners. The ends, after fiberglassing, should have on the outside a handle and a brace—the latter for a rope catcher on the diamond hitch. These are of clear pine or fir stock 1½ inches x ¾ inch. They should be installed with ¼-inch stove bolts, countersunk. For some years, I deliberately left off the leather straps that hook over the cross-pieces on a pack saddle, as a diamond hitch is actually sufficient to hold the boxes, if it is thrown properly; besides, the boxes are neater for shipping. However, for several reasons I later installed straps.

Mine are secured with two stove bolts (¼-inch) to each strap and tightened and riveted. A much better deal would be a pair of eye-bolts on the back of each box, with a swivel snap on the straps. That way, you could disengage the straps and place them inside the box for shipping.

Here is pattern Jobson used for his own panniers. Using bolts, bronze anchor nails, waterproof boat-type glue and plenty of boat-quality fiberglass, he achieved exceedingly strong construction. Originally, he left off the leather straps that hook over sawbuck saddle's cross-pieces, because diamond hitch is sufficient to hold panniers in place. For convenience, however, he later added straps (as seen in photo, page 193). He emphasizes that precise dimensions aren't critical if you want to build panniers according to this pattern. It's more important to make them sturdy and, when loading, to keep weight on each side of horse equal (about 60 to 70 pounds).

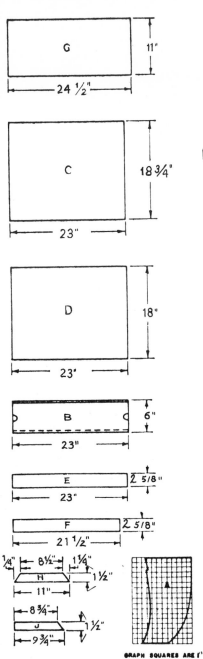

GRAPH SQUARES ARE 1"

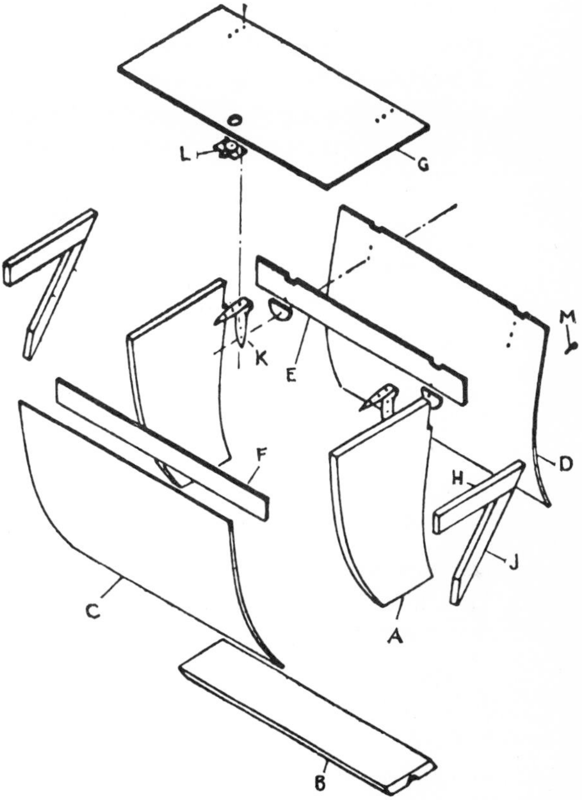

MATERIAL FOR A PAIR OF PACK BOXES			
PART	REQ	SIZE	MATERIAL
A	4	1"x12"x17"	WHITE PINE (STOCK SIZE)
B	2	1"x6"x23"	" " " "
C	2	18¾"x23"	¼" LAMINATED PLYWOOD
D	2	18"x23"	" " "
E	2	2⅝"x23"	" " "
F	2	2⅝"x21½"	" " "
G	2	11"x24½"	⅜" " "
H	4	1"x2"x11"	WHITE PINE (STOCK SIZE)
J	4	1"x2"x9¾"	" " " "
K	4	3"	STRAP HINGES
L	2		CABINET LOCK
M	4		EYE BOLTS

STOVE BOLTS, 1" BOAT NAILS, SCREWS, FIBERGLASS,
PAINT & LEATHER STRAPS TO SUIT INDIVIDUAL
REQUIREMENTS.

9

Other Modes
of Transport

Camping with Aircraft

I have been flying into and out of wilderness camping areas for a mighty long time. My first trip was in a flaming-red Curtiss Robin. That, my friends, was not three weeks ago.

In our modest Midwestern town not really very long ago, anyone who actually had camped via light aircraft enjoyed a notoriety in the same category as one school chum who had actually had a date with the star belly dancer of a vagrant carnival. I'm sure that my having flown over Canadian wilderness during summer vacation made me as famous as others who had accomplished prodigious feats of derring-do. In this more sophisticated and informed decade, legions of sportsmen and their families enjoy flying—yet there still is an old-fashioned apprehension about bush flying. I was talking with a doctor who was keenly interested in a Yukon trip until his spouse (a Smith graduate and you'd think she'd know better, poor thing) heard us employ the term "bush flying." She turned pale and declared, "No husband of *mine* is *ever* going to ride in one of those *light* airplanes!" That's the way they mostly put it. Huge, regularly-scheduled jet aircraft they accept, but a little plane, they think, is for suicidal chuckleheads.

Few notions are further from fact. These days private planes are as advanced as can be: easy to fly, safe and comfortable. If you hire a plane, either bush or air-taxi, your chances for longevity are much greater than if you habitually trudge up and down loose cellar steps. And learning to fly your own is a truly rewarding experience.

You can be in a bustling city, and in less than an hour be smack in the middle of the best camping, hunting, and fishing that the entire area affords. With your own plane you can (or could the last time I computed it) do this sort of thing for a cost of $.07059 per mile. Even if you hire your flying com-

Pontoon-equipped planes are being used with increasing frequency to pack campers, hunters and anglers into the wilds. This practice is especially popular in Northern locales where there are few roads but many lakes.

mercially, you come out very well indeed. My wife and I do all sorts of passenger flying, all the time. We just select a small airport on the edge of some good wilderness country. If the pilot can get us in either by landing at a wilderness airstrip or with floats on a wilderness lake, away we go. Generally, the flight averages about $15 to $50. For this we get a skilled pilot who, on a single trip, transports both of us and all our gear plus supplies to last for a week or so.

Going in, we sometimes make arrangements with the pilot to return for us on a specified date. Pilots are exceptionally reliable in this respect. Other times we hike out to the nearest ranch. Or we rendezvous with saddle horses (all prearranged). There are many variations and aircraft adapt to all. When your schedule is tight, particularly, a plane often enables you to enjoy leisurely wilderness camping that would be impossible any other way.

In this country, something like an old Cessna customarily takes in stride a couple or more passengers, with room for tent, bedrolls, other gear and grub. In Canada a larger DeHavilland Beaver can usually be chartered and these haul an enormous load, particularly if they are rigged for freight rather than a passengers. I don't mind sitting on a bedroll or pack box if I know I can take everything I need on the one flight. Enough to last us 30 days, say.

Above: Provisions for Jobson's party have just been unloaded from float plane, and journey into wilderness will continue by horseback. Top right: Author and friend beach inflatable boat equipped with outboard. Jobson rates Indian-style canoes and newest inflatables best for camping. Bottom right: Family sets up camp trailer and pumps up small inflatable canoe suitable for fishing or boating near camp.

Small Boat and Canoe Camping

Careful planning is vital when camping with boats. At the top of the list of rugged, dependable, lightweight, shallow-draft vessels are the traditional basic-Indian-design North American canoe and the modern inflatable craft with rigid floor and outboard-motor mount plus dependable oarlocks. These are becoming standard equipment in areas of the Far North with which I'm familiar. Now, any fool knows, and I know, there may be regional preferences for other suitable craft. If you wanted to probe deep into the Okefenokee Swamp you might select some form of john-boat. If you were going to camp upper New York you might, if lucky to find one, choose an Adirondack guide boat.

But a good canoe or an up-to-date inflatable craft will take you in and out safely and they will do more than any highly individualized design tailored for certain waters only. Both the canoe and the modern inflatable boat are extremely versatile; however, it might be noted that the canoe is by far the more versatile of the two. It is the most versatile craft in existence. But with either of these, I know I can go into and out of the Everglades (traditionally airboat terrain), the Okefenokee (traditionally john-boat or pirogue water) and the aforementioned Adirondack waters. What's more, with a good canoe I can cruise up the Inside Passage to Alaska and I can negotiate tumultuous, spume-throwing, murderously treacherous Northern wilderness rivers and streams.

Above: Campers beach their canoes among shadows of canyon walls on Colorado River. Right: Woodsman works his way down Big Duck Creek in Ontario. Good canoes are very maneuverable, yet stable in water when handled properly, and they hold enough provisions for extended journeys into wilderness.

A modern kayak will safely negotiate a lot of tremendously lively water and rough weather with its covered decks and beautifully efficient centuries-old Eskimo pliant construction and design. These are the sports cars of the light-boat world. You certainly can camp with them, and take astonishing journeys of thousands and thousands of miles. For big-game hunting the covered decks do handicap them somewhat, but they are fine for waterfowling and for many types of fishing.

Four good types of canoes are currently available: the traditional wood-and-canvas, aluminum, plastic and fiberglass. Many "dated" wood-and-canvas canoes are still in use after some 60 years of service. Which proves they're not so dated.

No canoe has a corner on the advantages. If you get one of adequate size for your needs and of genuine American-Indian low-prow *design*, it matters little which you choose. The lightest canoe consistent with strength is wood-and-canvas or wood-and-Dacron. Alloy canoes are impersonal to the "feel." You are not tempted to call one "she" or "old girl" as you do the old wood-and-fabric. Alloy canoes are noisy, at times, and they are cold to the touch in fall and hot during summer. On the other hand, they require little or no up-keep. My own canoe is of alloy.

Fiberglass canoes have their champions. They need little upkeep and are not quite so impersonal as alloy. I urge you, though, in buying a fiberglass to strongly consider construction of woven glass fabric. "Sandwich" construction of reinforced plastics with balsa core is rugged, and so is plain high-impact plastic. In fast water on *sharp* rocks most any canoe can puncture and hang up—but "obsolete" wood-and-canvas seems to slither over sharp rocks as readily as the other two.

If you're buying your first canoe, I advise you to shy away from the romantic little "one-man" 11-foot model. There are things a small canoe will do that no larger one can match, but, alas, it can*not* take a couple of buddies or a husband and wife with all their camping gear and food into wilderness and out again after two or three weeks in the bush. Nor will an 11-footer cross Windy Arm (at its worst) on Tagish Lake in the Yukon, carrying three men with all gear, as my own 17-foot did.

You might make your first craft a 15-foot if you want. My advice is the 17-foot for two people, 18-foot for three.

Single canoe carried this family with their cottage tent, bedrolls, propane stove and lantern, smaller equipment, clothing and food for long stay.

There is gear specifically designed for canoe-type use. There are canoeing tents, such as the rather complicated but effective Voyageur or Explorer's. Another good one for wilderness use is the Whelen lean-to with a mosquito bar. Any canoe tent should be bugproof. It need not be as lightweight as a good mountain backpacking tent; it should be a bit roomier as generally canoe country is wetter than in the mountains.

The best backpacks for canoeing are the big time-proven Duluth sacks. These have a tumpline and are the ticket for portaging and stowing supplies while canoeing. This same gear can be used for snowmobile camping, by the way, just as backpacking gear can be used for snowmobiling and canoeing. However, canoe equipment cannot successfully be employed in ambitious backpacking. Your 17-foot canoe can pack 1,200 pounds with ease, so you really don't have to go hog-wild on cutting down weight if you don't want to.

Here is the way I estimate meals on canoe trips, and it works splendidly for me. I figure out all the meals, each breakfast, lunch, and dinner per man-day. I then add 20 percent more days than I expect to be out. I increase the amount of the meals (amount consumed afield as against home) by *at least* 25 percent. Take twice the amount of sweets and fats as you imagine you'll need.

In remote North Country, author and his guide unload their gear from
big, modern aluminum canoe powered by outboard and designed for long excursions.

Allow plenty of candy bars, dried fruit, and peanuts for mid-afternoon and
mid-morning snacks.

About everything you pack (and particularly your dry groceries, lenses,
bedding, etc.) should be in stout, transparent plastic bags. I am a great one for
having plenty of tarps, and when I load the canoe I place one in the bottom,
put the load on that, and fold the ends over. It helps to circumvent the inevi-
table spray and water dripping in the craft. If you expect rough water, secure
part of the supplies (at least) to the canoe. The shoulder straps of the Duluth
packs can be disconnected and rebuckled around a thwart. Life jackets are
fine at any time, especially in temperate water. There is an odd saying up
North that their value is in helping rescuers to locate your soggy remains, but
it's still smart to take them along.

Canoe country often is porcupine habitat, and porkies look upon salty,
perspiration-soaked canoe paddles and gunwales about the the same way I'd
look upon bussing Miss Universe. A porcupine can ruin every paddle, axe
handle and wooden canoe trim in camp in a surprising short time. Try to
place this gear out of their reach.

On a canoe, I have never used an outboard motor larger than three-horse—and I prefer something smaller, like 1.7 h.p. Purists decry the use of a motor in wilderness. I like one. While most of the water will be covered by silent paddling, there comes the time when for safety's sake you need the added thrust of the motor to get you to shelter from a sudden storm. Waves can come up in a hurry. A motor will help you upstream. And your wife probably cannot paddle your rig out but she can run it to safety with the motor, if you come down with appendicitis or whatever.

With the little motors, if you plan to use them only in emergency, for most trips you can carry sufficient fuel. On long trips I hire a float plane to fly out in advance (in fact, I go with the pilot) and cache five-gallon cans of gasoline at strategic places along the route.

If you aren't well acquainted with the waters you contemplate canoeing, check several ways. One of the best is the *final* check—with residents on the spot. A float-plane pilot is one of the best sources, as he is taught to understand and communicate to others precise conditions of weather and water-surface, the currents, tides or whatever, and hazards such as rocks, shoals, mud banks. Other sources are commercial fishermen, guides, outfitters, trappers, etc. But long before you come to that, you should acquire as many useful maps as possible of your proposed route. Topographic maps are excellent, always, and charts. For the canoe country of Ontario and northern Minnesota, splendid maps and charts can be obtained from outfitters. As a matter

Rapids of this sort can't be recommended for beginners, but for those who can handle canoe deftly there's no finer sport than shooting white water. On unfamiliar streams, always check such stretches from bank before canoeing them.

of fact, these good chaps will rent you the whole works at a surprisingly reasonable rate: canoe, packs, tents, bedding, food, the works—including a guide if you like. Topographic maps can be obtained by writing the Geological Survey, Washington, D.C. 20025. Information on charts can be obtained from the Coast and Geodetic Survey, Washington, D.C. 20025. In some cases, the Forest Service and the National Park Service can supply specialized charts and maps. I have found that service-station road maps are valuable if used as an *accessory* to topographic maps.

I always take two compasses on a canoe trip. I keep one handy, for daily use, the other in reserve, sealed against the slings and arrows of outrageous whacks, bumps, wet, mildew and curious chipmunks. Another good thought about canoeing in strange country is to obtain the latest dope on fire permits, though in true wilderness there is not too much applicable law agin' it and it's up to the camper to be careful with fire, and burn only dead, otherwise-useless wood.

Always pack your unloaded canoe high above the highest visible waterline. I secure it with a nylon line, too, in case of wind. One time, having hastily landed and chased a black bear about 700 yards, I returned to find my empty canoe nearly out of sight on a big Northern lake, headed for the Arctic Ocean. There was only one thing to do and I did it: I swam and finally caught it. It makes my blood run cold now to think of how nearly I killed myself. I may do many foolish things, but losing a beached canoe will never again be among them.

Many chaps feel a canoe trip is a total loss if they don't shoot a bit of white water. I am fond of that sport, too. To start, always walk along the bank and check rapids. See if it's too much. Remember, skiers start on beginners' slopes. Same thing applies here. Empty the canoe and portage the gear around (especially the first-aid kit), and only then should you tackle the fine art of running the chute. When I hear a roar and see mist and spray, these days, I head for shore and check it out on foot.

I have never built a dugout canoe by chopping a log to shape but I've watched it being done from start to finish. You need a good axe and a couple of adzes. Also, I would concoct some sort of outsize calipers, made of plywood or even curved branches, to determine the thickness of the hull. You don't want it too thick (needlessly heavy) or too thin (dangerously weak). The natives I saw did not use calipers; they appeared to rely on the sound as the adze struck the hull.

A useful wilderness emergency canoe can be made by lashing together a frame and covering it with a large animal hide. In the North Country moose hide is often used.

This is log dugout described by author. While on safari in Africa, he watched natives build it with simple tools, relying on sound of adze to test hull thickness.

A craft which is useful for crossing a stream (though not for going its length) is the old Plains Indian bull boat. It's rather easy to make. You bend (by setting one end into the ground) pliant shoots of willow or some such. These can be lashed to a shape resembling a huge kettle drum. Over this the Indians affixed a hide, usually buffalo. These boats are rather unwieldy and hard to maneuver, but can be useful in a pinch. If animal hides are not available, you can use a heavy-duty tarpaulin for both the bull boat and the emergency bush canoe.

Driving with a Travel Trailer

Travel trailers tow easily and safely these days. And it's possible to buy an automobile equipped with a "trailer package" of extra features to provide better, more reliable towing. For little additional cost over a standard station wagon, you can be blessed with such devices as an extra-capacity radiator,

making it possible to conquer long and steep grades that used to appall trail-
erites. I know of trail enthusiasts who've driven hundreds of miles out of their
way to escape such impediments as Colorado's beautiful Monarch Pass. No
more! A trailer package may include transmission cooler, oversized fan, radiator cooler, special brakes, shocks, gear ratios, wheels, tires, springs—and a
wondrous trailer hitch that places much of the tongue-weight of the trailer-
bar on all four of the car's wheels, not just the rear ones. Some automobiles,
by the way, have an automatic leveling device, so you might ask if your
choice can be so equipped.

Loaded, it is very important that your car and trailer should both be riding level. Your car should not sag at the rear, nor should the tow bar dip. It is
dangerous to drive an auto-trailer in this condition! And it's hard on both
driver and equipment. There are several ways to beef up the rear of a car
properly.

My own feeling is that the trailer should be from 18 feet to 22 feet in
length and not more than about seven feet wide if you want it strictly for living afield. It is surprising where you can safely take one of these babies, after
you've driven one for a while. I have been through places with an 18-foot rig
where it has been impossible to get a 25-footer in and out.

John and Ann Jobson have used this rig on long Northern trips. He says hauling
trailer isn't as tough as it looks if loaded rig is level and you follow his tips.

Jobson's trailering instructions will help you back into spaces like this.
Among big trailer's attractions is space to carry such luxuries as folding chairs.

There is not much to learning how to back a trailer expertly. If getting it
into certain spaces is tricky, have an extra ball installed on the front bumper
of the towing vehicle. Then you can steer it in as easily as a forklift operating
in a warehouse. If backing a trailer confuses you at first, remember this cardi-
nal rule of procedure: Have all wheels pointed straight forward; place one
hand at the bottom of the steering wheel; move your hand right, the trailer
goes right; move your hand left, the trailer goes left. Don't practice in traffic
or on a city street. Catch yourself a nice big meadow, pasture, football field or
vacant lot. Set up a couple of bamboo poles (or some such) and practice backing between them until you do it smoothly.

When cornering, drive farther into the intersection than you normally
would without a trailer. When turning to the right, this keeps the trailer from
striking the curb; to the left, from striking a car waiting for the light in the inside lane. Always signal—way in advance so all traffic will know what you are
going to do. Stopping with a trailer is a trifle different from stopping with a
car. You must anticipate your stops and ease gradually. Gently coast to almost
a stop, then apply the brakes. If your trailer brakes are automatically connected with the car brakes, see if you can have them adjusted so they come on
a bit ahead of the car brakes. If you have a separate, manual control for the
trailer brakes, apply that lever judiciously a bit in advance of the car's brake
pedal. That straightens out your rig and keeps it from jackknifing.

When passing with a trailer, on the open highway, allow about twice the

Camp trailers eliminate some towing problems, and they require no
heavy-duty hitches or brakes, no special mirrors and no special engine features.

room you think you might need. A towed trailer can't be whipped in and out
of traffic like a sports car. Verve and *éclat* are fine in their places, but that
place is not with a travel trailer in traffic. By law you must go most slow with
a trailer—much slower than with a pickup and coach or a motor home.

About maintenance and service on the road: Expect that many service
stations look upon greasing your rig with the expression of a wine taster when
a foul odor suddenly assails his delicate nostrils. You will drive into a station
with no human in sight except two shiftless louts reading comic books. There
will also be one car in sight, the personal conveyance of one of these loafers.
It is hoisted up on the rack. As they indolently arise (as a big favor) they will
listen to your request and then point at the car on the hoist. "There's a car on
the hoist," they tell you. This explains why they cannot perform any work.
Another superb rejoinder is, "I'm alone." This type of station is run by an ab-
sentee boss. You will find many stations where the owner is there and unless
he is truly rushed he will accommodate you. And there are many well-trained
young men who'll help you—boss or no boss. The very best way to get service
is to head for the nearest big truck stop, where you may see a few short hair-
cuts and a lot of callouses on hands.

Another kind of "house" trailer is the folding or collapsible hard-walled
trailer. These have stout, rigid aluminum alloy or fiber walls and roof. They
easily erect for living, but fold for ease of towing. Some raise and lower,
others ingeniously fold like an intricate greeting card.

Reputable travel trailers are a bargain, and maintain a high resale and trade-in value. By law you must drive slower than with most rigs, and it's best if you have either a four-speed pickup or a specially factory-equipped auto to tow them. The camping trailers eliminate some of these problems. Camping trailers are the ones that are part-rigid and part-folding fabric. These are immensely and deservedly popular. They cost relatively little. No special car is required for towing. No special mirrors, heavy-duty hitches, or brakes. No added skill is required to tow them, except for just remembering they are back there, and there is no noticeable added strain on the car. Some places are lenient when these rigs exceed the usual uncomfortable "45 MPH with trailer" by a wee margin. Others *are not*. Virginia, I hear, is adamant regarding this regulation.

Driving with a Camping Coach or Motor Home

Life is surprisingly uncomplicated with a good pickup and coach. Winds and high-crown roads used to be sources of worry. No more. Not with the proper rig, that is. These new trucks are rugged and powerful. They accommodate high-centers, and the suspension and tires eliminate most excessive sway and tilt. They aren't infallible, of course. A zephyr that will blow away the roof off the high school gymnasium may damage your coach, too. The new breed of pickups, when loaded, will ride and handle like the conventional family automobile. They are comfortable, and a couple I have driven take no sass from modern autos on the highway. They will, in an emergency, do 90 with a loaded coach. They cruise at 65–70 if you want. And when you get on dirt roads, your camper pickup will run off and leave an automobile.

A popular kind of coach is the 10¼-foot slide-in. This is big enough for home-style living afield and yet it can be slid off when not in use, and the truck is free for other chores. Convenient loading and unloading can be accomplished with a set of jacks (preferably hydraulic). Many sportsmen leave the slide-in on the truck permanently, unless they get a good buy on haul-it-yourself fireplace wood or some such. Most coach owners I know go out about 40 or more weekends a year!

My current coaching rig has car air conditioning, AC coach air conditioning (great in the desert) twin propane bottles, LP refrigerator, LP gas range, twin sinks, pressure water, shower, toilet, waste-holding tank; 12-v, 115-v and gas lighting, foam beds that sleep four comfortably or six a bit crowded. We have a dining nook, twin water tanks, three gasoline tanks, twin batteries, 110–120 AC light plant and more than sufficient storage space. You

Jobson's slide-in camper coach is large enough for comfortable living afield; its features include air conditioning, gas range, refrigerator, shower and sinks.

can keep a rig like this loaded at all times, with camping gear and clothing plus all the canned and dry foods in place, water tanks flushed and filled, propane topped off.

Another type of coach has a couple of names, but the first was called a chassis-mount. The coach, somewhat larger than the slide-in, has the advantage of a walk-through, a bit more floor room and perhaps closet space but other than that has no more conveniences than a 10- or 11-foot slide-in. I've had both, and I like both. The walk-through is mighty convenient—but remember you can have a crawl-through with the slide-in.

It has been my experience that a well-mated truck-and-slide-in combo will outperform and outmaneuver the chassis-mount. It is just as comfortable for a couple (or a couple with two or three small children) and more convenient to drive on back roads. It parks easier, too, afield. The moment you turn off the ignition you have camp set up. A feature many sportsmen admire is that with a pickup coach you can tow, at separate times, a travel trailer,

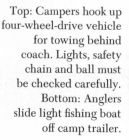

Top: Campers hook up four-wheel-drive vehicle for towing behind coach. Lights, safety chain and ball must be checked carefully. Bottom: Anglers slide light fishing boat off camp trailer.

camping trailer, a mobile home, boat trailer, snowmobile trailer or that height of efficiency afield, a four-wheel-drive off-the-road vehicle. Some fellows even lash a trail bike to the X or (less desirable) install it on one of the truck bumpers. If you install a steel rack up on the roof, you can lash a canoe and all manner of gear on top.

Of course, a late-model pickup and coach will not come cheap. There is the cost of the truck to consider. So some chaps prefer a camping trailer or travel trailer which can be towed behind the family car.

Now comes one of those things that sound more complicated in theory than in practice. When a pickup coach is parked, it's best to have the rig reasonably level. Through practice you can maneuver a bit and get your mobile love nest just right. If it doesn't seem just right place either a bowl containing water or an inexpensive two-way level on some flat plane such as the top of the stove. You ascertain at once from the tilt of the water which side or end of the rig must come up or go down. I usually maneuver a bit and drive a tire up on a short length of thick plank fetched along for the purpose. If things get

There are places you shouldn't try to negotiate with full-sized motor home, but you don't need four-lane highways; this is Jobson's rig on curving dirt road.

obnoxious I whip out my old 20-ton truck jack, a few blocks of wood, and have the coach or whatever right on the button with very little effort. If you have a shovel on hand, and you should, you can sometimes dig a shallow hole and run one wheel into it to level the outfit. I like the plank, it's easier.

Another excellent and relatively inexpensive motor home is the popular van-type rig. I see more and more of these afield and the owners seem pleased with them. They aren't the big motor homes, by any means, but they fill a need and have a legion of supporters. The little "walk-in" vans make into creditable living quarters. Usually, owners dream of some magic way to expand them, like the prospective yacht buyer who told his marine architect he wanted his craft built so it was 95 feet in length inside, and 47½ feet in length on the outside. Usually, the vans are stretched for "living" with folding fabric, and I've seen these little fellows blossom out in three directions at once. Generally the canvas expands up, so the breadwinner can stand without getting a crick in his neck.

Camping vans come in many versions, and some are expandable when set up for overnight stops. This one has wide door giving entry into spacious tent.

Well-built, well-maintained trailers can be hauled long distances over dirt or gravel. To keep dust out, close all its windows except front one or ceiling vent.

Tips on Coach and Trailer Travel

Old hands at touring with a pickup coach or trailer have learned a multitude of worthwhile little tricks. Take the matter of the water tank. Some are of galvanized metal with soldered seams. When fresh off the production line, it is not wise simply to fill them and use the water. Perhaps it's the acid residue from the solder (I don't really know) but using them uncleaned does not make for the best water. A cure is to fill the tank approximately half full, pour in a box of baking soda, and let that ride for a day or so. The sloshing action will thoroughly clean the tank, which can then be rinsed.

One of the sad facts of life is that this type of tank sometimes has an appalling habit of springing leaks. Having 15 to 25 gallons of unconfined water on the floor of the coach or house trailer does not put one's wife in the most cheery of moods, believe me. If the budget permits, specify a welded tank, preferably of stainless steel.

The lines and fittings of the propane-butane system should be regularly inspected. Vibration and abrasion can sometimes induce leakage. In transit the bottle-gas should be *turned off at the tank*. Should a leak develop *outside* the mobile home it isn't such a catastrophe. But if it leaks inside you are hauling around a potential bomb. If your refrigerator runs on gas, don't worry about it being off while traveling, as the ice cubes will keep it cool enough between stops. During lunch, for example, you can turn it on for half or three-quarters of an hour (which is usually sufficient until the next stop).

On gravel and dirt roads, dust can be a pernicious problem. The dratted fine silt enters the living quarters and seems to get into everything unless you close all the windows except the front one. This sounds a bit peculiar, but it works. If your front window doesn't open, try the ceiling vent (though this is not quite so effective).

If you are pulling a house trailer, by all means install a ball (for the trailer hitch) on the front bumper of the towing vehicle. When you have to back the trailer into a particularly tight spot, simply attach the trailer to the front ball. Most everyone finds that the ensuing chore is then much easier. You can see what you are doing, and the front wheels guiding the rig give the driver far quicker maneuverability. When not in use, cover the front hitch with a slit tennis ball.

I have finally got it into my head that the best dishware for trailers and coaches is the plastic variety. On rough roads, we have broken enough crockery to stock a Times Square cafeteria. One time in the spring of 1955 we pulled into Dawson Creek, B.C., with every dish, bowl, saucer and cup smashed to bits.

When traveling gravel or dirt roads, watch the trailer tires closely. I try to rig my huge rear-view mirrors so I can glance at either tire now and then. The reason for this is that on noisy gravel roads you can have a flat tire on the trailer and not realize it. The hazard is much more serious than merely a ruined casing and (perhaps) tube. Gravel can overheat a flat tire and cause it to burst into flame, thus setting the rig afire. This is as good a time as any to mention that a good fire extinguisher should be handy in the car (or truck) plus one in the living quarters.

The electrical connection between car and trailer should be something like the cannon-type that fits together only one way and then locks securely by threads. I have had exceedingly ill luck with certain other types.

After long storage, don't operate trailer or self-contained recreation vehicle until you check out its electrical connections, vents, fittings, brakes, tires, etc. This man found bird's nest behind vent.

On slick roads if you should feel a skid, hit the trailer brakes *first*—that will help to eliminate the dreaded, careening jackknife. If conditions are such that you do not have to stop, also press the accelerator. This little maneuver has pulled many of us out of more than one tricky spot.

When selecting a pickup coach, be sure it does not extend back past the truck's open tailgate. It's a good idea to equip the rear wheels with drop-center truck wheels (not the passenger-car type which can split). And it doesn't hurt a thing if the rear tires are eight-ply rated. For the front wheels, six or even four ply will do. The truck should have a good set of helper springs, and after the coach is installed and loaded for the highway, the whole outfit should be level. That is, it should sit level on level ground. If it doesn't, you'd better have extra leaves added to the rear springs and/or install heavier-duty shocks.

It is a snare and a delusion to go by "charts" because for one thing (and it grieves me to say this) some coach dealers have an exceedingly optimistic notion as to how little their coaches actually weigh, loaded. I know this, because I have weighed a few coaches. While a couple of hundred pounds or so among friends is not too important, what is important is that your truck rides level—and if the rear end needs beefing up, the best time to do it is before you leave home.

Besides your propane range in the coach or trailer, you might carry a gasoline camp stove. Propane sometimes has the deplorable habit of running out just when the Little Dove is smack in the middle of cooking a tasty meal. We like to carry 100 feet of good weatherproof "drop cord" in 25-foot lengths. This setup will come in handy, especially in sections of Mexico. It is wise to have a good battery lantern with a sealed beam spot plus an emergency red flasher or blinker, and you should have flares as well—just in case you have a breakdown.

A pair of wooden wheel chocks are a must. My garage man got mine for me. Keep them handy and use them instead of rocks (which are not always there when needed). I will never forget the time I parked on Trutch Grade on the Alaska Highway to take a picture. I put the rig in gear, set the brakes, etc., and was adjusting a tripod leg when out of the corner of my eye I saw the whole outfit merrily proceeding on its own. I caught it. If I had managed to run that fast in the 100-yard dash back in high school, I would be a legend to this day.

Stash cans of pure water in with the grub because in the Latin American countries, the Far North, and indeed even in the United States, it is not always possible to find water suitable for human consumption.

Pickup-coach aficionados do not seem to have this trouble, but for some reason when a trailerite stops curbside for a nocturnal nap within the city limits of seven towns out of nine, the trailer will draw the local Bobbies. Just as you are dozing comfortably for that much-needed hour or so of refreshing shuteye, these zealous constables on the night shift rap on the door (while rudely shining a flashlight through the window) and ask you to move on. So— when you're feeling drowsy on a long night journey, pull into the next truck stop. Most generally you are welcome there, and though it is noisy, you know that you are safe from traffic and will not be bothered. With the pickup coach, a city-side snooze on a quiet residential street can hardly be beat. Everyone on the block will figure you are a neighbor's friend.

If you are towing a trailer—house, boat, or utility—and for any reason you have to run through water with warm hubs, get them repacked with grease as soon as convenient. Don't ask me exactly what happens—probably some kind of osmosis. Enough to say that water enters the bearings and, if not attended to, results in a ruined assembly. Under certain conditions of travel this can make for a devil of a lot of wheel greasing, but it is far better than to be stranded, waiting for spare parts. Some of the newest types do not require this care.

After each stop it's very smart to perform this ritual: Take one last look into the coach or trailer and see that all is secure (cupboards shut, refrigerator closed, etc.); check the windows on each side to see that they are not only closed but latched; see that the trailer or coach door is shut and *locked;* turn off the bottle gas; if you're using a trailer, examine the hitch and safety chain and ask the bride to press the brake pedal and operate the turn signals while you watch the lights; finally, walk around the rig and look at each tire. On vacation I am as lazy as the next fellow, but I do all this without fail, and many times I have been happy I did.

The Four-Wheel-Drive

Many a good man has found himself impaled on the cruel horns of a dilemma: Should he or should he not invest in a four-wheel-drive vehicle? If you are what is known as an actual or potential two-car family *and* if you genuinely love the outdoors, then you should seriously consider making that second car a four-wheel-drive. These vehicles are exceedingly versatile. Great for shopping, herding dairy cattle, ferrying kids to school, going to beach parties, or a hundred and one other things. They can even plow the back pasture. But where they really pay handsome dividends is doing precisely what they are designed to do. And that is to take you and yours, in comfort, into spectacular

Jobson's four-wheel-drive vehicle is shown traversing region of Teddy Roosevelt's Dakota ranch. It will have no trouble leaving road to reach desired campsite.

country where you cannot go by any other practical, convenient means.

They will take you in for pennies, and they will take you back out. The sturdy little fellows will carry an astonishing amount of weight. They can and do perform feats like yanking loaded tanker semi-trucks out of muskeg-type mud. There is such a terrific margin of power and dependability inherent in the wee jewels! Indeed, aficionados sometimes get themselves into a sticky wicket by believing a four-wheel-drive can do *anything*. Of course, the vehicle won't. So, a hint for a new owner is to realize that your rig will go many places, with skillful driving, but it cannot climb Mt. McKinley.

Which type to buy? Well, there are truly luxurious ones if you always take the wife and kiddies. Some I know of have turbo hydra-matic transmission, power steering, power brakes and air conditioning. I have cruised in one for several days through the aromatic sage and dry-creek beds of Wyoming's Red Desert. Never have I ridden in such utter comfort over unimproved topography! It was a wonderful experience, and quite a revealing one. I'm an old hand with four-wheel-drives, and I guess I have been transported in them about as much as any sportsman. They have taken me to oddly assorted

Combination of 4WD car and trailered boat will take this vacationing family
of camping enthusiasts just about anywhere, on land or water.

places—up high mountains in Hawaii, through eight-foot-high elephant grass
in Tanzania and across tundra near the Arctic Circle. Where I have had my
most fun with them, though, has been in the contiguous U.S.A.

The four-wheel-drive as we know it now became justly popular because
of its great-uncle, the World War II military General Purpose Vehicle. I still
occasionally see a 1942 (or so) surplus Jeep doing Herculean service. Sportsmen demanded a civilian version, and there are now several makes. These are
the short-coupled, compact, highly maneuverable, rugged vehicles that, due
to their short wheel base, are the best for getting you over truly rugged terrain. They will crawl like a bug where a longer wheel base would get hopelessly hung up. They drive very well on the open highway, but some chaps
prefer to tow them by means of a yoke or tow-bar hooked to a better highway
vehicle. When road's end is reached, the highway car is temporarily retired
and the little "4WD" takes over.

There are many versions of excellent four-wheel-drives for those who
like to get way back in on roads too tough for an ordinary car or pickup, yet
do not particularly like to do an excessive amount of off-road travel. There
are regular-size station wagons, truck-type station wagons, and the big ¾-ton
or one-ton rated pickups. All the different types are useful, and all of them
will get you into country that will make your head reel with joy if, like me,
you love sports afield.

If you can swing it, useful extras on a "4x4" are a front winch, a steel
skid plate (the dealer will know), positive traction, and spare (built-in) gasoline tanks with changeover valves.

Trail Cycles

It is not possible for most people to trailer a saddle hoss from home to the Wild Yonder. One solution is to get a mechanized mustang—an inexpensive, utterly dependable modern trail cycle. If you rig your machine with a carrier, saddle bags, perhaps a scabbard for a gun or fishing rod or camera tripod, and if you own lightweight backpacking gear, you have a winning setup for adventuring afield. This combination will easily take you into places only suited for horseback or for hikers, and you can eat and sleep in comfort, being swiftly mobile and maneuverable. Trail cycling cross-country, off-roads, costs so little as to be inconsequential.

I'm thinking primarily of the wire-wheeled machines that look superficially somewhat like small conventional motorcycles. There are also disc-wheeled trail *scooters*, which are wonderful within limits. If all you plan to do is ride exclusively on rough trails, you ought to investigate the scooters before deciding on a purchase. But they're considerably lower-slung and smaller-wheeled, so the larger bikes are more versatile, much better able to negotiate rugged terrain.

Now, I am not discussing the Hell's Angels type of road machine. I'm not even talking about the competition bike or the so-called "scrambler" machine, neither of which to my thinking, is useful afield. They are too noisy, too damaging, often too heavy, far and away too powerful. You do not require much engine power on a good trail cycle. You want low gears, a small, quiet, muffled engine. It has to be light enough so that *you* handle *it*, it does not handle you. And you want to sort of crawl along in a dignified manner, not blast off.

Make certain your muffler almost silences the exhaust. (A noisy bike is an abomination afield, and will gain you more enemies than friends.) Also make certain your muffler does one other thing: It absolutely must arrest sparks. I have never seen sparks flying out of any trail bike, but apparently it's a possibility, because a U.S. Forestry-approved spark arrester should be fitted if your machine is to be used in a National Forest. Make sure your muffler is hung high, so it doesn't hit trail obstructions.

A good trail bike is an uncomplicated device, basically being two wheels on a welded frame that's engineered for abuse it likely will never encounter. This frame will hold the engine and it will have a drive system, suspension system, electrical and brake system. What makes the modern trail bike so outstanding is the way all these component parts have been perfected, and the way they've been made to work together.

I have used several different types of trail bikes and have found all of

Trail cycles, like snowmobiles, have been accused of damaging woodlands, but when used judiciously they're harmless, enjoyable machine for back-country travel.

them dependable and reliable. Some have a mechanical clutch requiring a control (mine is by hand) and others have the easily-operated automatic which cuts in as the throttle is opened. Both work to beat the dickens, so whether you select the centrifugal or friction clutch (or whatever) depends on personal preference. These trail cycles usually adapt to grinding up trails or flashing along paved roads by changing the gear-sprocket ratio. Some have two sprockets on the drive (rear) wheel and you switch the chain from one to the other, depending on whether you're off-road or on-road. At least one other has a lever on the gear box which accomplishes this in a second.

I like my own trail cycle light enough so I can lift it in or out of my old station wagon (admittedly grunting mightily when I do so) or put it in or out of the bumper rack on a pickup truck. Both four-cycle and two-cycle engines are available. Always air-cooled, they are vastly reliable though a bit heavy for the power output.

Unless you should for some reason want to, it is no longer necessary to pre-mix oil and gasoline for the two-cycle engine fuel. On my own bike I put the oil into a reservoir, the gasoline into the tank, and some cunningly contrived gadget automatically meters the flow for proper combustion. Call me a sissy, but I would not use a trail cycle that did not have electric starting. This has saved the day for me a time or two when I carelessly stalled the engine in a tight spot and needed both hands and both feet for other pressing chores. I think lug tires are a necessity, and we all wear safety glasses (my tempered shooting glasses serve) because if there is a machine ahead of you sometimes little projectiles fly back. Also branches can whip you, so you should to protect your eyes. I like a really powerful headlight, a speedometer and odometer (very important), a comfortable, adjustable seat, wide handlebars, waterproof ignition system and good brakes that come on easy, gradually.

Probably because they resemble at first look a conventional street motorcycle, and because motorcycles have a reputation for being dangerous if carelessly or recklessly handled, I often am asked if trail cycles aren't hazardous. No, they are not even as dangerous to your person as riding a horse. Or driving your car in traffic. They go slow, and unless you're very careless it's pretty tough to get hurt using one. They are easy to ride. I am no mechanical wizard but the first time I got astride one, a pal showed me the clutch and the throttle and off I went with nary a bobble. They balance easier than a bicycle. When you buy a trail cycle, you get a manual with it giving trail tips and little details that help. Also how to care for it.

It goes without saying that no real sportsman will have a noisy bike, nor will he cut up vital watersheds or harass wildlife with his bike. Some fellows dearly love their trail bikes. I have found that people who disparage these machines have never owned one.

Snowmobiles

A mere handful of years ago, before the current snowmobile explosion, any intrepid adventurer taking his family into the boondocks in midwinter, far from roads, for a spot of overnight camping was apt to be considered temporarily deranged. Now all that has changed.

Snowmobiles are no longer in the experimental stage. They are dependable work horses and I strongly doubt that winter camping with one is any more hazardous than summer camping with a canoe. It is a wonderful experience, I think. A snowmobile is about as reliable mechanically as an outboard motor. These machines have made it over the polar ice cap to the North Pole, and to the best of my recollection everyone got back safe and sound. And those were not the latest or most powerful models available, by any means. Eskimos have seized upon snowmobiles with the tenacity of a dedicated Border Patrolman locating two kilos of grass. They are substituting these won-

Snowmobilers now enjoy such accessories as special insulated suits and felt-lined boots. Tool kit, spare gas and oil should be carried by snowmobile campers.

derous little rigs for dog teams—and if there are any more practical folks than Eskimos, when it comes to coping with rigorous conditions afield, I can't think offhand who they'd be.

Ranchers in Wyoming and Montana use snowmobiles to feed cattle and to locate livestock in inclement weather. No longer need anyone be snowbound. Backwoods or isolated doctors employ them. So do law officers. But most of them are purchased for recreation. Among the fun is camping. It's getting increasingly popular; people who timidly try it once generally become hooked.

Snowmobile accessories such as special clothing can now be bought and what I've seen is functional, particularly the felt-lined boots. So far no camping equipment unique to snowmobiling has shown here in the Wasatch Range but other gear serves admirably. If you have backpacking equipment, such as a good two-man tent, small mountain stove, contoured down sleeping bag, lightweight nested cooking and eating kit, you're all set. With a supply of freeze-dried and dehydrated food as a reserve, and with a pair of good snowshoes lashed aboard, you're in shape for a rewarding solo trip. It is not the worst notion in the world to have a buddy along with his own fully-equipped rig, and some areas require it.

A tool kit should be included to keep the tracks from tightening too much and to keep the skis parallel. Spare gas and proper motor oil has got to be toted. If you mix gas and oil afield, be sure it is sloshed around for a seemingly interminable time, as when cold it does not readily amalgamate. And please—don't heat gasoline near a campfire, as I have seen done.

Where to carry all this gear depends on your individual machine and needs, but it is easily done. Even if part of it is on your back in your alloy pack frame. For a family outing, of course, the logistics will have to be figured out carefully.

The way it seems to work best here in the West is for each adult to have his own machine. Tots can ride behind Mom and Dad. Heavier camp gear is called for, usually, than in summer. This does not mean *really* heavyweight automobile camping tents, cots, etc., but somewhat larger shelters, a two-burner stove and a greater variety of food. This is carried in a sled towed by the snowmobile, and it is wise to use one recommended by the manufacturer of your machine. Not that I have not seen some pretty fruity home-grown sleds dragged along—one memorable beauty being an old beat-up toboggan with the front slightly raised so it would not skitter on turns.

At least one ideal way to camp with a snowmobile is to locate long stretches of frozen rivers and lakes. There the going is smooth and pleasant. Come late afternoon you duck into the timber, set up camp, make a small cooking fire (reserving your stove for emergency). Maybe later in the evening you'll enlarge it to a social council fire. Everyone is snug and warm. The faithful machine stands by, and the sight of it is reassuring. You yawn, take one last lingering look at the glittering heavens, duck into the cozy tent, zip the flap and crawl into the fluffy down bag. Surprisingly fast you're toasty warm. You extinguish the little folding lantern, snuggle around a bit and soon are in deep slumber. It is one of the good things in life.

Horse and Wagon Camping

Camping by means of a horse team and farm wagon (indeed, even horse and buggy) used to be popular in portions of this country. A good many people in their late forties and early fifties recall with acute nostalgia those unhurried days afield. The experience is unique.

Folks who have read classics such as *The Covered Wagon* have wondered now and again what camp life was like for the people of the old-time wagon trains, and especially how a large group made out. The mechanics of wagon-train camp life is well recorded. We know, for example, that the ideal camp-

Old-fashioned wagon-train camping gives modern recreationists chance to capture feeling of westering pioneers as they set out across unfamiliar country. This is nostalgic adventure without really "roughing it," and experience gives campers new appreciation of pioneers' freedom, courage and self-reliance.

site was near palatable water (they carried barrels of water for dry camps), a place with ample feed for the stock to graze, and wood to burn. The women-folk generally slept in the prairie schooners, the men tossed their bedrolls under the wagons or near the fires. Usually, each family cooked for itself. In hostile country a night watch was maintained—for protection of the stock, mostly, as it was uncommon for Plains Indians to attack the *people* of a wagon train at night. The train was managed like a small community, with minor influences of military discipline and procedures. There was the wagon master, who was roughly a combination of mayor and general. He had his scouts (guides) and outriders. Usually there was a committee approximating a village council. All citizens had their responsibilities.

I never expected to participate in a wagon-train camp. Then I got an assignment to learn all I could about camping attractions in the beautiful Great Smoky Mountains which repose in splendid purple-blue-green majesty across western North Carolina. There a member of the Department of Conservation and Development asked if we'd like to spend a day with a real old wagon train. My jaw dropped in astonishment. The wagon train with which we became temporarily connected was no fanciful escapade. Carefully planned and sponsored by the Macon County Wagon Train Association and the Western Carolina Riding Club, its purpose was to point the need for scenic routes through the mountains.

People and livestock are still people and livestock. We heard much the same sounds, sniffed similar if not identical odors, enjoyed nearly the same sights as pioneers would have in the mid-1800's. The wagon train camped in a

beautiful large meadow near fresh water. Each family selected its own camp-site. All hands performed certain necessary chores. The stock was unhar-nessed and let out to graze. Wagons were partially unloaded. Water was car-ried, fuel gathered. Fires were built and soon the intoxicating scent of blue woodsmoke laced the fresh mountain air.

I need no crystal ball to know I can expect criticism of this essay: "Why in the hellfire tarnation do you write about such a passé subject as wagons and horses? There are better ways of camping these days."

I am aware that there is no *need* to employ a horse and wagon, even for a single camping trip. There is likewise no *need* for paddling a canoe, with our excellent outboard motors engineered for every conceivable requirement. There is no *need* to shoulder a good pack frame and trudge deep into wilder-ness country that can be reached by no other surface means. You can see the country from aircraft. The joy of at least one camping trip with horses and wagon is purely nostalgia, a way to experience an element of the American scene rapidly disappearing. There are a few ranchers and farmers around these days who will get a kick out of the adventure. There are still isolated ranches with a team and wagon that will "camp you out" for a fee. I'm sure most serious camping enthusiasts have a strong appreciation of the romantic. I know that I am deeply grateful that my father had the patience to endure a wide-eyed little kid on some of his cherished team-and-wagon hunting-camp-ing trips. He was wise in many ways; with his perceptive insight he undoubt-edly knew that not only would the experience be thrilling and educational for me—it would afford a priceless storehouse of memories.

10

Where and When

Locating Campsites and Campgrounds

We have close friends in our little hamlet who own a gorgeous camper, a chassis-mount model costing upwards of $7,500. They know the back country, which is at our doorstep, and they know how to get along in the wilderness.

Come the weekend, what do they do? They drive up to a tiny man-made lake quite near home, one not particularly noted for anything, including shade and fish. There they consort with other truck-coach and travel-trailer aficionados, all crowded together like kippers in a can. They have a wonderful time and come Monday are back on the job refreshed in soul and spirit, keen of eye, springy of step and anxiously looking forward to the next weekend for more of the same.

Personally, I would hate to be caught at that miserable little reservoir. My wife and I do just about the opposite. We seek out the loneliest places we can find, and we are pretty good at it. So good that if we see one human over the weekend we get severe shooting pains and our eye muscles may flicker with the onset of a tic. We are not gregarious when camping. Our friends have a ball, and so do we—each doing what he likes best. The idea of camping is to have fun, and the choice is yours.

But many a beginning camper is hazy about the campsite essentials to look for. The camp must be pitched at a reasonably proper site or upsetting incidents occur. Among them: collapsed tents, disturbed rest (because of sloping beds or snuffles from the dank woods) or, heaven forbid, an unexpected flood could wipe you out.

The best campsite is an unused one. Old ones often are populated with rodents and bugs (including bedbugs). The best firewood is gone, and there is evidence of garbage, buried and otherwise. Your entire campsite ideally is fairly level, with just a gentle slope. Earth is preferred, but if you're forced to pitch a tent on humus or sand, special stakes or logs and boulders may be used to secure the tent's bottom perimeter.

Some campers are gregarious souls who like to seek company of kindred spirits at organized campgrounds such as at Whycocomagh on Nova Scotia's Cape Breton Island (above). Others prefer solitude of secluded sites like those above Moraine Lake in Banff National Park, Alberta (left). Best spots to camp depend partly on your choice between solitude and camaraderie.

Excluding a desert "dry" camp, the classic, traditional campsite is near stream or lake water, but not right on the shore. Camp should be respectably above the highest detectable waterline. Up in the prevailing breezes, which have such salubrious effects as discouraging mosquitoes while keeping tent, bags and clothing well aired and dry. In hot weather, the slightest breeze is cooling. Wily old-timers try to catch a campsite that is sunny during the morning, yet shady in late afternoon. Try north and east of trees, a hill, or some such, but don't make camp under an outsized tree or steep cliff. Trees drip water interminably after showers, plus sap and bird lime. Cliffs dislodge rocks and slabs. Be far enough away to be safe and yet enjoy the long afternoon shadows. It is better to pack water a ways to camp and to stroll down for fishing and swimming, rather than being too near the waterline. In the West, incidentally, never pitch camp in a gulley. A dry wash can suddenly become the channel for a flash flood.

You'll read that prevailing breezes can be predicted with some expertness. True. In the Rocky Mountains, however, winds capriciously swap ends within seconds. By breezes I don't mean a gale, such as I've encountered in parts of Wyoming where the zephyrs can whisk a tent to soaring heights. Better not to camp on such a site, but if you must, be in a basin or some other protected area.

The tent and possibly the kitchen area should be level, but the whole site should have a gentle slope to drain not only rampaging water, but moisture as well. Seashore campgrounds notwithstanding, a healthily functioning camp is a camp of dry fabrics. It's better to be on a knoll than in a hollow, normally. Streamside it matters little, if you attain campsite height via a steep bank or a long sweep so you are high enough to escape bugs and chilblains.

Whether or not you cook with it, the heart of the best camps is a cheery wood fire. I hesitate to recommend your ringing the fire with rocks unless you know about them. Some when heated can blow apart like a grenade. If they're sooty and black from long use, and if they're dry, probably they're okay. Never build a fire on any sort of forest-floor humus, moss or ground cover like needles or dry prairie grass. Cleared mineral soil or sand is best. I've never had a fire get away on me, but I've seen it happen enough times to know it's a hazard. Shovel out an ample space, below the roots.

About the problem of underbrush and thick weeds, my advice is not to camp in or near them. If your camp must abut brush, chop it, as this thick growth does harbor dratted insects and reptiles.

It is said that the mountain men (and the superbly knowledgeable Plains Indians from whom they learned) looked for a campsite with "wood, water and grass." This is still a good rule of thumb, if you add "level" for the tent.

Even at resorts like Cape Breton, with its popular organized campgrounds (shown on page 229) inquiries will often turn up beautiful, uncrowded spots like this.

A basic latrine or outside privy can be contrived by digging a hole between two trees and lashing a couple of sapling poles across at seat height. A square of light scrap canvas can be artistically festooned about, for convention's sake. From habit (my parents did it) we sprinkle lye and some loose dirt into the cavity from time to time, but perhaps nowadays there is something better than lye. Whatever you use, the rules of sanitation should be preserved, and flies and odor discouraged afield.

Now, when on the road and seeking a camp*ground*, long experience has taught my wife and me not to fret if space is unavailable at the nearest public or private facilities. If we keep our attitude on the light side, and our thinking flexible, these dilemmas seem to resolve themselves. If all the places seem to be filled up and you don't know where to stay, don't be afraid to ask around. Good sources are the service stations (particularly the small, "homey" ones) and country stores. Police are extremely helpful. Ranger stations and state-trooper barracks are good—and we've never failed with the small-town officer. It bears repeating that emergency "overnights" for self-contained rigs include big shopping-center parking lots and quiet residential side streets where

Campgrounds near roads often can accommodate trailers or camping coaches. (Jobson's rig is shown above.) For backpackers like Jim Kern and Tom Montoya (right) some camping meccas offer trail shelters. This one is on Florida Trail at Gold Head Branch State Park. There are also sites, as at Gushues Pond Provincial Park in Newfoundland (far right) equipped with fireplaces, benched tables, wooden tent floors, firewood and even toilets.

general parking is permitted. It is not recommended to drain water or leave other impolite evidence.

Privately owned campgrounds and public conventional campgrounds are not coping with the hordes of campers, though they're making valiant computerized efforts. Most people head for the most popular and most accessible spots. Thus the easily available camping meccas are a shambles from overcrowding, whereas many side-road campgrounds—even at the season's height—stand empty. Learn to travel the back roads, for that's where they are (though sometimes within earshot of a busy super-highway). Camping congestion breeds congestion. Seek the lonely places and chances are excellent you'll find a place to camp where you can relax, fish, hike, enjoy zesty campfire meals and breath the good air.

There has been a tremendous upsurge of privately owned campgrounds, and a few take reservations. But remember to arrive early as there seems to be a current practice of overbooking, just as airlines and hotels overbook.

The best camping routine while traveling, especially, is to leave at the crack of dawn and pull in around 3:30 or 4:00 in the afternoon. You'll have less trouble, and will sometimes find space at popular federal and state campgrounds then. If the "SORRY—FULL" sign is up at a National Park campground, have a talk with the ranger. He may quietly direct you to an "off-limits" spot where you can nest on an emergency basis.

Now and then my wife and I find it rewarding to go straightforwardly up to a farmer or rancher and ask him if we can camp on his back property if we behave ourselves, do not make a nuisance and obey his informal rules. *This is probably the best casual camping* left to the family or weekend camper. If you can get a rancher or farmer on your side, you may find yourself camping with ease, grace and genuine unhurried pleasure at streamside, under lofty shade trees in rich green meadows.

Also get and make a habit of using a good up-to-date newsstand guidebook to campgrounds. This tidal wave of camping popularity has resulted in a profusion of just about everything suited to camping needs, and these guidebooks are among the goodies.

Great Circle Routes

Friends in New York City motor to the Adirondacks on Interstate 87, and re-turn the same way. From Salt Lake City, other pals regularly make the pleas-ant jaunt to Glen Canyon and always follow the identical Interstate Highway there and back. This saddens me. I'm not really criticizing it, but there are other ways of having tent-camping auto-traveling fun. In plotting our itin-eraries, we look upon our quaint little love-nest as a point on the rim of a great wheel. We can with but slight additional expense go around the perim-eter, seeing fresh sights and yet ending up where we began. In a manner of speaking, each day of driving we're simultaneously departing from and head-ing for home.

There are hundreds, likely thousands, of combinations of excellent *circle* trips in North America. One of the best we've taken was a loop that brought us through the Theodore Roosevelt National Memorial Park, on the site of T. R.'s Elkhorn Ranch. It's a place you ought to visit sometime, even if you don't live along our "rim." (We reside in the Salt Lake Basin.) Our trip was inspired by the burning urge to cavort through western North Dakota and bits of neighboring states. Roosevelt himself was responsible for the urge. I've been a palpitating hero-worshipper of Teddy Roosevelt ever since, as a boy, I read his wonderful outdoor stories. The locale of many of these superb tales is near the whistlestop of Medora, which has not changed too much. It is the gate-way to a bizarre, captivating land. T. R. had two ranches near Medora and one (of which he was part owner), the Maltese Cross brand, is easy to reach; we've been there several times. The other, his own favorite and to me the more intriguing, is the site of the Elkhorn brand spread, on the Little Mis-souri. This place can be difficult to reach.

Over the years I had been nearly consumed with a desire to tread that hallowed terrain, the focal point of some wondrous T. R. adventures. As we wheeled out of the driveway, I said forthrightly, "Mamma, we're not coming home until we walk upon the Elkhorn. Even if I have to hock the homestead and hire a helicopter." She gave me a sideways look, knowing I just might try it. We did it without becoming airborne, but it was necessary to travel some poor roads, and stay off them if rain was predicted. That gumbo will ensnare a bulldozer. We had to ford the Little Missouri at T. R.'s old ranch crossing. This entire park is exceedingly interesting—one reason it is a park—and if you're among those who admire Roosevelt's outdoor stories, the Theodore Roosevelt National Memorial Park will surely fascinate you.

There is excellent camping there and near there. Throughout this entire circle trip we found bountiful and excellent campgrounds, most of them but

Jobson's 4WD is shown fording Little Missouri, near Teddy Roosevelt's Elkhorn Ranch, during combined camping and historical sight-seeing trip described in text.

fractionally occupied. Unspoiled, uncrowded, free. My wife Ann and I casually tossed our minimal, basic, but sufficient gear into a 4WD. We didn't want to be bogged down with tiresome equipment, nor did we desire to spend hours and lots of Jobson perspiration erecting and striking camps. Our shelter was practically a backpacker, a splendid bush tent of the long-proven Explorer design, six feet two inches high for ease of dressing—with a floor 7½x7½ feet. Up or down in a minute or so. Change of wash 'n' wear. Two light sleeping bags and high-density foam pads. Nested cooking kit, cooler, small camp Dutch oven. Dishes, utensils, one-burner Coleman stove, propane lantern, insulated bottle for morning coffee (in bed) and waterbag. Hatchet, shovel, a few other tools, camera (with changing bag, tanks and chemicals to develop afield test rolls of film). Also a metal detector and a pet .257 Roberts with 500 rounds of handloads for varmint shooting.

Our first stop was at the ghost towns of Atlantic and South Pass on Wyoming's historical South Pass. Good camping and stream fishing among the sage. Meandering to Devil's Tower, the Black Hills of South Dakota, Twin Buttes, Medora, Valley of the Yellowstone with the Custer battlefield and Pompey's Tower where carving remains from Lewis and Clark. Here it is no feat to duck in and out of the Bighorn Mountains, which we love. Next, the drive from Montana over the towering Red Lodge Highway into Yellowstone Park. I've eyeballed the Alps six times and doubt if they contain superior alpine meadows. From around in here, it's easy to journey to Glacier National Park and *then* over the Red Lodge Highway, Jackson Hole, Pierre's Hole, back into Utah with its unique parks and multiple charms. If you admire Western scenery, try Monument Valley on the Arizona-Utah border. This all makes a dandy circle trip—one adaptable to shorter or longer routes.

Here's one of Jobson's Far North rigs as it nears Whitehorse, after trip on Alaska Highway; mud reaches almost to racked canoe but there was no mechanical trouble.

Alaska Highway and Other Points North

A camping trip over the Alaska Highway is not for everyone. I ought to know. I've made 13 round trips over it, involving travel with all types of recreational vehicles—trailers, slide-in coaches, chassis-mount coaches, motor homes, van, and one trip with a station wagon and tent-camping gear. People in Whitehorse or Valdez used to shout at us, "Have you *moved* up here?"

A trek over the Big-A is the stud of all North American motor-camping ips. Interest (for most true outdoorsmen) far exceeds Mexico, but not everyone will enjoy the experience, I'm now convinced. My wife and I have always had fun in the North, and in getting there. Gravel roads hold no terrors for us, as I was raised in country where a graded, maintained gravel road was the height of gracious motoring. In spite of: washouts (on one trip, 21 portions of the Big-A evaporated into limbo on us); dust so thick it would make an Egyptian sirocco seem pellucid as the Big Hole River; mosquitoes and no-see-ums; some of the settlement odors (all of which do not assail the nostrils like attar of Jacqueminot); the nuisance of getting anything done far from town (or in), like car repairs; the flying rocks kicked into your windshield or radiator by big trucks; plus plenty of other hazards and discomforts—all the little vicissitudes pale into insignificance compared with the pleasures of camping amid or in sight of towering, ice-clad mountains so awesome they halt your breath. The scent of resinous northern spruce campfires by clear, salmon-choked streams under the radiance of blazing constellations set in velvet heavens swept by Northern Lights. The sight of grizzly bear, white sheep, bull moose over seven feet high at the shoulder. The Far North holds unique attractions for the camper.

Yet I'd be less than honest not to say that I've seen visitors from as far away as Florida leave Dawson Creek, B.C., Mile 1, determined to drive to Fairbanks, quit and turn around 40 to 60 miles after the end of the hardtop, which doesn't last too long. There is not much pavement on the Alaska Highway in Canada, more than 1,000 miles of gravel, though at the Alaska-Yukon border you're back on blessed hardtop. Some people make it from Mile 1 to Fort Nelson but no farther before calling it quits. A percentage of good folks cannot take the pounding, the noise of rough corduroy, chuck-holed gravel, the lack of a center white line and the absence of safety shoulders.

But say your mind is made up to do it. The first thing you ought to get is a book called *The Milepost,* $3.95 postpaid from Alaska NW Pub. Co, Box 4-EEE, Anchorage, Alaska 99509. I cannot think of any worthwhile information concerning travel over the Alaska Highway and all connected roads that isn't between the covers of this one source.

The Alaska Highway is a living thing. It never is in repose and cannot be classified as being either this way or that. The weather, seasons, traffic, maintenance all affect the Big-A. I have never (in 26 trips over it) seen it the same twice. Sometimes the road surface is soapy-slick as grease on certain curves. I've seen cars and trucks slither off on the straightaway, due to the high crown of that section. The answer is to drive slower, no faster than 45 mph when the roads are dry and good, slower when they're wet or unusually rough. The key to successful driving here is *patience.* Never hurry or become over-restive. *Never* speed. Some do, but they have tire failure, ruined rigs and, sadly, wrecks.

Best time to go? I'd say July, August and part of September. The salmon make spawning runs then, and the bugs are either gone or mostly gone. Washouts from spring floods have been repaired, the Big-A is dry (mostly) and it's far easier to cope with dust (turn on headlights and go *slow*) than with a soapy road surface. I find winter is second best for travel but not for camping. Spring is the worst; it can be pretty awful.

You may be surprised at the luxuriance of flowers and berries in the North. I love the fireweed but also admire the forget-me-nots, wee rhododendrons and a type of orchid. Good low-bush berries include blueberries, huckle, raspberries, straw, lingon, cranberries, plus salmon berries, crow, bear and nagoon. My wife bolsters our meals with platters of a delicious wild mushroom, resembling a morel, which conveniently grows roadside in the Yukon. Investigate clam digging and the availability of crab and shrimp in Alaska. The Indian dried fish often is excellent.

You'll have to begin, if you're driving, at Dawson Creek, B.C. Some get there from the West, through British Columbia and the Hart Highway. Others come in through Alberta. A pearl of a notion is to drive only one way over the Big-A, and take an Inside Passage ferry the other way. For information on this delightful gambit, write: Alaska State Ferry System, Pouch, Juneau, Alaska 99801. For Canadian boats: British Columbia Ferries, 816 Wharf St., Victoria, B.C.

There are two stratagems for getting aboard a State of Alaska Ferryliner. Say you're heading north, and want to travel part of the way by boat, via Prince George and Hazelton (Highway 16) to the tidewater port of Prince Rupert, B.C. The Alaska Ferry runs from there to Skagway-Haines, Alaska. There you head the bus north 150 or so miles to Haines Junction, Yukon Territory, where the Haines Highway intersects with the Alaska Highway. This portion of the Alaska Highway to the Alaska border, many feel, is the most scenic of the Canadian portion, with the awesome, spectacular, mighty St. Elias Coastal Range off on your left (as you head north). The Haines Highway, incidentally, is among the very loveliest of all Far North roads.

But if you don't feel like driving from Haines to Haines Junction, you can put your rig on a flatcar at Skagway and take the picturesque narrow-gauge railroad to the capital of the Yukon Territory, the city of Whitehorse, where you likewise intersect the great Alaska Highway. At Whitehorse, you might investigate taking off on the "Mayo" road to Dawson City, Yukon. Dawson was a Klondike Gold Rush metropolis at one time. It is not abandoned, by any means, but compared to its former glory, it is a ghost town.

In this general area you'll discover an occasional side road beckoning the more adventurous. It's best to ask a reliable local citizen before taking off on one. Pursuing further the matter of this "Marine Highway" north, by taking a State of Alaska Ferryliner at either of its terminals (Skagway-Haines, Alaska, and Prince Rupert, B.C.), we have told you that you can drive your rig to Prince Rupert, going north. But you don't even have to do that. A short drive from Seattle will take you to the town of Port Angeles or Anacortes, Wash., or Vancouver, B.C. From either place it's a short ferry ride to Vancouver Island. From Port Angeles or Anacortes you'll probably ferry to Victoria, B.C., or from Vancouver you can ferry to Nanaimo. You then can motor (from Victoria, about 220 miles) to Kelsey Bay, where you can board the British Columbia Ferry System's *Queen of Prince Rupert* which will cruise you to Prince Rupert, B.C. At Prince Rupert, as mentioned, you transfer to an Alaskan Ferryliner for the trip to Skagway, Alaska. Incidentally, on this ferry you can explore, if you like, Juneau, Sitka, Petersburg, Wrangell, or Ketchikan. It's wise to have advance reservations.

Motor camping in Alaska is wonderful. The network of excellent highways will easily "whisk" you to varied climes and scenery. I'm fond of the Kenai Peninsula, the trip to Valdez and Mt. McKinley, the cities of Fairbanks and Anchorage and towns like Seward and Homer. The great rushing rivers and towering mountain ranges are unforgettable. You may well luck into excellent fishing virtually at roadside.

The great Trans-Canada Highway (from the Pacific to the Atlantic) is over 5,000 miles long, and is well worth seeing. It isn't a truly "Northern" road, but more an up-to-date transcontinental highway and super-highway. The Trans-Canada Highway is useful in getting to wilderness roads. Say you live in the East. A rewarding gambit is to drive to Quebec City, enjoy that, head west over the scenic Trans-Canada until you get to Calgary. At Calgary, turn north, through Edmonton, Valleyview, Whitecourt and Grande Prairie to either Dawson Creek—Mile Zero of the colossal Alaska Highway—to the wee hamlet of Grimshaw, Alberta, which is Mile Zero of the Mackenzie Highway, that mostly graveled ribbon of highway running true as a ruler to Yellowknife, a modern city on the shores of Great Slave Lake. My feeling about the drive to Yellowknife (and side trip to Ft. Smith) is that an expert and dedicated camping enthusiast should take it, if only to visit Yellowknife and get some of that excellent angling. For folks residing in our Mountain States and on the West Coast, a pleasant way to reach Mile Zero of the Alaska Highway is over the Hart Highway (#97), reached via British Columbia's scenic Cariboo Highway (through Williams Lake and Quesnel).

A relatively unknown road is one of the best for the lover of wilderness motor-camping. It's the road from Williams Lake, B.C., across the Chilcotin Plateau, through Riske Creek, Alexis Creek, Tatla Lake, Kleena Kleene, Anaheim Lake, Tweedsmuir Park, Stuie, and into Bella Coola, B.C., at tidewater. Some of the best angling in the world is at and out of Bella Coola. There is, much of the time, also excellent grizzly hunting from there. It is not a trip for the casual weekend camper, as some of the road can be rough. Standard cars make it all the way to Bella Coola, but I don't advise it. I always use a four-wheel-drive, specifically a Land Rover 109, often with coach. But I might tackle it with a new pickup. The road is marvelous in interest. Across the plateau it's much like Jackson Hole, Wyo. (in the early days). There are grizzly, moose and caribou on that plateau and exceptional trout fishing. There

Above and at near right are scenes
along Alaska Highway. Mountains toward
which trailer is heading are part
of St. Elias Range. Rest stop in lower
picture is at highway "water
hook-up," where most valuable camping
accessory is wife with strong back.

With motor home or coach, camping trip across
U.S. or Canada is one long scenic adventure—an adventure
John and Ann Jobson and thousands of other campers
have experienced and then repeated with many fascinating
variations. Recorded here (from top) are stops
at Yukon Border, at bilingual campgrounds in Quebec, and on
Mackenzie Highway near Peace River in Alberta.

are descendents of Sioux who ventured as a war party from the Great Plains and were so enamored of the area they decimated all the men of the indigenous tribe, took to themselves the women and never returned to the faraway Dakotas. It's a land of heady, aromatic sage; of evergreens and aspen—high, the air crisp to the point of smelling "brittle." Then, as you proceed, hold your hat, for all of a sudden you descend a roller coaster, down around thrilling hairpin curves—down until you level out in the wondrous, somber, cool, tranquil solitude of the incredible Coastal Rain Forest, an astonishing place! Prodigious, lofty trees, hanging moss, vines, gigantic ferns seemingly out of a science-fiction movie such as *The Lost World*. Lush undergrowth, all interlaced with fantastic rushing rivers at times teeming with salmon and steelhead, and fresh grizzly tracks on the sandbars. Over all, benignly surveying this scene, the towering, eternally glacier-clad peaks. Off-the-road, via chartered boat or bush aircraft, there's outstanding trout fishing on waters such as the Dean River. I've motored and camped on every connected Northern road, to the ends of them all. My wife and I have employed all popular means for camping and we have arrived at one final conclusion: For our maximum enjoyment our rig must be self-contained—a good 10½-foot camper coach, though we've gone with great chassis-mount rigs and a 27-foot motor home. The vehicle should be in excellent condition, with new tires. If the tires are tubeless I install tubes, regardless.

There are conventional public campgrounds all over the North but with a proper rig you camp just about when and where you please. The first trip North I worried about it, for after all I had a trusting little city-bred wife with me, not to mention a highly valued friend, my exceptional dog Casper. The second time around I worried vaguely, intermittently, discovering I was the only one who did. On the next dozen trips I worried not at all. While some campgrounds and campsites are more desirable than others, I feel that in the end the true secret of mastering the fine art of Far North motor-camping is to leave home with a dependable car-and-trailer, pickup coach or motor home, completely self-contained.

Mexican Camping

A well-planned camping trip throughout the mainland of Mexico is nudging the very top of any list of worthwhile vacations readily available to North Americans. (To Mexican nationals, by the way, we are not "American." We are *North*-American, *por favor, señor.*)

If you haven't yet been there, or haven't read extensively about the country, probably you are in for some pleasant surprises. Strangers to the land conjure up the classic scene of a *peon* drapped with *serape, sombrero* over his eyes, sleeping in the sun with his faithful burro standing by. In the background is an organ-pipe cactus. Well, this scene is there, all right, but it is an infinitesimal part of Mexico.

Mexico is a foreign land. It is just as foreign as Spain or Italy when you get well away from the border towns or the larger established resorts frequented by *norteamericanos.* Mexico is a series of geographical (and other) contrasts. There are mighty deserts, lush rain forest, monkey-filled jungles. Within the physical tropic zone, you will drive through coniferous forests complete with crystal-clear trout streams. There are countless palm-fringed beaches and lagoons awaiting you—and this can be subtropical and tropical camping at its best. The word for "camp" is pronounced *campanMENto,* by the way.

Mexico has exceedingly high mountains (the Continental Divide) running through a section of its middle from the U.S. border to the extreme southern border at Guatemala, and they get lofty indeed. As an example, Mexico City sits in a *valley,* and it is somewhat over 7,000 feet above sea level, as I recall. Below Mexico City, farther into the tropics, are mountains covered with snow. The farther south (south and southeast, to be technical) you journey, the narrower Mexico becomes, so you have two oceans plus a great many climatic zones at your fingertips. You can be high in coniferous forests and within a few hours return to tropical or subtropical beaches.

If you belong to the AAA, try to obtain its book on traveling in Mexico. It's the best I've ever seen. Oil companies furnish excellent road maps of Mexico, but if you hit a snag an easy out is to buy a Rand McNally road atlas.

The Mexican highway system is well marked and amply endowed with hardtop, and a great many campers see Mexico without leaving hard-surface roads. When the *paviemento* ends, though, boy, it really ends! Some of the secondary roads make the Alaska Highway look like Wilshire Boulevard. The highways generally are satisfactory by *norteamericano* standards. They can be a bit narrow for some tastes, and some of the bridges *are* so narrow they would be classified as one-way in this country. It is best never to drive at high speed, and I do not advise driving at night in the boondocks. For one thing, black cattle like to snooze on the sun-warmed hardtop.

Fishing is wonderful, and presents no problems that I know of. There is freshwater angling, but Mexico is noted for its superb saltwater game fish. What we call the Gulf of California (and they call the Sea of Cortez) is one gigantic fish trap. I have never gone saltwater fishing at any spot on either ocean, in Mexico, and failed to score heavily.

Another favorite Jobson jaunt is through sparsely settled rural areas of Mexico, where author says necessity has taught people how to load pack animals. In this arid locale, be prepared for rough, hot-weather camping.

Mexico has conventional campgrounds, for a fee, and some are quite satisfactory. Better, though, are the trailer parks such as, for instance, those at Acupulco, Mexico City, Guadalajara, Mazatlan, Guaymas, etc. The location of either campgrounds or trailer parks can be elusive; quite often they are not where the traveler desires them to be. You learn to cope by approaching the *policia* or the *Jefe* in the smaller towns, in quest of information. Ask at hotels. They are often extremely cooperative toward trailer and pickup-coach travelers and for a small fee will allow you to park, use an electrical extension cord and have bathroom privileges.

Unless you are traveling with a caravan, I urge you never to roadside camp overnight away from habitation. People do it (I have done it) and get away with it. Others have miserable experiences. Some of those stories about Mexican bandits are true. I do not think a tent is the best means of camping throughout Mexico. A trailer or pickup camper is safer and more versatile.

If some earnest soul tells you to go ahead and drink the water, suspiciously view him thenceforth as a bumbling lackwit. He is the type who falls down wells and gets stuck between floors in elevators. Boil the drinking water, or purify it by other means. Suit yourself but *I* ain't agoin' to eat fresh fruit or vegetables that cannot first be peeled. I do not eat raw vegetables (like lettuce) unless my wife first soaks them in a strong halazone or permanganate solution (and then thoroughly rinses them in purified water). Bottled water is good when you can get it. So are beer *(cerveza)* and soda pop *(refrescos)*. Take plenty of insect repellent. You can purchase it there, but somehow I have a notion our own is a bit more effective. Mexico has a couple of ticks (the *garrapata* and the *pinolilla*) which I do think are among the meanest anywhere. You may require a smallpox vaccination, by the way.

If none of your party speaks Spanish, I cannot put too heavy an emphasis on imploring you to learn key phrases. A surprisingly small number of them, coupled with gestures, will get you by nicely. Most Mexicans, incidentally, warm to a person trying to speak their tongue. They may laugh, but they laugh with *simpatico*—with you, not at you as in some countries (notably France).

If you can, tune your car for low-grade fuel. The gasoline in Mexico often is low octane, making the family bus sound like the clashing of sabers in a 1930 swashbuckler movie.

U.S. auto insurance is valid, but showing a U.S. policy to a rural Mexican cop is akin to showing him the wiring diagram of the space lab. Buy reliable *Mexican* auto insurance at the port of entry. You can obtain your Tourist Permit, valid for six months, at the same time (or you can obtain it in advance by writing to the nearest Mexican Consul).

Hot-Weather Camping

Most summer family vacations are planned a good bit in advance and unless Dad is the seventh son of a seventh son, it is impossible for him to prophesy precisely what the weather will be. Instead of temperate pre-Labor Day weather, he could run into a spell of sizzling "dog days" hot enough to prostrate a camel. The entire family will benefit if proper procedures are learned and equipment is added to the gear to cope with sweltering heat waves.

I'll lay on you here a factual, heart-rending tale of the time I took my bride to a bosky campsite complete with singing creek and tuneful waterfall near the adjoining borders of New York, Massachusetts and Connecticut. Great leafy forests abounded and tremendous cumulus clouds cruised a faultless azure sky. Woodchucks were so plentiful we had a pet one coming into the tent, and whitetail deer came shyly to our fireplace to nibble crackers. We stumbled upon a fellow raising (for a hobby) prize-winning beef cattle who took a liking to us, and sold for a pittance all the prime aged T-bone steaks we could grill. We explored untrammeled dales and mossy glens ringed with maples that knew the Mohawks. And we hiked to resin-scented mountain crests. Not the least of our good fortune was taking the wrong trail and running onto a lonesome moonshiner who'd once guided Babe Ruth on some deer hunts and whose name was just Tom. All was idyllic when without warning we got a series of days so scorching that nothing moved in field or forest. Our camping neighbors, mostly city people, left in droves. We witnessed

more than just a few cases of heat exhaustion, cramps and heat prostration. They didn't know how to adapt to it, or ride it out. I did, as I'd camped on the plains.

The first tip will happily cost you nothing. It's simply to know your equipment and how it works. It can be (literally) murder to set up camp during a heat wave. If you can swing it, add a fly, an added roof, to your sleeping tent. That flow of air between the tarp and the tent's roof is a marvelous insulation. For cooking and dining in hot weather, latch onto a canopy. Some chaps go further and get a breezy bugproof kitchen tent with canvas roof and floor and netting walls. If possible, sleep on uninsulated canvas (Army type) folding cots. Canvas "director's" chairs are excellent, as are mesh lounges and the old-fashioned mesh hammocks.

During a heat wave it is not wise to do any cooking at all over campfire or charcoal. Use a camping stove and stand back as much as possible. The one hot meal should be in the evening; during a trial by heat, cold cereals and sweet rolls suffice at breakfast with cold-cut sandwiches and spreads okay for lunch. Drink instant iced tea and coffee rather than hot.

Some campgrounds have no shower facilities, or occasionally you may be near a water supply (like a dangerously swift river) in which you cannot bathe properly. Take the time we were on a remote. Mexican beach. The ocean was great, but it had some wee varmints in it that clung to the skin and stung us. So we tooled over to the nearest town and bought an ancient shower

Hot-weather camping can be very dry in Utah (left) or very humid
in some parts of Florida (above). Either way, if you follow advice in
text, you'll stay safe, healthy and much more comfortable than
novices. Heat exhaustion, heat cramps and heat stroke can be avoided.

head, the kind you pull a string to turn on. The local welder brazed a flange
to it, with a matching flange and four bolt holes in each. With homemade gas-
kets, we put this on the bottom of an oversized canvas duffle bag and rigged it
so we could lower to fill, then hoist aloft. It was hot there on the Sea of Cortez, and we'd never have made it without that blessed shower. I've seen five-
gallon cans rigged up similarly. You can buy little cabanas, now, to enclose either a shower or a toilet, but another good way is simply a spare tarp and four
poles. I urge you not to overlook the immense benefits of regular showers during hot weather, as they not only are cooling but discourage all sorts of rash
and fungus.

When out of ice, an old trick is to keep wet cloths around perishable
items. The evaporation cools nicely and is the reason that canvas waterbags
and unglazed pottery *ollas* keep water palatable. If you are near cold water
you can sink perishables in lidded containers, although sometimes bears and
raccoons find them.

Hot weather, unfortunately, is the season for insects and plants that attack. Learn to recognize poison ivy, poison oak and poison sumac—and avoid
them. But if contact is made, wash with soap and water, and *thoroughly* wash
your clothing. Don't scratch. In emergency, coat with a flour-and-water
paste. Some aspirin usually helps substantially. Extreme cases require imme-
diate medical aid. If bugs are bad, either spray (garden spray helps) or fog the
entire campsite.

If you heed the foregoing, you probably won't become ill, but it's good to know that for heat *stroke*, the symptoms are high body temperature (101° or more); dry, hot skin; and sometimes nausea, vomiting and dizziness. Remove the patient to a cool spot with cool bath and rubdown. Do *not* use ice unless you're a doctor, as this can complicate matters. This condition is sometimes fatal, so (a) cool the patient and (b) get a doctor.

Heat *exhaustion* is often a collapse due to overexertion in hot surroundings. Sweating can be heavy at first, and the patient is wan, pale, weak and clammy to the touch. Body temperature is normal or below. If the latter, add hot packs, and keep the patient in a cool place. He may faint, and/or have headaches for days.

Heat *cramps* come from profuse, sustained sweating without sufficient intake of salt. If you're drinking lots of water, salt pills usually are indicated, although your own doctor knows best regarding your salt intake. It's smart to have a checkup and ask him about such matters before the summer camping season begins. In the event of heat cramps, keep the patient cool and, if in doubt, administer at least a little salt.

Years ago, various establishments used to give away fans of stiff cardboard or palm, imprinted with advertising. These are a real aid while relaxing. If you own a beach or lawn umbrella, by all means try to fetch it along. Remember that a conventional bumbershoot is vital to good photographs afield, to shade both you and the camera. Films and loaded cameras should be kept in a camp cooler. Inexpensive wide-brim porous straw hats are a blessing under an unrelenting sun.

Cold-Weather Camping

Winter camping is not foremost among the popular outdoor activities today and that is a shame in a way, for most of those who indulge swear it is just as much fun as summer camping. There are long weekends and school vacations during the colder seasons. A fellow has little competition for choice camping spots during the off-season. The bugs and snakes are gone. The woods often are under a virgin mantle of bright, clean snow and there is a peaceful *quiet*. The blemishes and eyesores of careless summer campers have magically disappeared. Instead of hot, muggy days, the temperature is crisp and invigorating. And if a chap goes with the correct equipment he is eminently comfortable at all times.

The most pleasant days are moderate ones—but suppose you hit some zero-type temperatures? We can take a few tips from the Eskimos. Have your

If you can retreat to professional A-wall tent, warmed by sheepherder's stove and perhaps an additional heater, cold-weather camping becomes cozy experience.

clothing multi-layered and loose. Eskimos often wear two parkas; one of unborn caribou, fur side in, the other heavier, of caribou or seal, fur side out. Loose and flappy, so moisture is expelled by a circulation of air rising from the parka bottom out the neck and sleeves, if there's the slightest hint of overheating. The number one rule afield in this regard is to *avoid excessive sweating*. Prevent that at all costs if you're very far from camp. The Eskimos make excellent "sun glasses" from driftwood, but better for us (giving much greater peripheral vision) are dark green or gray shooting glasses, for prevention of snow blindness.

It's wise to keep your head, feet, hands and kidney region comfortably warm. Effective for keeping your feet warm are loose-fitting "mukluk"-type ½-inch felt booties over a couple pairs of wool stockings, the whole encased in rubber-bottom, leather-top pacs. Many people swear by insulated boots, rubber or leather. The soles of our feet exude heat, so does the head and neck area. Hands get cold easily because they're extremities. Often, if you'll heat up your head, your feet will grow warmer, and vice versa. Worthwhile protection for the hands are gloves inside mittens. Again, taking a tip from the Eskimos, make a harness running across your shoulders, out each sleeve, securely fastened to each mitten. Losing one could be tragic and it is easy to do, as you often shed the mitts for some chore or other.

The greatest cold-weather tent for North America is the Plains Indian tepee. It is the one tent in which you can have an open campfire, and the heaviest snow will slide off its steep sides. Pretty good, too, is the familiar A-wall tent with wood-burning stove. Such a stove will keep a tent nice and warm as long as you maintain the fire. When it goes out, as it rapidly does at

Good supply of seasoned firewood is great comfort in winter camp, but fetching it from pile can be painful. Effective way to keep hands warm is to wear gloves inside mittens (right). Snowmobilers (below) generally wear well-insulated boots and windbreaking, hooded coveralls with down-insulated garments underneath.

bedtime, and a sort of marrow-congealing polar front descends on your little nest, you are glad to be in that warm bedroll with only your nose exposed. A sneaky gambit here is to lay in a supply of either pitch wood or fuzz sticks before retiring. In the morning grit your teeth, leap manfully out of the sack, and with one quick match start the fire.

Whatever heater you use, if your bed is toward the rear of the tent and the heater by the front opening, have a razor-sharp knife handy. If the tent (heaven forbid) catches fire, trapping you, *cut* your way out. I know of seven men who were burned severely while escaping a tent that had not been treated with flame retardant. Their knives were not at hand.

There's a wonderful array of tent heaters, working on a variety of fuels. They are safe and reliable if the manufacturer's directions are followed. The key instruction is never to use them in an unventilated tent. Certain tent heaters are capable of getting the inside temperature up from freezing to 60° in short order. Family "umbrella" tents are best heated for most uses with a commercial tent heater, but a wood-burning stove can be installed. I've seen it done, and done it myself.

Pitch your tent out of the wind, like the Blackfeet of Montana-Alberta who wisely camped in the stream bottoms and let the blizzards howl harmlessly over their heads. Find a sheltered site and you've got the cold more than three-fourths whipped right there. Scrape the tent area free of snow. Put down building paper or old tarps, and erect the shelter on that. Then bank snow around the canvas—it's great insulation.

Your bedroll should be insulated with plenty of something like Dacron fiberfill or down. Five or six pounds of fiberfill is not too much. My own down bag (90″x90″) has five pounds of down, and it is not too much for winter in the mountains, believe me. Like the Eskimo, sleep near the ground with an overabundance of insulating padding *under* the bedroll: a tarp, then a Space Blanket, mattress (or if you prefer, foam), folded blanket, then the fluffed-up sleeping bag. Wear a stocking cap and wool stockings, down booties or felt boots. Air your bag daily, and don't sleep in your clothes unless necessary.

Pure water can be obtained by melting snow in a can. A good kind is the five-gallon can in which cooking oil is sold to restaurants. Cut out the top and set the can near the campfire. You will find (again like the Eskimo) that you require more fats in your diet when active in cold weather. Allow more food than for summertime menus. We use a lot of freeze-dried meals. The scrambled eggs are great, for instance. Unless we have our big A-wall tent, we like to eat facing the campfire, where it's warm, with a tarp rigged behind us.

In winter driving, have tire chains, a handyman jack, some milk cartons of sand and a couple of shovels (so if you get a helper, you can both work).

Propane-fueled catalytic heater (below) is worthwhile winter accessory. Woodburning cookstove (right) is worth all the firewood you have to split. In addition to cooking fine meals it radiates welcome heat.

Ordinary five-gallon salad-oil can has many camp uses. Snow can be melted in it for pure water or, as shown here, it can be pressed into service as improvised stove, fired with that old stand-by, canned heat.

Taking the Family Pet

I know of an author who advises potential campers that they definitely must leave their dog in a kennel when on a camping trip. If this isn't enough to afflict one with the vapors, I don't know what would. The advice is sometimes correct. I take umbrage at his sweeping statement that *all* affectionate, loyal dogs should be put in kennels. There are all sorts of dog-owners and all sorts of dogs.

Undoubtedly there are a few campers who would benefit the world if they did clap their dogs in the pokey before taking off for a public campground. A busy campground or beach is no place for a dog off a leash, or one that barks, howls, bites or is careless about where he goes to the powder room. As a ranger once told me, the main trick about having dogs in campgrounds is to realize that a dog can't read and doesn't know all the rules. It is the responsibility of his owner to educate him.

You will encounter busy public campgrounds that do not allow dogs, even well-behaved and on a leash. There are legions of campers who, when encountering this situation, go elsewhere, taking their dollars with them. The notion that if you are taking a long trip it is better for the dog to be placed in a kennel ("for his own good") is in many cases strange logic. I have observed dogs placed in kennels while their master blithely take off for Alaska or some such. When the owner is out of sight the dog nearly has a stroke, and in many cases refuses to eat or drink. If you have an older, well-trained dog and you love him, my feeling is that it's much better to put up with the slight inconveniences of having him with you. The pleasure of his company more than offsets the little nuisances, and the dog is going to be much happier. My friend Jack O'Connor disagrees with me. He feels the pet is much happier in a kennel, where he is calmer. Jack is a very smart man. Perhaps it depends upon the individuals involved.

I had a dog named Casper who was 19 years old when he died. Several experts feel Casper was quite possibly the most land-traveled dog alive. He traveled many times north of the Arctic Circle and deep into the tropics. He was in 49 states, all the provinces of Canada (plus the Territories) and most states in Mexico. He took about *15 lengthy wilderness pack trips.* Never did he cause us real trouble or make us wish we'd left him in a kennel "for his own good." I never knew Casper to be a nuisance in a public campground, either. A look from either my wife or me would silence him, and he was as "sanitary" as a human.

If you decide to take your dog with you, and I hope you do, here are a few tips. Have a leash handy and put him on it at stops near a public highway

In photo below, author and his old friend Casper are steaming up British Columbia's Inside Passage to Alaska. Camping must have agreed with Casper, since he lived to be 19, and he never got into trouble in wilds or caused any annoyance at campgrounds. Hikers shown at right, in Oregon's Willamette National Forest, would agree that properly trained dog is better off in camp than kennel.

or road. When you pull in for gas, take your pet for a short walk away from the station. I try to pick a station with a nearby field or adjacent vacant lot. Have his water dish handy and a canteen. If he looks uncomfortable, try giving him a drink, rather than waiting until the next stop. Dogs can get very thirsty all of a sudden. Never overfeed. We find commercial dog food best—not table scraps. Make certain he has a comfortable place to lie, while traveling. And, of course, he must get his rest at night.

In the Yukon on nights so cold that hoar-frost formed on anything damp, I would partially open my down bag and let him lie next to the opening, partially covered. He slept like a babe. Some dogs are fearful of thunder. We carried a little bottle of tranquilizers and gave him one when the heavens were booming and crashing. We don't consider Casper unusual just because he was so good about traveling. Before him, we had a Brittany spaniel named Skeezix who traveled with us for 14 years.

11

Emergency Measures

Camp Safety

A well-organized camp is among the safest plots of earth known to man. Mishaps occur, as they do any place, especially when a person is either unprepared or unaware. An example concerns one of the best wilderness campers in the world, a long-time pal of mine, a part-Indian who for decades was considered by many to be the top outfitter in the Yukon Territory and the best sheep guide in the world—a man of infinite resource and experience. One autumn after the dudes were gone he and two of his top wranglers went with a pack train into the mountains to get the winter's meat supply. Homeward bound with loaded packs, they camped on the beach of Tagish Lake. The only trees were short, thick poplars, not the lodgepoles of the high country. With red-blooded ingenuity, fore and aft they stoutly rigged a single imposing tree trunk with plenty of rope as an improvised but secure way to pitch their big A-wall tent. One day away from home, it was a careless and hasty camp. Tired and worn, they slept deeply until a grizzly invaded the nearby cooking equipment. The enthusiastic bashing of tins and buckets made a tumultuous din.

"Wake up boys!" shouted the outfitter. "There's a bear in camp!"

"I'll get him," cried the first wrangler. Rifle in hand, head down, he charged the flaps like a Green Bay lineman. Mournful, ominous groans ensued. "The bear got him," observed the outfitter calmly, in the manner of General Terry reflecting upon the Custer debacle. To the rescue, the second wrangler tore into the night; a sickening thump, then silence, and the outfitter shrewdly said to himself, "By golly, that bear is standing there waiting."

He craftily commandoed under the rear of the tent. His .30-06 at the ready, he surreptitiously eased around the front corner to witness the bloody carnage. There was none. The bear had fled and the heroic wranglers were laid out one over the other, knocked comatose by ramming their heads into an unexpected and unyielding object—that stout tree trunk.

Guy lines make handy clotheslines, and using them that way adds safety. With towels and clothes hung like warning flags, people are less apt to collide with ropes.

This true anecdote illustrates as well as anything that even experts can come a cropper if each camp is not organized, neat, tidy and familiar.

This is all important, and the first rule of successful camping is: With lines (ropes) in camp, day and night have some light-colored objects attached to them, even strips of white rag. Garroting and broken necks have been suffered by vacationists running into unseen clotheslines, and people trip over tent and dining fly ropes. Some campers feel so strongly about the danger, they take down unused clotheslines. In certain parts of Canada they suspend clotheslines some 15 feet aloft with tiny pulleys.

A common source of mangled toes, skinned shins and debilitating falls are tent stakes and old-fashioned guy ropes. Again hang something visible on all the guylines. Purists sometimes touch up stakes and canopy poles with luminous paint.

It is no secret that bears and lesser beasts come into camps where there is any odor of food. Do not ever have any sort of food smell on a bedroll or pajamas. Do not eat in the sleeping tent, dropping crumbs, or leaving chocolate, ham, or bacon traces on the sleeping bag. In bear country have the kitchen away from the sleeping shelter. Before retiring, scrupulously wash pots, pans and plates. All foodstuffs should be hermetically sealed in lidded plastic containers or screw-top tins. A bear can smell these if they're under his nose, but they do not exude an aroma into the forest.

Never have garbage in camp overnight. At the least, mice, rats or something like raccoons will move in on you. If sealed-cover refuse cans are not available, burn containers until the food smell is gone. I've mentioned that the latest accepted technique is to pack these out—logic being if you can tote

These pictures illustrate important safety rules:
Camp axe should be kept very sharp so that it
won't glance or skip; fireplace should be safely
distant from tent, and shovel should be near fire;
tent should be above high-water line, and childen
should be supervised; in snake country, first-aid
gear should include snake-bite kit.

them in full, it is no big deal to carry out the empties—but in virgin wilderness this may not be possible. In which case burn them, and bury with lavish sprinklings of lye, under the dirt. This usually kills the scents that attract animals. Such cleanliness also keeps pestiferous insects to a minimum.

Keep camp knives and axes extremely sharp—the proverbial "razor's edge." They are much, much less dangerous this way, and a keen blade makes for efficient chores. Dull cutting edges slip, skip, bounce, glance and wander, yet can slice tender human anatomy with astonishing ease. Contrariwise, sharply honed tools bite into the job and go where directed. Knives and axes should be in leather sheaths when not in use. Many good folks unexpectedly draw blood while rummaging in the utensils, and a leather scabbard prevents this. When using an axe, stay free of overhanging branches, clotheslines or anything that could deflect the head into yourself or an innocent bystander.

The heart of camp is the fire, but it should not be near family tents. Heat and flying sparks can damage canvas and bedrolls. For campfire cooking, have a shovel, long picnic-style forks and spoons, sturdy gloves for the men, asbestos mitts for ladies, pliers, wire, extended handles for fry pans, hooked rods for manipulating Dutch ovens and pots. There is no reason ever to burn yourself at a campfire. Especially for conventional family camping, keep fires small and easily contained. Away from fireplaces in public campgrounds, never build a fire on humus of the forest floor. It's much better on sand, rocks and/or mineral soil, with a shovel handy. Firewood is best prepared a bit away from the cooking area.

Unleashed water is a potential source of annoyance and danger. For the tent site, select a well-drained area away from dry streambeds, overhanging cliffs and trees taller than the rest. (Tall trees attract lightning.) At a shore or beach, camp above the highest high-water mark. Avoid depressions under the tent—water collects there. It's fashionable to declare that a shallow trench with a leadoff around the tent is passé. Baloney. Unless it's against the law, or if you're in a conventional campground where judicious construction makes it unnecessary, it is still a fine idea. Just fill the little trench again before departing. Check for rotten trees, or poised boulders high on a slope, with you in their path if wind and rain start them toppling.

With small children, of course, it's better not to camp near bogs, swamps, cliffs, high-speed rivers or heavy tides. Any mother will tell you it's impossible to watch toddlers every minute. Small fry must be instructed not to enter either water or woods alone.

What to do, short of moving camp, if you discover "hard-case" insects like scorpions, ticks, virulent spiders, etc.? My advice is to spray them discreetly. When camping in certain areas, you'll want to pack a snake-bite kit, of course, in addition to the standard items in your first-aid kit. And in almost any region, you'll want insect repellent. In this beloved field for 30 years, I have with my peers labored both openly and behind the scenes for proper use of the environment, not only for mankind but for the birds and beasts of the field. Like many others who have for decades been worried, I would give a lot to eliminate the countless tons of insecticide mercilessly and callously dumped upon this nation. Insecticide is a nasty word these days. But until there is a law against it, I would rather have a little spray in my tent than scorpions, spiders and cockroaches.

It is prudent, once you achieve a camping layout that you like and are comfortable with, to adopt a routine and have all your camps similar. Make camp with everything in relatively the same place. In this instance familiarity does not breed contempt.

Bear!

Anytime people are in contact with bear there is a chance of trouble. Mostly such incidents are minor, a few humorous. But there have been tragedies—the killing of two helpless girls in Glacier Park a few years ago and the forester in Idaho who was "ripped to pieces." National Park officials have ways of dealing with troublesome bruins (most of which are black bears, the clowns of the woods). Generally, the difficult ones among them are marked, trapped and removed. If they persist in being obnoxious to park visitors they are destroyed.

Grizzly bears are something else. There are few left in the contiguous U.S. Most of these are in Glacier and Yellowstone, and in the rugged mountain country between the two parks. (In passing, let me add that Montana grizzlies often have short tempers for some reason.) Grizzlies in our parks are exceedingly scarce and extremely shy. Most of them are nocturnal and greatly fear man.

There are many reasons why a grizzly becomes dangerous. It might be a wounded one or one that has been teased and greatly annoyed. It can be a protective mamma grizzly with a squalling, frightened cub. Odoriferous food can bring a grizzly into camp, and no mistake. One time in the Northern wilds we were boiling a pot of cabbage on the beach and someone looked up and said "Hey!" Here came a grizzly on a dead run. We had to kill him.

I have scarcely ever been in a wilderness camp in grizzly country that I didn't have some incident. One time my wife had a mother grizzly with two cubs in her camp for 10 nights running. I was off at a remote jack camp hunting sheep. The bear never bothered her—mainly, I think, because our dog

Never feed tame-looking park bears, as all bears are dangerous, and don't unwittingly invite them into camp by leaving any food or garbage uncovered.

Casper raised a furor. Once we had a grizzly try all night to get into our coach. I sat up with a loaded .338 waiting for him to come in. Another time we had a grizzly enter a tent, knock down the poles, and the canvas collapsed around him. He got exceedingly annoyed.

Grizzly bears that are so wild they do not know man, and consequently have little fear of him, are dangerous. Likewise, grizzlies that have for other reasons lost their fear of man are dangerous. But *something* generally provokes a grizzly to actual attack. He doesn't do it for amusement. Nor do grizzlies *customarily* eat men or belabor the body cruelly after they feel the victim is dead. When you go into National Parks having a substantial bear population, you will be handed a little folder instructing you about bears. Follow the directions, regardless of what you see others doing. Do not feed "tame" park bears. It is quite dangerous, actually. Do not sleep in exposed sleeping bags near where you or others have eaten. Never tease bears, in any way. What *you* think is fun may provoke *him* to an attack. Some of the antics I see in Yellowstone and Glacier parks make my blood run cold. One father was caught smearing his child's face with honey so he could get an 8mm movie of the bear *licking it off.* That the youngster didn't immediately lose his face is a miracle. Many parents try to get snapshots of their offspring riding a bear. This is akin to playing badminton with dynamite caps.

Lost!

Getting lost is, at best, highly irritating. At worst, it can be tragic. I think a better word for being lost is "confused." It makes one feel better right off to know he's merely confused and not *lost*. By following basic rules and some simple learning, I seldom get directionally confused afield. But it's happened, and I did not like it a bit. I was hunting Rocky Mountain goats with two Indian fellows, one my outfitter (a good one) and the other his camp helper who came along for the stroll. We had a 22-foot boat that we parked in a cove at the foot of some awesome cliffs. Ascending them, finding, stalking and harvesting a goat took most of the day, so the outfitter suggested that while they processed the trophy and packed the meat, I should hustle back to the boat and keep a big driftwood fire going to guide them in after dark. Also, I could have supper ready. I soon found that I'd been trusting the guide entirely and had not paid attention to directions. I also found that there were many coves besides "ours" and that a fog was rolling in. To make up for being stupid, I began *hurrying,* which was sin number one. Brought to a halt in a thick patch of alders where I'd fallen, I first was exasperated, then humiliated and next, exceedingly angry. All normal so far. Then a peculiar aura of being "alone" set in, difficult to fight off. Next I felt helpless and finally—I have to admit it— frightened. But I quickly got a grip on myself and we all met at the boat at daylight.

Right then I learned that the main hazard of being confused afield is a person's own emotions. The primary danger of your being lost, and quite likely the *only* danger, is mental—your emotions and outlook. Knowing this in advance, you can guard against it.

So, suppose you have the misfortune to find yourself amid unfamiliar surroundings not certain of your whereabouts. If you have companions in camp, as most will, the first thing to do is remember the wilderness expert who never was lost: He was *here,* it was the s.o.b'ing *camp* that was temporarily misplaced. Gather a plentiful supply of firewood, more than you'd likely need, and build a fire. Right away, you have escaped panic by establishing your own camp, and you have a sense of ownership and pride in it.

Sit for awhile, cogitate a bit and see if you can figure out what went wrong. Tell yourself that at this point you can't be very far from camp, and more than likely only a hundred yards or so from a trail! So stay there, and don't go running about thinking that if you "hurry fast" you'll find familiar surroundings faster. It doesn't work that way. You may well travel clear out of the search area where they'll be looking for you. Don't yell (unless you hear someone) or soon you'll be hoarse and lose your voice when you most

If you think you're lost, first thing to do is sit, rest, and think about
where you went wrong. Chances are, you'll discover you're not lost after all.

need it. Don't waste ammunition by firing shots in sets of three, unless you
hear gunshots close by, signalling you. Hang on to that precious ammo!

When your little camp is set up nicely and you've built a rudimentary
lean-to shelter of poles and boughs in front of your warm fire, look around for
high points where you can climb and look at the countryside. At this stage, be
sure to break the tips of branches along your route so you easily find your way
back to your emergency campsite. At nightfall, if you're still there (searchers
generally get serious the second day, so plan on that) eat half your lunch
(candy, raisins or whatever) and *save half* for breakfast. This is *important*.

Go to sleep. Next morning you'll either be rescued or you'll have re-
called where it was you went "wrong." If you have camped alone and cannot
expect rescue, in wilderness country follow a stream downhill; rills run into
rivulets, thence to creeks, to streams, to rivers—and there you'll find habitation. In semicivilized country, like a Michigan swamp, for example, just
travel a straight line, either by compass or by continuing to line up visually
three objects in a row, never less, and proceed that way until you come to a
road. Otherwise, you will invariably wander in a big circle.

Personally, I would never leave any camp these days without a couple of
gadgets. One is an extremely lightweight little kit that fits on the belt and carries two signal flares with self-contained launcher, a self-operating red-smoke

Many public camping areas are posted with information signs and maps showing roads, water, campsites, main trails and shelters. If, in spite of these aids, you become confused about your location, climb to high vantage point and look for familiar landmarks.

signal, a sure-fire fire-starter and an ingenious signaling mirror. The other is a plastic waterproof match holder containing kitchen matches and a candle stub, with a compass on one end and a loud whistle on the other. Every camper should have something similar. The whistle saves you from shouting and subsequent loss of voice. And this is a far more practical match carrier than metal ones which you cannot open with icy-cold fingers.

Remember that even if you're a city man, you can learn to navigate the woods and plains like a native. At first, use compass, paper and pencil to lay out your route. This is just about what woodsmen do, only they do it in their noodle and so can you eventually, but use paper and pencil first. I think it was Townsend Whelen who said that if a fledgling woodsman will mark down roughly that he has, for instance, traveled three hours north and then three hours east, all he has to do to reach camp is to travel about four hours (or so) southwest. Simple!

And, when you're meandering along, look back often, as all terrain looks much different from a reverse angle. Another big help is to observe all landmarks such as hills or a very tall tree. If a situation arises where you have two streams flowing closely side by side, be sure you identify the one you want. Following the stars is great fun. So is watching the wind direction and having a touching faith in tree moss, the sun in the heavens and other ancient modes of navigational skill. But it's better to rely on a rough sketch, compass and timepiece. That way, even in a fog you ought to be able to home in on camp so accurately you may walk right into the tent before you see it!

Falling in Chilly Holes

One day I got a letter from an engineer in Maryland who was about to go camping in the North Country. He wrote that an old experienced buddy had warned him against "snow crevasses." Since he had never seen much of this hazard mentioned in hunting yarns, he wondered if the pal were not being oversolicitous of his welfare. Come to think of it, I haven't seen much written about it, either—in camping articles or in general stories of hunting and other sports afield.

I do think the hazard of tumbling into such an opening is of more direct concern to alpinists and mountain climbers. Nonetheless, when a fellow is camping or hunting in timberline country, above timberline or around glaciers, there is always the off-chance he might become a statistic in this way.

A crevasse is a deep crack or fissure. I imagine what is meant by "snow crevasse" is one filled with loose snow with a crust, perhaps, on top; or one not filled with snow, loose or otherwise, but with a crust over and concealing it; or maybe a simple little ol' snow bridge over a creek. While not as dramatic as the romantic-sounding crevasse, these snow "bridges" do occur. Watch any gully or ravine filled with snow. There may be a creek course below that has eaten away the snow, leaving a void. Over the top, caused by successive melting and freezings, is a hard crust which holds its shape. That is, it holds its shape until walked on by you or your horse. It is not necessary to

On Northern pack trips, watch for snow-covered gullies and creeks or suspicious patches of snow. There may be thin crust over hole that can cause bad fall. Dismount and lead your horse cautiously over any spots that look chancy.

plunge end over end into a fathomless pit, with your rapidly diminishing screams of horror making a sound-chamber echo, in order to get hurt. You and your horse can get banged up by unexpectedly falling 20 feet, 12 feet or even six feet.

When on foot, you can simply test any spot that doesn't look right, and sometimes a brief detour solves a potential problem.

When on horseback, if you come to a patch of suspicious-looking snow, dismount and gingerly lead your horse over it. You may do this 789 times and not have it give way. You may blithely try to ride over it once and fall in. When there is more than one rider in the group, it usually suffices if the first man leads his horse over—then the rest of the chaps ride over *one at a time*.

Getting Unstuck

Some real forward thinker (he was a cola truck driver in Baja California, as I recall) once sagely observed that very often on poor roads (or on no roads at all) if you can coax your vehicle to go just one more yard, it then is an uncomplicated matter to drive it onward 10,000 gloriously triumphant miles. But it is astonishingly easy to get your vehicle ignominiously bogged down. It can be dangerous. At best, it's frustrating, time-consuming, arduous—and, believe me, the labor expended can make snow-shoveling seem like fly tying.

You can generally get trailer
or camper through bad spots
like these if you're a careful,
skilled driver, but you
should carry equipment that
can be counted on to
extricate you from deep mud,
sand or soft earth.

I'm sure that over the years you have read much advice about extricating the bus when it becomes balky. The classic strategy, something I've done at least 19,376 times, it seems like, is the rocking technique. The driver sets up a back-and-forth motion by rapidly shifting from forward to reverse. The trick is to keep increasing the distance the vehicle will move backwards, then forwards, until momentum is built up sufficiently to pull out of the bad spot. This works a lot of the time. If you can recruit a gang of stalwart buddies to help push, this is particularly effective if they'll really give it the heave-ho fore and aft and, as the driver senses he is about to successfully move forward, the pushers all grunt loudly. It seems to help.

Then we've all heard that in sandy soil, especially, if you'll deflate the tires around 50 percent, it imparts greater traction and out you go. Some sages advise packing along containers of sand, cinders, ashes, spray-chain, rock salt; or conveying old gunny sacks, pieces of carpeting, lengths of steel mesh GI foxhole shovels and hanks of parachute-shroud lines. Sometimes this pays off but not if you are stuck within my definition of the term, which is: The vehicle is down, boy. Down to the axles—to the *frame*.

If you are going to do much off-road driving, sooner or later you're going to get stuck badly. It is no sin, nor anything to be ashamed of. The best four-wheel-drive pilots in the world get halted now and then. I have seen professional hunters in Africa who drive every day afield for nine months of the year go through it. You'll discover that while you can learn to "read" back roads and off-road terrain, a spot that looks okay (and is, 98 percent of the time) occasionally can be treacherous. I came to an inglorious halt for five hours in my own driveway, one time.

When, alas, the fateful time arrives and Loyal Betsy slithers into a fathomless fen and settles with a horrible metallic sigh on her axles, you can look upon the incident as more of a bloody nuisance than as a calamity. *If* you have prepared in advance.

Anyone who plans rough-country driving should put together a "package" of vehicle-extricating equipment. It is relatively inexpensive and, while not needed on every trip, when required is one of those good things in life whose value is not measured in money. There are several ways of going at this but since my own gear works as well as any I've ever seen, I'll describe it. When departing for the boondocks I toss in a 30- to 35-foot length of good "log" chain. This isn't the fragile type sold by auto-accessories stores for a buck or two. A length of chain like this will cost much more. Have a hook installed on each end. Some fellows prefer steel cable but I find that chain takes less space. I just feed it into an old gunnysack. And it's easier to handle than cable. Next, a good pointed-type shovel with a "D" handle. A stout pair of gloves (not fabric). A full-sized utility barnyard axe (weight is not much problem in this instance). A buck saw if you don't have a camper's chain saw. Don't forget the saw! A set of tire chains to fit the drive wheels. If possible and legal, a set of snow-mud tires with studs, mounted on extra wheels when you are running with summer tires. If you find it inconvenient to put on and take off full tire chains (some folks are baffled by it) you might try the strap-on emergency type. They are better than nothing.

Even skillfully driven
four-wheel-drive can get
mired down. You
should always have good
high-rise jack
stowed in vehicle.

And now the most important item: Get a professional *high*-rise jack. Not one of the toys given with new automobiles. Your jack can be worked like a winch, also. In the Yukon I have seen one of these jacks pull a car and loaded boat trailer (22-foot boat) out of 12 feet of water.

In addition, an exceedingly useful little rig—lightweight and something I would not be without—is a puller-hoist. If you graduate, as a lot of sportsmen are doing these days, to a four-wheel-drive vehicle, what really pays off is a front-mounted winch. Installed by the dealer, many of these obtain their power from the vehicle's engine. Other winches are available powered electrically from the vehicle's 12-volt system. Some chaps may vary this equipment list a bit—for example, they may pack along strips of steel mesh to go under the wheels. But the stuff I've listed will give you peace of mind, knowing you can venture into rough country and get out again!

Peace of mind—that's an important thing, an important part of the joy of outdoor living. I hope I've added to yours by sharing these tips and techniques, distilled from many years of camping experience. This is a big country as well as beautiful, so perhaps there isn't much chance that we'll ever meet personally. All the less chance because Ann and I enjoy the serenity of remote campsites. But just on the off-chance, we'll look forward to the feeling of camaraderie that campers experience when they meet people who share their enthusiasms. So if you spot our campfire, sit a while and have a snack with us before going on. Meanwhile, have a good trip. Better yet, have many.

Index

Picture Credits

In addition to the photographs by the author, pictures for this book were supplied by the following photographers and organizations, listed in alphabetical order.

Bill Browning: jacket and page 173.
Canadian Government Travel Bureau: title page, 5 (top), 116, 161, 229, 231, 233.
Canadian Pacific Railway: 201.
Robert Elman: 39.
Florida News Bureau: 247.
Florida Trail Association: 232 (bottom).
Michigan Department of Natural Resources: 79 (top).
Bert Popowski: 47 (top).
Leonard Lee Rue: 23, 47 (bottom), 73, 79 (bottom), 204.
U.S. Bureau of Outdoor Recreation: 257 (top right), 263 (bottom).
U.S. Fish & Wildlife Service,
    photo by E. P. Haddon: 260.
U.S. Forest Service,
    photos by Jim Hughes: 120, 254 (right);
    photo by Ray Manley: 137 (top);
    photos by Bluford Muir: 3, 7;
    photo by W. L. Poulson, 65;
    photo by B. R. Van Gieson: 41 (top right);
    photo by George R. Wolstad: 41 (top left).
Utah Travel Council: 108–109, 246.
Weyerhaeuser Company: 121, 147 (top).